The Ultimate Wine Lover's Guide

2006

Sterling Publishing Co., Inc.
New York

The Ultimate
Wine Lover's
Guide 2006

FRED DuBOSE
EVAN SPINGARN
WITH
NANCY MANISCALCO

The Ultimate Wine Lover's Guide 2006

Published by Sterling Publishing Co., Inc.
387 Park Avenue South, New York, NY 10016
© 2005 by Sterling Publishing Co., Inc.
Distributed in Canada by Sterling Publishing
c/o Canadian Manda Group, 165 Dufferin Street
Toronto, Ontario, Canada M6K 3H6
Distributed in Great Britain by Chrysalis Books Group PLC
The Chrysalis Building, Bramley Road, London W10 6SP, England
Distributed in Australia by Capricorn Link (Australia) Pty. Ltd.
P. O. Box 704, Windsor, NSW 2756, Australia

10 9 8 7 6 5 4 3 2 1

Photography and illustration credits are found on page 272
and constitute an extension of this copyright page.

Sterling ISBN 1-4027-2815-8

For information about custom editions, special sales, premium and
corporate purchases, please contact Sterling Special Sales
Department at 800-805-5489 or specialsales@sterlingpub.com.

Publisher: Barbara J. Morgan
Copy Editor: Alexandra Koppen
Design: Richard J. Berenson
               BERENSON DESIGN & BOOKS, LLC
               New York, NY

CONTENTS

Welcome!

*G*ETTING TO KNOW WINE is an adventure, and few journeys are more leisurely, interesting, and fun—something you, as a wine lover, probably already know. If you're a beginner just striking out, get set for a wonderful trip. Even the most seasoned connoisseur will find new territory to explore, and this book is a companionable guide.

Wine is typically enjoyed—and is best understood—in the company of food. That has been its traditional role from the feasts of the pharaohs to the banquets of ancient Rome to the wealth of choices on the modern restaurant wine list. Some people even think of wine as a sort of condiment for food, an endlessly variable "sauce" of sorts that uplifts both the dinner and the one who dines. With this in mind, each description of the 1000+ wines in *The Ultimate Wine Lover's Guide* includes a food-pairing suggestion.

In 1992 Nancy Maniscalco (pictured at right with Evan Spingarn) opened Nancy's Wines for Food on the Upper West Side of Manhattan, sparking a wine boutique trend that continues to this day. Small, friendly, and welcoming, with its wines lined invitingly against the walls and tagged with handwritten cards describing them, the store offers scores of terrific wines, many under $10; unusual finds from all over the world; and a philosophy that personal taste and enjoyment always trump the worship of labels. The shop was, and remains, a place where any wine snobbery should be left in the wet umbrella stand by the front door.

The same philosophy underpins this book. Nancy, her expert staff, and co-author Evan Spingarn (wine educator, writer, and former wine manager of the store) have sifted through twelve years of wine-buying (and many more of tasting!) to recommend their favorites in each price range—and in so doing, expand the consumer's horizons. More than a mere shopping list, *The Ultimate Wine Lover's Guide* is an introduction to wines you don't want to miss.

Some of these wines are famous, and justly so. Others are bargains, simple and pleasing. But beyond the advertised brands and the flashes-in-the-pan lies another tier, a category of wines that as yet fits no

marketing plan. They are first and foremost food wines. Such wines appear in the carafes and tumblers of bistros as well as the dusty cellars of a château. Wherever they may hail from, we can search them out: the hidden gems, the true originals, the wines that have something to say. When you find them, you come to understand the difference between wines made for the collector or trader or swigger and those made for that luckiest of creatures—the enthusiastic wine lover.

How the Book Works

In the interest of practicality, the book groups wines by price bracket, from the least expensive to the most.

    ❧ In the Primary Red Grapes and Primary White Grapes chapters, grapes like Cabernet Sauvignon, Merlot, and Chardonnay are featured because their wines are what most American wine lovers drink.

    ❧ Chapters featuring the wines of secondary, or lesser known, grapes—Other Choice Reds and Other Choice Whites—introduce you to some of the best blended and single-grape wines out there, while a chapter on sparkling wines ventures well beyond the borders of

Champagne. Fittingly, the book ends with an eclectic and tempting collection of fortified and sweet wines.

❧ A Country and Region special index enables you to locate at a glance the book's Burgundies, Bordeaux, Valpolicellas, Riojas, Sancerres, American wines, Australian and New Zealand wines, and a scattering of those from other parts of the world.

❧ A Wines for Food special index guides you to the wines that pair well with meats, cheeses, pizzas, egg dishes, vegetables, salads, and more.

❧ Separate appendices provide contact information for every North American winery represented in the book, as well as for importers of foreign wines.

Terminology

Wine has a language much its own, meaning you're likely to come across some puzzling terms. What's an appellation? What's the translation of foreign terms such as *terroir* and *garrigue* and *Grand Cru* and *cuvée*? The Glossary (pages 217–222) will help make sense of the standard wine vocabulary, so don't forget to turn to it as necessary.

WINESPEAK

A century ago, wine vocabulary was based on social class, with wines described as noble or well bred. The descriptors later shifted to terms based largely on gender—feminine, delicate, and soft as opposed to manly, muscular, and robust. It wasn't until the 1970s that comparisons to fruits, vegetables, and minerals came to the fore. This approach is more politically correct, but picking the right word remains a challenge. General terms like "floral" and "fruity" may sketch a wine's basic character but lack useful detail. Writerly terms like "crushed seashells" or "nutskins" can intimidate readers—or just make them laugh.

So that we don't get too nutskins ourselves, we've tried in this book to steer a middle course. For the classic "green apple" taste of Mosel Riesling, for example, we've kept that term, hoping most readers will find it familiar. Where a wine's flavor seems less specific, we've used less specific language, like "herbal" or "citrusy," which gets the idea across but leaves room for welcome interpretation. Coupled with each note's food recommendations, which everybody relates to because everybody eats, our descriptive approach should help readers come to each wine with enthusiasm, not bewilderment. (See also "'Barnyard' and Other Curious Terms" on page 162 and "So What's a Cru?" on page 186.)

Reading the Wine Descriptions

The descriptions of the wines recommended in *The Ultimate Wine Lover's Guide* follow the same format, and the sample entry shown here will familiarize you with it.

Note: While naming the wines also follows a set format, the names may not be exactly as they appear on the wine label. The aim is to give you all the words you or a wine merchant will need to identify the wine, with the key words set in capital letters.

1. Winery/Producer	**La Tunella**
2. Type of wine	**CABERNET FRANC**
3. Body and nutshell description	**Medium-bodied. Succulent and meaty on the palate.**
4. Description and food suggestion(s)	Vintner Livio Zorzettig's enticing Cabernet Franc smells of sweet herbs, tastes like ripe berries, and works with food as few other wines can. Vegetables, tomato-based dishes, and hearty pastas are perfect partners for this darkly sensuous Italian red. Drink it young.
5. Price	$12–14
6. Place of origin	*Friuli, Italy*
7. Importer	*Imported by William Grant*

1. Winery/Producer
It may be the boldest or the smallest name on the label, but this is the most important piece of information you need to identify a wine. It is the legal title of the estate or co-op or person who created the wine.

2. Type of wine
In Europe, wines are generally named for where they're from, such as Chianti, Bordeaux, or Rioja. In the United States and other countries, wines are most often named for the grape from which they're made, such as Cabernet, Chardonnay, or Riesling. (See also page 86.)

3. Body and nutshell description
The first boldface notation gives the impression of "weight" in a wine, whether full, medium, light, or somewhere in between. (Remember that a wine can be light-bodied, but still "full" of flavor.) The second boldface notation usually refers to mouthfeel, but mainly serves to make it easier to compare one wine to another within a price bracket.

4. Description and food suggestions

The description of the wine, which also often notes something of interest about the vineyard or winemaker, will vary in length. The food–and–wine suggestions are based on either regional tradition, our actual experience with the wines at the table, or both. Please remember that these suggestions are meant to be merely representative of the kinds of foods the wine pairs well with, not by any means the only appropriate choices. Your palate is the final judge.

5. Price

The prices given are ballpark figures. They are based on a standard retail mark–up (generally 50%) from known wholesale prices, confirmed by prices found in actual stores and on the Internet.

6. Place of origin

Where the wine was made. U.S. wines specify a region as well as a state when possible. If no region or town is given, it is because the grapes for the wine came from more than one place. For example, if half a wine's fruit came from Napa and the other half from Monterey, its appellation is simply "California," the common denominator for both appellations.

7. Importer

Foreign wines can have multiple importers on a national level, so although the importer we name is one source for the wine, it may or may not be the source in your area. For an explanation of how an importer might help you find a wine, see page 227.

Locating Wines

Your friendly local wine merchant is your best information source when you're unable to locate one of the wines described in *The Ultimate Wine Lover's Guide* (and any other publication, for that matter). As a backup, all of the North American wineries and overseas wine importers are listed, starting on pages 223 and 227, respectively. Also check out the special feature "Find That Wine!" on page 198.

If all your efforts come to naught, there's another tack to take: Describe the elusive wine's characteristics to your wine merchant and see what he or she recommends as a substitute. It's true that no two wines are identical, but you know your taste in wine. The time and effort you put into wine appreciation may reap unexpected rewards.

CHAPTER ONE

Primary Red Grapes

The high-flying grapes of red winedom are a multicultural bunch—among them, Cabernet Sauvignon and Merlot from France, Nebbiolo and Sangiovese from Italy, and Zinfandel, an honorary Californian by way of Eastern Europe.

What makes reds red? The inclusion of pigment-rich grape skins during the fermentation process. With rare exceptions, grape flesh is too pale to give wine even the blush of a rosé, much less the blackish red of a Syrah.

Cabernet Franc

This early-maturing black grape has been cultivated in France for more than five centuries. A major component in the wines of Bordeaux, it comes into its own in the Loire.

ABERNET FRANC is the gentle grandfather to Cabernet Sauvignon's red-blooded *bon vivant*, yielding wines with a bit less body and tannin. As a matter of fact, the grapes are indeed close relatives: Recent tests at the University of California at Davis found Cabernet Franc and Sauvignon Blanc to be Cabernet Sauvignon's ancestors—and whether because of cross-breeding or a happy accident of pollination is anyone's guess.

Native to France, Cabernet Franc is frequently blended with Cabernet Sauvignon and Merlot in the wines from the Médoc, Graves, and St. Émilion districts of Bordeaux. In the Loire Valley, however, Cab Franc stands alone, creating fruitier, lighter wines than those of Bordeaux and typically graced with aromas and flavors redolent of raspberries, bell peppers, and herbs.

Cabernet Franc–dominant wines have what is called in wine lingo "lively acidity"—a characteristic that works in their favor at the dinner table. Cab Francs are versatile across a spectrum of roasted meats, fatty fish like salmon and tuna, and vegetables. Yet despite their many charms, searching for quality Cabernet Francs from any country or region is no easy task. If a wine store stocks them at all, they are likely to be outnumbered ten to one by Cabernet Sauvignon.

Outside France, Cabernet Franc has long been grown in Italy, especially in the northeastern region of Friuli. In the United States, it is found in the cool, inland climates in which it thrives—mostly California's Napa and Sonoma valleys, the Pacific Northwest, and New York State.

Under $12

Caves des Vignerons
SAUMUR-CHAMPIGNY
Light-bodied.
Nicely fruity and juicy.
This "bistro red"—casual, inexpensive, and meant for immediate drinking—comes from a quality-minded cooperative of French growers. Serve it lightly chilled with appetizers or spicy fare. $6–8
Loire, France
Imported by House of Fine Wines

Jacky et Fabrice Gasnier
CHINON "Les Graves"
Light- to medium-bodied.
Soft yet lively, with a bright finish.
Hints of earthiness and cedar waft from this raspberryish wine, which has surprising length of flavor. It's a fine choice for herbed fish or greens. $10–12
Loire, France
Imported by Sussex

Mionetto
CABERNET DEL PIAVE
Medium-bodied. Succulent, fruity, and fairly intense.
The largest Prosecco maker in Italy also turns out food-friendly reds and whites, with this Cab Franc/Cab Sauv blend a prime example. Herby, berryish, and lively on the palate, it enhances the flavor of classic Mediterranean ingredients like olives, peppers, and tomatoes. It's also an excellent red to serve with fish. $10–12
Veneto, Italy
Imported by House of Burgundy

Domaine Saint Vincent
SAUMUR-CHAMPIGNY
"Les Trezellières"
Light- to medium-bodied.
Succulent and well balanced.
This Cab Franc is the red wine you imagine you'll sip while sitting in a café in Paris, perusing the newspaper and snacking on a baguette or omelet. $10–12
Loire, France
Imported by Winebow

Domaine du Roncée
CHINON
Light- to medium-bodied.
Vibrant, zesty, and full of fruit.
This reliable bargain Chinon sports red currants and cherries all over. It's all the more delightful with a light chill. Think cold cuts, ham sandwiches, and traditional or veggie pâtés. $10–12
Loire, France
Imported by Langdon Shiverick

$12 to $20

La Tunella
CABERNET FRANC
Medium-bodied. Succulent and meaty on the palate.
Vintner Livio Zorzettig's enticing Cabernet Franc smells of sweet herbs, tastes like ripe berries, and works with food as few other wines can. Vegetables, tomato-based dishes, and  hearty pastas are perfect partners for this darkly sensuous Italian red. Drink it young. $12–14
Friuli, Italy
Imported by William Grant

Domaine des Roches Neuves
SAUMUR-CHAMPIGNY
Medium-bodied. Rich and elegant, with a long finish.
The reverberating red fruits and earthiness of this wine are propelled forward by mouth-watering acidity. It's one of the most versatile food wines in the world, spanning the culinary map

from pork roasts to broiled fish, steak tartare to baked vegetables, roast chicken to chimichangas. The estate's fuller-bodied **"Terres Chaudes"** ($20+) is an unheralded masterpiece. $12–14
Loire, France
Imported by V.O.S.

Clos Roche Blanche
TOURAINE ROUGE
"Cabernet"
Medium- to full-bodied.
Big, dense, and mouthwatering.
Made 100% organically and shot through with black fruits and minerals, this is high drama for a Cab Franc. In  its first year in bottle, it's a vivid partner for herbed lamb and beef. After that, the wine starts to soften, the berries and jam emerge, and it becomes amazingly versatile with white meats, grilled fish, and vegetables. $13–15
Loire, France
Imported by Louis/Dressner

Pellegrini
CABERNET FRANC
Medium- to full-bodied.
Abundantly flavorful and finished with oak.
An impressively constructed red whose ample oak is usually matched by enough black cherry and blueberry fruit to back it up. Wines like this suggest the potential in Long Island for the production of world-class Cab Franc. Good, curranty wine for beef and lamb. $16–18
North Fork of Long Island, New York

Hagafen
CABERNET FRANC
Medium-bodied.
Fruity, firm, and kosher.
Though this kosher wine is loaded with tasty red cherry and cranberry fruit, it shows oak treatment that borders on the excessive in many vintages. Still, it's the best kosher Cab Franc on the market and an elegant partner at the Passover table with brisket and other traditional fare. $17–19
Napa

Charles Joguet
CHINON "Cuvée de la Cure"
Medium- to full-bodied. Rich, powerful, and often tannic.
This wine is an expression of its superbly situated vineyard, the small and essentially organic Clos de la Cure. The winery suggests keeping this violet-scented and raspberryish Chinon for a few years before drinking, and so do we. Pork loin pairs well with it, as do pâtés of duck or goose liver. $17–19
Loire, France
Imported by Kermit Lynch

Pierre Breton
BOURGUEIL "Les Galichets"
Medium-bodied. Vividly juicy and scintillating on the palate.
This completely organic wine is about as pure an expression of *terroir* as you'll find in the middle Loire. It's a serious wine for foodies, with mouth-watering acidity and pronounced fragrances of green tea, bell pepper, and raspberries. One of the few reds that can handle asparagus, it's also ideal for bell pepper and eggplant dishes. Pierre Breton makes several other wines, all worth trying. $18–20
Loire, France
Imported by Louis/Dressner

TWO SKY-HIGH ST. ÉMILIONS

HE BIRTH of your first child . . . your golden wedding anniversary . . . It takes either a very special occasion or a very fat wallet to enjoy **Château Cheval Blanc,** of the St. Émilion appellation in Bordeaux. The 2000, 1998, 1990, and 1982 vintages of this Cab Franc–dominant wine, blended with Merlot and a bit of Malbec, will set you back anywhere from $150 to $1,000.

Cheval Blanc's costliness is partly due to the fact that its annual production is much smaller than that of other Bordeaux wines, including Haut-Médoc's Château Lafite Rothschild. But it is its potential to age into the most exciting Cabernet Franc in the world that sends the price soaring. Cheval Blanc is good enough to drink right away, with scents of ripe black fruits, exotic Asian spices, minerals, herbs, and a hint of eucalyptus. But with bottle age it becomes a beguiling symphony of scents and flavors—magic in a bottle! At the table, it's a spectacular match with roasted leg of lamb.

Another premium St. Émilion is **Château Ausone,** with new releases costing around $400. Its dense black bramble fruits, barrage of violets and truffles, and cedary high notes are all pleasant, but it's the wine's unmistakable minerality that captivates. The best vintages, including 1996 and 2000, have a cellar potential of up to fifty years. A perfect partner? A stuffed veal roast. *Both wines imported by Diageo*

CHÂTEAU CHEVAL BLANC
Iᵉʳ Grand Cru Classé
1989
St Émilion Grand Cru
APPELLATION SAINT-ÉMILION GRAND CRU CONTROLÉE
Mis en bouteille au Château   13 % BY VOL.
Stᵉ CIVILE DU CHEVAL BLANC, Hᵗⁱᵉʳˢ FOURCAUD-LAUSSAC
PROPRIÉTAIRES A ST-ÉMILION (GIRONDE) FRANCE   750 ml
PRODUCE OF FRANCE

Olga Raffault
CHINON "Les Picasses"
Medium- to full-bodied. Rich, solid, and built for the long term.
For some tasters, the Olga Raffault estate represents the benchmark for Cabernet Franc in the Loire. Complex but tight in its youth, Les Picasses should be softened either by aging or by being splashed about in a decanter. Try it with lamb chops or aged goat cheeses. Also look for "La Poplinière" ($15–18), a delicate but stunning (and less costly) single-vineyard release. $18–20
Loire, France
Imported by Louis/Dressner

$20 to $40

Yannik Amirault
BOURGUEIL "Quartiers"
Medium-bodied. Savory, with beautiful concentration.
This wine comes from one of the great producers of the tiny Bourgueil appellation, which lies on the north bank of the Loire in the western part of the Touraine; its wines are typically more aromatic and tannic than those of nearby Chinon. Pure, fragrant raspberries are the theme of this Bourgueil, with subtle murmurings of sweet herbs, mint, and minerals. At the table, it's sheer elegance with steak au poivre. $23–25
Loire, France
Imported by Weygandt/Metzler

Philippe Alliet
CHINON "Vielles Vignes"
Medium- to full-bodied.
Intensely flavored, rich, and deep— and a big finish to boot.
Black fruits and roasted coffee run wild in this well-regarded French interpretation of Cab Franc. Because it's so vintage-sensitive, it isn't released in the U.S. every year. The wine is superb with grilled vegetables, meat-and-mushroom dishes, and anything gamey. Alliet's "Coteau de Noire" bottling ($28–32) is denser and benefits from cellaring. $24–26
Loire, France
Imported by Daniel Johnnes

Schneider Vineyards
CABERNET FRANC
Medium- to full-bodied.
Polished and fruity, with a zesty finish.
Bruce Schneider put New York State Cabernet Franc on the map the moment he started making it in 1994. His attractive version, blended with a small percentage of Merlot, is judiciously oaked and loaded with blueberry and sweet cedar flavor. A natural with Long Island duckling. $24–26
North Fork of Long Island, New York

Paumanok
CABERNET FRANC
Medium- to full-bodied.
Big and bold, with lots of oak.
Made in America and more Bordeaux than Loire, this richly put-together Cab Franc is especially tasty in the 2001 vintage. It's pricey for its type, but the quality is evident; anyone who likes good St. Émilion should enjoy this wine. Goes well with red meats, especially lamb. $28–30
North Fork of Long Island, New York

Cabernet Sauvignon

The best-known grape to millions of wine drinkers reigned for centuries in the heart of Bordeaux, then reinvented itself in the vineyards of California.

CABERNET SAUVIGNON began its storied ascent in the area called Bordeaux, on the banks of the Gironde and Garonne rivers in western France. The Romans planted the grape, the French nurtured a great wine from it, and the English shipped it to every far-flung port of their empire. But just what is it that makes Cabernet so perfect for winemaking?

When carefully tended in the right climate on gravelly, well-drained soil, the Cabernet grape can make wines of impressive body, dark color, high tannin, and deep flavors—predominantly black currant, cedar, and bell pepper. Blended with Merlot (which lends softness) and Cabernet Franc (which offers acidity), Bordeaux wines strike an ideal balance: They're rich and lengthy; they keep and develop further complexity with age; and they're exceptionally able to reflect the soil and environment in which they are grown—the quality known as *terroir*.

Until the 1970s, Cabernet Sauvignon's chief interpretation was this Bordeaux blend, the best examples of which came from the wealthy estates of the Médoc and Graves growing areas. Then, in California, winemakers discovered the next great stomping ground for Cabernet wines: the Napa Valley. Here the grape was vinified on its own, creating huge, powerhouse reds packed with sweet fruit and aged extensively in new oak barrels. A few vintners who decided to continue pursuing the Bordeaux–style blend also found success, coining the term "Meritage" for their opulent wines; these have since become some of the highest-priced wines in the world.

Happily, most Cabernet is not of this rarefied sort. Today's wine lovers find bottlings that cost under $20 (most ready to drink upon release)—and they come not only from California and France but from Australia, South America, and elsewhere. The best of these are fruity, balanced, and show the grape's classic flavors. In a few other cases, the wines achieve the kind of extraordinary quality and dizzying prices commanded by the top wines from Napa and Bordeaux, upholding Cabernet's unparalleled international reputation. For many collectors, "King Cab" remains the benchmark by which quality wine is judged.

Under $12

Carta Vieja
CABERNET SAUVIGNON
Light- to medium-bodied. Ripe, smooth, and true to the grape.
This Chilean find is an amazingly consistent bargain and is easily mistaken for a $15 red. Berry fruit abounds, with little or no oak in evidence. Pour a bit into whatever you're cooking and drink the rest with dinner. $4–6
Maule, Chile
Imported by Frederick Wildman

Château Tour de Goupin
BORDEAUX ROUGE
Light-bodied. A fruity, buoyant Bordeaux with a good dollop of Merlot.

This organically grown, cherry-scented sipper finishes with a pleasant, minerally tang. It's good company at cocktail parties with light appetizers. $8–10
Bordeaux
Imported by Baron François

Viña La Rosa
CABERNET SAUVIGNON/ MERLOT "La Palma"
Medium-bodied. Dry, elegant, and nicely textured on the tongue.
The style of this 60% Cab and 40% Merlot from Chile is more akin to Bordeaux than the New World. Coffee, earth, and savory dark fruit are its themes. A true bargain that goes well with fun fare like burgers, sandwiches, kebabs, and fajitas. $8–10
Rapel, Chile
Imported by Viña La Rosa

Château de Ribebon
BORDEAUX
Medium-bodied. Savory, with balanced fruit and a good dose of Cabernet Franc.
Wine lovers everywhere should be thankful that there are still wines like this left in Bordeaux. An exercise in elegance, it offers raspberries, herbs, and honest complexity for an affordable price. A great match for pâté, cold cuts, or stuffed mushrooms. $8–10
Bordeaux
Imported by Serge Doré

Castle Rock
CABERNET SAUVIGNON
Medium- to full-bodied.
Rich and polished on the palate.
This increasingly popular Napa Cabernet, dominated by black cherries and pipe tobacco, is surprisingly gutsy for the price. Fine with burgers but worthy of sirloin steaks. $10–12
Napa

Blackstone
CABERNET SAUVIGNON
Medium-bodied. Easy on the palate, with an oaky finish.
This is probably what most people are looking for in a California Cab. Sourced from vineyards halfway between San Francisco and Santa Barbara, it's a pleasing mix of cherries and milk-chocolatey oak. Try it with cheeseburgers, franks, or a meatloaf sandwich. $10–12
Monterey, California

Cartlidge & Browne
CABERNET SAUVIGNON
Medium- to full-bodied.
A classic California Cab.
Mocha notes from oak are balanced gracefully with lively, black currant flavor in a Cab that is better (and lower-priced) than

many of its western cousins. A terrific steak and grill red. $10–12
California

Villa Maria
CABERNET/MERLOT
Medium-bodied.
Savory, juicy, and light-handed.
New Zealand's cool-climate take on the traditional Bordeaux blend. Cedary, herby, red curranty flavors mesh well with herbed poultry and roasted vegetables. $11–13
Hawkes Bay, New Zealand
Imported by Vineyard Brands

$12 to $20

Powers
CABERNET SAUVIGNON
Medium-bodied. Well-balanced, smooth, and judiciously oaked.
Washington wines grow in near-desert conditions, which render the reds a bit more curranty and acidic than most California Cabs and Merlots. This example is a tasty partner to any grub with a good char, including grilled burgers and chops. The vineyard's high-end flagship "**Mercer Ranch**" ($18–20) ages well.
$12–14
Washington

Monterra
CABERNET SAUVIGNON
Medium-bodied. A particularly ripe, satiny wine that washes smoothly over the palate.
It's cherries, cherries, and more cherries in this Cabernet for Merlot drinkers. It needn't be drunk with food to be enjoyed, but simple chicken dishes, chops, and hard cheeses would find it a nice complement.
$12–14
Monterey, California

Dalton
CANAAN RED
Medium-bodied. A fruity, lip-smacking blend.
Cabernet Sauvignon, Merlot, and Shiraz form a unique trio in this Israeli kosher wine, a good choice for dishes with sweet or salty flavors—say, cabbage stuffed with raisins or peppery meats. The straight **Cabernet Sauvignon** ($26–28) offers a richer, drier style. $16–18
Galilee, Israel
Imported by Allied Importers

Pagor
CABERNET SAUVIGNON
Medium- to full-bodied. Great taste driven by fruit, not oak.
Exquisitely ripe black cherry and mocha flavors define Ed Pagor's Rolling Hills Vineyard boutique Cab (sometimes hard to find), with fruit sourced from the Temecula Valley. Great with highly seasoned meats. $16–18
South Coast, California

De Loach
CABERNET SAUVIGNON
"Estate"
Medium-bodied. Mellow yet mouthfilling, with tannins on the soft side.
Formerly labeled "Los Amigos," this is one of De Loach's most easily enjoyable wines. It's at its best after three or four years, and the '99 is spicy, cherryish,  and still drinking great. The pricier **O. F. S. Cab** ($28–30) is mostly just oakier. Try the basic estate wine with a skirt steak smothered in garlic and parsley. Yum! $16–18
Russian River, California

Alexander Valley Vineyards
CABERNET SAUVIGNON
Medium-bodied. Plump and friendly mouthfeel.

One of our favorite affordable Cabernets out of California

year after year, this wine features delicious cherry fruit with hints of mint and milk chocolate. For Mom's meatloaf or cheesy casseroles. $18–20
Alexander Valley, California

Cape Mentelle
CABERNET SAUVIGNON/MERLOT "Trinders"
Medium- to full-bodied. Well-rounded, fruity, and flavorful.
This popular red (60% Cabernet, 40% Merlot) comes from the estate that put Margaret River on the map. Intended for immediate enjoyment, it's a boatload of blackberries dusted with spearmint—a flavor profile typical of the appellation. It sings with minted lamb. $18–20
Margaret River, Western Australia
Imported by Clicquot

Bleasdale
CABERNET SAUVIGNON "Mulberry Tree"
Medium-bodied.
Sweetly ripe and satiny.
It seems this Down Under winery can't produce anything but fabulously jammy, minty red wines with explosive finishes—which is perfectly all right with us. Their Cab is particularly tasty when enjoyed with saucy, spicy fare like barbecue. $18–20
Langhorne Creek, South Australia
Imported by Southern Starz

Domaine Mosse
ANJOU ROUGE
Full-bodied. Dark, densely layered with flavor, and more savory than sweet.
This 100% Cabernet Sauvignon (unusual for a Loire wine) is full of ripe raspberry fruit, with pepper, moist earth, herbs, and licorice serving counterpoint. It's complex stuff—and frankly magnificent. One of the world's most "adult" lamb partners, it's also a good match for pepper steak, hearty stews, and stuffed green peppers. $18–20
Loire, France
Imported by World Wide Wine

Pheasant Ridge
CABERNET SAUVIGNON
Medium-bodied. Smooth, fleshy, and balanced on a dime.
This Cab leads the charge of quality red wines emerging out of the American Southwest. A touch gamey

and full of prunes and cherries, it's a cheeky, oaked New World–style wine that's a terrific pick for barbecue aficionados. Yee haw! $18–20
Lubbock, Texas

Pellegrini
CABERNET SAUVIGNON
Medium- to full-bodied. Dark, dense, and moderately tannic.
A carnivore's wine from Long Island, with black currants, mulberries, and tarry, smoky oak nuances coming through. A rolled pork roast would excel as a partner, as would a hickory-smoked rack of ribs. $18–20
North Fork of Long Island, New York

$20 to $40

Murphy-Goode
CABERNET SAUVIGNON
**Medium- to full-bodied.
Pleasant and polished, with a
ripe fruit core.**
Murphy-Goode has long been one
of the Alexander Valley's biggest
names, and their winemaking has
changed for the better. As of 2001,
the oak-like wines of yore were
replaced by those with less time
in wood, fabulously ripe fruit of
the maraschino cherry variety,
and reasonable alcohol levels.
Enjoyable young, this Cab brings
out the best in duck. $20–22
Alexander Valley, California

Tim Adams
CABERNET SAUVIGNON
**Full-bodied. Satiny, plush,
and multidimensional.**
A limited-production Australian
wine (and winemaker) with a
following. Aged in a combination
of French and American oak, it
surges with blackberry, blueberry,
and cocoa; in some years, it's
distinctly minty as well. Underpriced compared to its peers, and a
flashy match for barbecue. $20–22
*Clare Valley, South Australia
Imported by Orientate*

Philippe-Lorraine
CABERNET SAUVIGNON
**Medium- to full-bodied.
Elegant, subtle in its power,
and very dry at the finish.**
This extremely small-production
Napa Cabernet, with its earthy but
understated palate, is about as
close as California ever gets to the
Médoc. It's often a good bet in
modest vintages. Uncork, let
breathe, and serve with rack of
lamb, roasts, and even good old-
fashioned beef Wellington. $20–22
Napa

Devil's Lair
CABERNET BLEND
**Medium- to full-bodied.
Strong and firm, with seductive
and mouthfilling fruit.**
This Cabernet-dominant blend
from Western Australia varies
from year to year in its
proportion of Merlot, Cab Franc,
and Petit Verdot, but it's always
strapping, fruit-driven, and fun.
Deeply cut with black currant,
black cherry, and cappuccino
flavors, it's amazing with grilled
lamb chops or other meats bound
for the barbie. $24–27
*Margaret River, Western Australia
Imported by Southcorp*

Château de France
GRAVES
**Medium- to full-bodied.
Velvety and mouthfilling.**
The flavor of this rich, red
Bordeaux is layered with sweet
herbs, red currants, and cherries.
Excellent for drinking young,
it's good with mild meats like
brisket or braised short ribs.
The producer's **Le Bec En Sabot**
second label ($12–14) is an
outstanding value. $25–30
*Bordeaux
Imported by Bayfield*

Château Les Ormes de Pez
SAINT ESTÈPHE
**Medium- to full-bodied.
Tannic and meaty.**
This wine—typical of St. Estèphe
in its earthiness—remains one
of the best values in Bordeaux.
It's a treat for Francophiles and
anyone who likes
a hint of turf in a
wine. A hearty
companion to
charred steaks
and game.
$25–30
*Bordeaux
Imported by Diageo*

WHERE EAGLES DARE

It feels like the set for a John Ford western, but inside the old ranch house at Barnwood Vineyards, winemaker Eric Hickey is making some of California's tastiest Cabernet. Working from mountain vines perched 3,200 feet above the Cuyama Valley floor, he allows no chemical treatments and employs whole-berry fermentation to make bold, deep-fruited wines utterly distinct from his Santa Barbara neighbors'. **Barnwood Vineyards Cabernet Sauvignon** ($18–20) is forthright, berryish, and smooth—and a terrific value to boot. Hickey's superb deluxe blend of Cabernet, Merlot, and Syrah, called **Trio** ($24–26), is aged longer in oak and is more structured. Try the Cab with sliced duck in peppercorn sauce or anything off the grill; the Trio goes best with beef.

Château Les Barraillots
MARGAUX
Medium-bodied. Mouthfilling, with a clear expression of fruit.
With its savory array of black fruits, subtle violets in the nose, and complex earthiness, this is everything you could wish for in Margaux—and a natural partner for filet mignon. Foodies might like to try it with sautéed wild mushrooms drizzled with truffle oil. $25–30
Bordeaux
Imported by Bayfield

Best's Wines
CABERNET SAUVIGNON
"Great Western"
Full-bodied. Multiflavored and firmly textured.
Worthy of long-term cellaring, this blue-chip collectible Cabernet from the low-lying Grampian mountains of Victoria, Australia, represents great old-fashioned style. Its black currant fruit is topped by delectable layers of berry compote and bittersweet chocolate. Great for game. $30–35
Grampians, Victoria
Imported by Epicurean

Heitz Cellars
CABERNET SAUVIGNON
Medium-bodied.
Ripe-fruited and understated, yet meaty at the end.
Fans of this legendary estate mourn the loss of Heitz Cellars' formidable founder Joe Heitz, but classy Cabs are still made from his Napa properties. Enjoy the basic release with lean steaks and chops. The "Trailside" ($50 and up), with its endlessly deep palate and nose like a fresh pot of coffee, stands up well to crusty, dry-aged porterhouse. $35–40
Napa

Woodward Canyon
CABERNET SAUVIGNON
"Artist Series"
Full-bodied.
Black, burly, and dramatic.
Considered one of the foremost wineries in Washington, Rick Small's twenty-five-year-old estate turns out this great, shambling Kodiak bear of a wine year after year. Cellar it or serve it with something you just shot. $35–40
Walla Walla Valley, Washington

$40 to $60

Château Talbot
ST. JULIEN
Medium- to full-bodied.
A bit oaky when young, but soon
blossoms with sweet fruit and a
soft mouthfeel.
We love this estate for its extraordinary consistency and the
approachability of its wines.
Cherries, strawberries, milk
chocolate, and roses swirl through
the mouth in practically every
vintage. (For new wine lovers,
this is a great introduction to fine
Bordeaux.) Superb with short ribs
and roasts of pork or veal.
$40–45
Bordeaux
Imported by Diageo

Château Pontet–Canet
PAUILLAC
Very full-bodied.
Richly tannic, inky,
and built to last.
Not a wine for
wimps, Pontet-
Canet packs in as much black
fruit, stone-and-flint aromas, and
strong ripe tannin as possible.
Hot-weather vintages like '89 and
'96 take years to come around, so
we advise proceeding as follows:
a) Cellar the wine as long as
possible; b) decant it and let it
breathe for two hours or more;
and c) serve it with rare, fat-
marbled beef. $45–50
Bordeaux
Imported by Diageo

Bernardus
MARINUS
Full-bodied. Luxurious and full-
flavored, with a smooth finish.
Some vintages are better than
others, but overall this proprietary
blend of Cabernet and Merlot

from California's Central Coast
is elegant and delicious. Dense
plantings, tiny yields, and
Bordeaux-style vinification are
the secret of its success. Ready
to drink young with leg of lamb
and lean cuts of beef.
$45–50
Carmel, California

Cosentino
MERITAGE "The Poet"
Full-bodied. Deeply fruited and
opulent, especially when young.
In 1986, Mitch Cosentino's The
Poet became the first so-called
Meritage (Bordeaux-style blend)
in California.
About two-thirds
Cabernet, it's
formulated like a
Bordeaux yet
remains distinc-

tively Californian in its in-your-
face ripeness and drinkability.
Gratifying with double-thick pork
chops or steak in rich sauces. Also
look for the winery's less pricey
Crystal Valley line, which features
a decadent, cassislike Cabernet.
$45–50
Napa

Penley Estate
CABERNET SAUVIGNON
Very full-bodied. Complex,
densely layered, and structured.
Kym Tolley's deservedly famous
Cabernet, easily the best of its
class in Coonawarra, offers deep
veins of ferrous earth and black
fruit laced with ribbons of
caramelly French oak. Serve
with lamb, beef, or game hens
stuffed with porcini mushrooms.
$45–50
Coonawarra, South Australia
Imported by Old Bridge Cellars

Forman
CABERNET SAUVIGNON
Full-bodied. Rich and complex, like a fine Graves made on California soil.

Ric Forman, a pioneer Napa vintner, makes monumental Cabernets. They're generally plump and giving, with black currant, blackberries, minerals, and hints of cedar threaded intricately into the mix (shades of Château Haut-Brion). Worthy of a standing rib roast or a late-evening session with some aged farmhouse cheddar. $50–60
Napa

Clos du Marquis
ST. JULIEN
Full-bodied. Velvety on the palate and particularly ripe and expansive.

Crafted by the talented Michel Delon, this hedonistic Bordeaux leaves you smacking your lips from its sweet kirsch finish; you would also be hard-pressed to find a bad vintage. Glorious with prime rib but versatile with roast pork and poultry as well.
$50–60
Bordeaux
Imported by Diageo

Château Gruaud Larose
ST. JULIEN
Medium- to full-bodied. A suave wine with a long, perfumed finish.

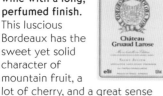

This luscious Bordeaux has the sweet yet solid character of mountain fruit, a lot of cherry, and a great sense of completeness. An exquisite partner for rare roast-beef.
$50–60
Bordeaux
Imported by Diageo

Over $60

Duckhorn
CABERNET SAUVIGNON
Medium- to full-bodied. Impressive, penetrating on the palate, and very black.

Founded by Dan and Margaret Duckhorn in 1976, Duckhorn Vineyards is one of California's perennial stars. Though best known for Merlot, the winery also produces an outstanding mineral-rich Cab, mostly allocated to restaurants. The wine should be cellared—but if you can't wait, let it breathe for two hours and enjoy with a Black Angus steak. $60–70
Napa

Darioush
CABERNET SAUVIGNON
Medium-bodied. Savory and elegantly understated.

This has to be the heaviest wine bottle in America. Yet for all the heavy packaging, Persian-American winemaker Darioush Khaledi crafts a surprisingly gentle Cab built not for power but for complexity and subtlety. (The 2000 was A+.) Let the wine breathe and serve it as a thoughtful complement to slow-cooked meats, mushrooms, root vegetables, or hearty casseroles. $60–70
Napa

Caymus
CABERNET SAUVIGNON
Full-bodied. A great big wine best enjoyed after cellaring.

Chuck Wagner's celebrity Cab is worthy of its reputation, but it's made in a very specific style. A distinctive prune, espresso, and smoky character is strapped in by a battery of strong tannins, challenging tasters who prefer

A MIDDLE EASTERN DELIGHT

In 1930, the estate of Château Musar was established just north of Beirut by the brave and irrepressible Gaston Hochar. His son Serge, a winemaker since 1959, continues the tradition. Undaunted by war, border disputes, and Syrian tanks parked in the vineyards, the estate continues to create a unique blend of Cabernet, Cinsault, and Syrah that combines the roastiness of the Rhône with the savor of left-bank Bordeaux. Medium-bodied **Château Musar Red** (around $40, though up to $100 for older vintages) is marvelously supple, subtly tannic, and usually mature at release (current release: '96). A knockout with food, it's a beautiful partner for game birds and aged crumbly cheeses. *Imported by Broadbent*

fruity reds. What to eat? The best steak you can find. Caymus's **"Special Select"** ($130–140) is even bigger, overpriced for most budgets, and harder to acquire. $70–100
Napa

Spring Mountain
CABERNET SAUVIGNON/MERLOT
"Miravalle–La Perla–Chevalier"
Full-bodied. Richly made, expertly balanced, and Bordeaux-like.
This Napa blend (75% Cabernet and 25% Merlot) comes from three historic adjoining estates on Spring Mountain resurrected in the early 1990s by Tom Ferrell. Made in minuscule quantity, it displays the intense blackberry aromas that seem to be the signature of this appellation, with chocolate, dark cherry, coffee, and earth nuances preceding a graceful finish. Though extra bottle-aging by the winery gives this Cab complexity, you also can cellar it for many years. Decant and serve with a stack of lamb chops or a filet mignon en croûte. $80–100
Napa

Château Lynch Bages
PAUILLAC
Very full-bodied. Consistently one of the deepest and densest Bordeaux.
This is an insider's Bordeaux— and a tremendous value even in "off" vintages. Look for the classic cedar aroma and the elusive

"dusty" quality detectable in Pauillac, along with sweet black fruit and rich cassis. Beef of any sort will do, but a rarest-of-rare grilled porterhouse is a spectacular choice. Lynch Bages's second label, **Haut–Bages Averous** ($32–35), is usually superb. $80–120
Bordeaux
Imported by Diageo

Château Léoville Barton
ST. JULIEN
Full-bodied. A weighty wine with impressive breadth of flavor.
This wine, with its intensely sweet fruit and liqueurlike richness, comes from what is generally considered one of the top ten estates in Bordeaux. Still, the 2000, albeit excellent, is a shock at $150 (surprisingly, older vintages can be found for almost

half that). Try the '95 or '96 with fatty beef cuts like rib eye. $90–120
Bordeaux
Imported by Diageo

Joseph Phelps
INSIGNIA
Full-bodied. A dense, lavish powerhouse of a wine.
This Cabernet-based blend from California pioneer winemaker Joe Phelps, with 10–15% Merlot and a spoonful of Cab Franc, is one of the premier American wines for collectors. It also needs to be cellared. Aromas of black currants, vanilla, and fruitcake follow through gorgeously on the palate. Steak spoken here. $100–125
Napa

Château Pichon Longueville Comtesse de Lalande
PAUILLAC
Full-bodied. Sensationally rich, complex, and almost creamy.
This Bordeaux is good in every vintage, but at its best in warm years when it becomes positively thick with flavors of black currant, milk chocolate, and espresso. The tannins give it gravitas but never knock you

flat. The overall effect is of velvet sliding over the tongue, capped off with a pleasing cigar-smoke nip. Serve with crown rack of lamb. $100–200
Bordeaux
Imported by Diageo

Château Haut-Brion
GRAVES
Full-bodied. Powerful, with a very Cabernet-driven palate.
Readily identifiable for its unique bouquet of dusty earth, flowers, and exotic Asian spice, Haut-Brion offers one of the purest expressions of *terroir* in the world. A must-have in any serious cellar, it's always interesting and often

sensational. Its sister wine, **La Mission de Haut-Brion** ($80–100), is sometimes flashier but remains the less important wine for collectors. Both partner well with firm, aged cheeses, but an old-fashioned holiday roast might be the most classic pairing of all. $150–300
Bordeaux
Imported by Diageo

FIRST AMONG FIRSTS

Given all the associations connoisseurs have with it, it is hard to find words to describe the legendary first-growth **Château Latour.** At $300 or considerably more, it cannot live up to its own hype (no wine could). Yet taken on its own terms, one can say that this very full-bodied Bordeaux reliably offers an opulent, show-stopping, luxurious glass of wine, virtually regardless of vintage or maturity; it invites the taster to concentrate hard and rewards the effort many times over; and it speaks eloquently of the place from which it comes. As such, we place it above its peers as our favorite Premier Cru Bordeaux. Serve it with good cheeses, pâté, or the simplest preparations of beef or lamb—the fewer distractions the better. *Imported by Diageo*

Gamay

Perhaps no wine grape is so identified with a particular place as Gamay, which succeeded in putting a rocky region of east central France on the map: Beaujolais.

WINE LOVERS can always depend on wines from Beaujolais to be light-bodied, fresh, fruity, low in alcohol and tannins, and pleasantly juicy—the perfect quaffing wine. Most of the other wines made from Gamay (full name Gamay à Jus Blanc) have never made as big a splash, though a few from the Loire, Auvergne, and Burgundy—of which Beaujolais is a part—stand out.

Until recently, it was thought that Gamay grew widely in California but, after DNA testing, the grapes known as Napa Gamay and Gamay Beaujolais proved to be different varieties altogether. For practical purposes, true Gamay is grown only in France.

Most of what Americans see from Beaujolais is called Beaujolais-Villages. These wines come from throughout the appellation, but the best are grown in the granite soils of the northern end of the region known as Haut-Beaujolais.

In Haut-Beaujolais, thirty-nine communes are entitled to the Beaujolais-Villages appellation, whereas ten communes just north, the Cru Beaujolais, are more prestigious and brand their wine with their own names: Brouilly, Chénas, Chiroubles, Côte de Brouilly, Fleurie, Juliénas, Morgon, Moulin-à-Vent, Régnié, and Saint-Amour. Connoisseurs enjoy debating their differences, but in general, Cru Beaujolais are deeper in flavor than the Villages wines and often bear a close resemblance to Pinot Noir.

Whatever their origins, wines made from Gamay are generally best drunk soon after bottling. The flavors most often attributed to the wines are strawberry, raspberry, and banana. The banana scent in Beaujolais comes from the cultured yeast used by many producers during vinification. Small artisanal producers often opt for natural yeast (also called wild or ambient yeast) because the resulting wine will reflect the local style and *terroir* more effectively.

Under $12

Pascal Chatelus
BEAUJOLAIS NOUVEAU
Light-bodied. Fantastically fruity and lively.
Consistently our favorite Nouveau every November, this small-production seasonal specialty jumps with aromas of red berries, taffy, bananas, and cherry cola. It's sheer fun with brunches, appetizers, spicy stuff, and salty snacks. $6–8
Beaujolais
Imported by Alain Junguenet

Domaine du Pavillon
CÔTE ROANNAISE
Light-bodied. Grapey, ebullient, and enticingly aromatic.
In good years, this 100% Gamay—sourced close to the head of the Loire River in central France—is everything you want in a light red: great fruit, sweet aromas, modest alcohol, and bright, juicy acids. It's a café wine ideal for quiches, omelets, and light sandwiches. $8–10
Loire, France
Imported by V.O.S.

Pierre et Paul Durdilly
BEAUJOLAIS
"Les Grandes Coasses"
Light- to medium-bodied. Meaty and mellow, with a long, plump finish.
This expertly balanced Beaujolais has tons of dark-tasting cherry flavors yet boasts a palate that avoids feeling heavy. The winery's **Beaujolais Nouveau** ($7–9) is invariably excellent as well. Great with chili or barbecue. $10–12
Beaujolais
Imported by North Berkeley

Château de la Salle
BEAUJOLAIS
Light-bodied. An extremely fruity and easy-to-sip kosher wine.
From Abarbanel, producer and importer of kosher wines, this version of France's classic quaffer mixes jam and cherry-soda flavors in soft, balanced harmony. Sip it lightly chilled at lunch or before supper with appetizers. $10–12
Beaujolais
Imported by Abarbanel

Clos Roche Blanche
TOURAINE ROUGE "Gamay"
Medium-bodied. As rich and "serious" as Gamay gets.
If it didn't sport that strawberry Gamay nose, you might mistake this wine for Cab Franc. It's a bold, dark, vibrant choice for fatty meats and creamy stews like paprikash. $11–13
Loire, France
Imported by Louis/Dressner

Vissoux
BEAUJOLAIS "Pierre Chermette"
Light-bodied. Beguilingly perfumed and delicate.
Produced organically in very small quantities by a maverick vintner who has a strictly back-to-basics approach to the production of Beaujolais, this is a lovely red to serve with hors d'oeuvres, light fish dishes, and sushi. The **"Vielles Vignes"** ($14–16) drinks like a great Cru Beaujolais. $11–13
Beaujolais
Imported by Weygandt/Metzler

Over $12

Jean-Paul Brun
BEAUJOLAIS "Terres Dorées"
Light-bodied. The driest Beaujolais and one of the purest.
Uncompromising organic production, sourcing from vines

BEAUJOLAIS NOUVEAU

*W*HETHER YOUR HEART races when you see the posters that go up in wine shops each November trumpeting *"Le Beaujolais Nouveau est arrivé!"* or you merely marvel at the marketing genius of the French, there's no denying that Beaujolais Nouveau is the beloved tipple of millions of wine lovers. Perennially delicious, this fresh and fruity wine is bottled fast, then rushed to markets around the world via airfreight to arrive in wine stores on the third Thursday in November—its official first sale date.

And what leads up to this yearly ritual? Each year in the days immediately following harvest, many wineries in France's Beaujolais region select a portion of their production to undergo a special type of fermentation called carbonic maceration, which captures the freshness, charm, and grapiness of the year's Gamay fruit. And, unlike aged wines, Nouveau is released when only seven to nine weeks old. (Tradition says it was the wine made for the vineyard workers to enjoy at the end of the harvest.)

Because it's an uncomplicated wine meant to be consumed in the first six months after release, Nouveau's appeal is universal. So, come November, plan a visit to your local wine merchant to pick up a few bottles and join the fun.

Price Note: Beaujolais Nouveau that is shipped by air to arrive on the third Thursday in November is typically priced around $9 or $10 per bottle. A week or two thereafter, boat shipments arrive in retail shops and the bottle price drops a bit. The most universally available Beaujolais Nouveau is made by George Duboeuf, but many other fine examples are its equal or better.

over forty years old, and a shockingly dry palate of complicated earth and mineral tones make this perhaps the most "adult" Beaujolais. A highly traditional choice for escargots and steak tartare. $12–15
Beaujolais
Imported by Louis/Dressner

Thierry Puzelat
LE P'TIT TANNIQUE COULE BIEN
Light- to medium-bodied.
Pungent and complex.
Defiantly organic winemaking by Thierry Puzelat, the younger of the two brothers who run the family estate in the Loire, turns out, as one might

expect, a totally different kind of Gamay: earthy and *sauvage*, with aromas driven by sour cherry and barnyard (see page 162). What a wine for mustardy meats and sausages! $13–15
Loire, France
Imported by Louis/Dressner

Domaine de Peyra
CÔTES D'AUVERGNE
"Vielles Vignes"
Light- to medium-bodied. Rustic and full-flavored yet surprisingly gentle.
Some bottles of this fruity, floral, fascinating wine (100% Gamay grown at the headwaters of the Loire in central France), show a light haze because the wine is organically produced and unfiltered. But don't worry: Lightly chilled, it makes a perfect foil for flavorful fare—everything from Szechuan noodles to pungent cheeses to seafood gumbo. $14–16
Auvergne, France
Imported by World Wide Wine

Domaine du Clos du Fief
JULIÉNAS
Light- to medium-bodied. Fresh-tasting, balanced, and layered with flavor.

Michel Tête's elegant Cru Beaujolais from his small estate in Juliénas is full of fresh berries and minerals. It's a traditional charcuterie partner but is just as good with poultry and vegetables. Tete's **Beaujolais–Villages** ($10–12) is equally classy and reliable. $14–16
Beaujolais
Imported by Louis/Dressner

Château de Pizay
MORGON
Medium-bodied. Concentrated fruit that's bold in the nose and on the palate.
A consistently fine Cru Beaujolais, with black plum and berry fruit packed into its buoyant, balanced frame. The estate's **Régnié** ($13–15) is just

as good, and its **Beaujolais** ($9–11) is a bargain. Both the Morgon and Régnié make especially fine partners for ham and saucy, salty meats. $13–15
Beaujolais
Imported by Martin Scott

André Rampon
RÉGNIÉ
Light-bodied. Fragrant, silky, and exquisitely delicate.
This wine stands above even its Cru Beaujolais contemporaries. With a modest 12% alcohol, it's redolent of fresh cherries, it's true to its *terroir*, and it's about as graceful as red wine ever gets—in a word, perfect. You'd be hard-pressed to imagine a better red wine for fish. $16–18
Beaujolais
Imported by David Bowler

Henry Marionnet
TOURAINE ROUGE
"Premiere Vendange"
Medium-bodied. Intensely aromatic, with amazing depth of flavor and a long, complex finish.
Perhaps the greatest Gamay we've ever tasted. Imagine a Beaujolais reduced to its essence, shot through with the minerals of the Loire Valley soils. It's completely organic, less than 12% alcohol, and has no added sugar or sulfites— just wild blackberry and boysenberry fruit and the "funky" quality that wine drinkers either love or hate. Bring on the sausages, pâtés, and sweetbreads. $18–20
Beaujolais
Imported by Weygandt/Metzler

Grenache

The primary grape of the wines of Châteauneuf-du-Pape,
Grenache is most often used in blends—the reason
it's one of the most widely planted vines in the world.

*I*F WINE GRAPES got report cards, Grenache would get an
A for "gets along well with others," lending, as it does, strength
and sweet fruit to thousands of international blends. But on
its own, its grade slips to B− because the wines made from it are
frequently overburdened with alcohol. The 100% Grenaches among the
wines we've chosen here are the impressive exceptions.

A hot-weather variety, Grenache thrives throughout southern
France and Spain (where it is called Garnacha), Morocco, and other sunstruck climes. In France, it is often blended with Syrah, Mourvèdre, and
Carignan, a group that wine writers call "the usual suspects." In Spain, it
partners with the Tempranillo grape or shines on its own in the formidable red wines of Priorat. Italy joins the growers' club with Guarnaccia

on the isle of Ischia and Canonau in
Sicily. But Grenache's spiritual home is
France's Southern Rhône, where it
heads a gang of thirteen grape varieties
in the wines of Châteauneuf-du-Pape
and its neighboring appellations.
Whenever you buy a bottle of red Côtes
du Rhône, what you're most
likely getting is a blended wine based
on Grenache.

Other interpretations include the
inexpensive jug wines of France's
Languedoc and California's Central
Valley, tongue-tingling rosés from all
over, and some intense late-harvest sweet wines (see pages 208–215).

Growers in Australia and California have taken a liking to the grape
and some produce 100% Grenaches. But without the addition of other
varieties for balance, Grenache's alcohol and tannin remain a bit of a
problem. As a result, those who want a stand-alone wine will usually do
better with a Shiraz/Syrah from either place.

Under $12

Campo de Borja
BORSAO RED
Medium-bodied.
Sweetly ripe
and fun to drink.

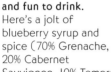

Here's a jolt of
blueberry syrup and
spice (70% Grenache,
20% Cabernet
Sauvignon, 10% Tempranillo)
that borders on outright sweetness in warm vintages. It's a
great choice for pizza with the
works or an overstuffed burrito.
$6–7
Campo de Borja, Spain
Imported by Tempranillo

Bodegas y Viñedos del Jalon
VIÑA ALARBA
Medium-bodied.
Ripe and mouthfilling.
This 100% old-vines Grenache,
grown south of Rioja, is whole-
berry fermented to accentuate
the fruit. Bursting with roasty
red cherries and sweet coffee
flavors, it's a treat not only with
Spanish rice and beans but also
with pepperoni pizza, burgers,
and meatier Chinese dishes.
$6–8
Calatayud, Spain
Imported by Tempranillo

Bodegas Sucesores de Mañuel Piguer
CARIÑENA "Lelia"
Medium-bodied. A cherry bomb.
Here's a very fruity Garnacha
from northern Spain—a red to
party hearty with. Or go native
at the table with chorizo, mole,
or pimientos. $6–8
Cariñena, Spain
Imported by Frontier

Domaine des Jougla
SAINT CHINIAN
"Cuvée Tradition"
Medium- to full-bodied.
Opulently ripe and pungent—
a "peasant red."
This meaty blend of Grenache,
Syrah, and Mourvèdre is a good
choice for wine lovers who
enjoy a little funk in their reds.
A great partner for sausages,
raw milk cheeses, and
traditional French country fare.
$10–12
Languedoc, France
Imported by Baron François

Vinicola del Priorat
PRIORAT "Ónix"
Medium- to full-bodied.
Thick, sweet, and rustic.
A 100% Grenache that could
almost pass as dessert in most
vintages, this purple wine is a
big cherry-berry fruit bomb.
It cries out for hearty fare
like barbecue or thick-cut fried
pork chops. $10–12
Priorat, Spain
Imported by Tempranillo

$12 to $20

Château de Pech-Redon
COTEAUX DE LANGUEDOC
"La Clape"
Medium- to full-bodied.
Big, earthy, and opaque.
Black as Texas crude, this rustic
red is made from 50% Grenache,
30% Syrah, and 20% Cinsault.
Its barnyardy aromas may not
be for everyone, but this wine's
the real deal from southern
France—the kind the locals
drink with peppery meats,
country pâté, charcuterie, and
hearty stews. $12–14
Languedoc, France
Imported by House of Burgundy

Château du Trignon
CÔTES DU RHÔNE
Medium-bodied. The quintessential Côtes du Rhône— dry, dark, spicy, and satisfying.
This blend of Grenache, Syrah, and Mourvèdre is a super value in every single vintage.
Teeming with black cherries, licorice, and

black currants—and usually slightly tinged with oak—it's terrific with barbecued meats or burgers topped with a thick slice of smoked cheese. $12–14
Rhône, France
Imported by Kermit Lynch

Domaine l'Ameillaud
CAIRANNE
Medium- to full-bodied. Hearty and satisfying, with bold, spicy flavor.
This big Côtes du Rhône Villages smells as if someone tipped the contents of a whole pepper shaker into the fermenting vat. It's also one of the best consistent values on the market. A winner with meat stews of any sort. $12–15
Rhône, France
Imported by Daniel Johnnes

Domaine de Fontenille
CÔTES DU LUBERON
Medium-bodied. Starts gently, then fills the mouth with enticing flavors.
This smoky dark wine from Provence (half Grenache, half Syrah) is redolent of *garrigue*, the aromatic mix of lavender, turf, and herbs that perfumes the local countryside. Try it with sausages and peppers, chicken Provençal, or pepper jack cheese. $13–15
Rhône, France
Imported by Weygandt/Metzler

Buil & Giné
PRIORAT "Giné Giné"
Full-bodied. Rustic, with a distinct impression of sweetness.
This Grenache/Carignan blend tastes like a molasses fruitcake studded with figs and cherries. It's too syrupy for some and a delirious pleasure for others—but whatever your taste, you'll do well to have some sweet glazed ham or barbecue on hand when you open the bottle. $16–18
Catalonia, Spain
Imported by Think Global

Joän d'Anguera
MONTSANT "La Planella"
Full-bodied. Very dark and satiny.
Montsant, formerly part of the Priorat appellation, is home to

---

GOOD-VALUE CÔTES DU RHÔNES
From the Rhône Valley in southern France, **Domaine Les Grands Bois Côtes du Rhône** ($11–13) is a reasonably priced red that's complex, savory, dry, and elegant. Its flavor? Roasted fruit accented by earthiness. When drunk young, it's lovely with roast chicken or picnic foods. Another bargain Côtes du Rhône from the same estate, **"Cuvée Gabrielle"** ($16–18), is supple, sweetly ripe, and teeming with strawberries—a great fondue wine. The estate's deluxe bottlings, **"Cuvée Mireille"** and **"Cuvée Maximilien"** ($18–$22), are superb examples of Rhône *terroir* and outclass many pricier wines we've tasted. Both are worthy of your finest roasts, ragouts, and ribs.
Imported by Weygandt/Metzler

huge, sun-roasted reds based on Grenache and Carignan. Case in point: this overwhelmingly luscious, barrel-aged, 100% Grenache. Its cassis-syrup finish is irresistible with fruit-sauced roasts of pork or duck. $17–19
Catalonia, Spain
Imported by De Maison

Domaine Alary
CAIRANNE
Medium-bodied. Solid, savory, and lengthy.
This unfiltered blend of 85% Grenache and 15% Syrah boasts the classic Rhône roster of tarry, herby, smoky nuances and packs them snugly into every corner of your palate. It's a surefire partner for Provençal ragouts and smoky cheeses. Also look for this estate's **"La Grange Daniel,"** a super $10–12 *vin de pays*, and **"La Brunote"** ($20+), beautifully crafted and full-blooded. $17–19
Rhône, France
Imported by Weygandt/Metzler

Domaine Chaume–Arnaud
VINSOBRES
Medium-bodied. Succulent, graceful, and silky-soft on the palate.
There's an elegance and balance in this blend (Grenache, Carignan, Cinsault, Syrah, and Mourvèdre) that recalls Burgundy more than the Rhône. Its soft berry fruit, allspice, and earth flavors work nicely with winter vegetables and white meats. $18–20
Rhône, France
Imported by Daniel Johnnes

Domaine Le Mas de Collines
GIGONDAS
Medium- to full-bodied. Extremely elegant, with deep fruit and great complexity.
This wine is late-released, so current vintages tend to be about four years old. It's worth the wait: The first blast out of the glass is ripe plum fruit, followed by an alluring mélange of dried strawberries, sage, and sweet earth. This is a deluxe dinner red at a more-than-fair price. Enjoy it with stuffed pork, veal, or poultry. $18–20
Rhône, France
Imported by Bayfield

$20 to $40

Domaine Bressy Masson
RASTEAU "Cuvée Paul Émile"
Full-bodied. A concentrated wine for people who like it "chewy."
A blend of 70% Grenache from hundred-year-old vines, 20% Syrah, and 10% Mourvèdre. A defiant non-sipper, it demands the richest and fattiest of birds, beef, and game. If you want something gentler with more fruit, try **La Souco d'Or** ($18–23) or the estate's regular bottling, **Rasteau–Villages** ($14–16). $20–24
Rhône, France
Imported by Daniel Johnnes

Alvaro Palacios
PRIORAT "Les Terrasses"
Medium- to full-bodied. Subtle for Priorat—drier, more elegant, and almost Bordeaux-like.
Young Alvaro Palacios has conquered Catalonia with his wines from Priorat, a hotbed of "big reds" eighty-five miles southwest of Barcelona. This isn't his most expensive or famous Priorat, but it is splendidly

OLD VINES, FINE WINE

Châteauneuf-du-Papes bear the mark of distinction, but **Domaine des Pères de l'Église "Le Calice de St. Pierre"** stands out among its peers: It consists of 85% Grenache (90+ year-old vines), 3% Syrah, 2% Mourvèdre, and a 10% field blend of over 100-year-old vines. One of the great wines of the Rhône, it's medium-bodied, graceful yet complex, and priced at a surprising $35–40. The 2000 vintage, the first under the estate's current winemaker, was the breakthrough, and '01 was even better. The wine has all the bacon, wood smoke, and roasted fruit you could wish for, couched in a gentle mouthfeel; its long, fruit-driven finish is barely brushed with tannins. Cellar it or serve with pâtés and terrines, delicate game hens, a glazed ham, or even a hearty salad of romaine hearts, walnuts, and blue cheese. *Imported by Weygandt/Metzler*

balanced, subtle, and complex, with soft but lasting tannins and a knockout palate of figs, earth, and tobacco. Enjoy it with slow-cooked meats, a filet mignon wrapped in bacon, or a platter of Spanish cheeses and thinly sliced *jamón ibérico,* the prized cured ham of Spain. $25–30
Catalonia, Spain
Imported by Rare Wine

Clos du Mont-Olivet
CHÂTEAUNEUF-DU-PAPE
Medium- to full-bodied.
Classic Châteauneuf of fine strength and depth.
Sourced from old vines (75% Grenache), devoid of new oak, and unsparing of tannin, this is about as traditional as Châteauneuf gets. It is fragrant and almost musky, with red fruit, incense, and wood spice notes. Stick to top vintages like 2000, then bring out the rare roast beef. Try the estate's **Côtes du Rhône "Monteuil La Levade"** ($10+) for everyday sipping. $30–35
Rhône, France
Imported by North Berkeley

Bonny Doon
LE CIGARE VOLANT
Medium-bodied.
Surprisingly light on its feet for such a richly flavored wine.
Randall Grahm, the winemaker-cum-philosopher of Santa Cruz, steals wine lovers' hearts every vintage with his California tribute to Châteauneuf-du-Pape. Poised, welcoming, and elegant, it offers baked earth and spices to spare, a suave fig-and-cherry center, and subtle tannins. Ideally a duck wine but not bad with a Thanksgiving turkey. For kicks, try Grahm's juicy, fruity **Clos de Gilroy** ($12–14). $30–35
California

Domaine le Sang des Cailloux
VACQUEYRAS
Very full-bodied. Thick in the mouth, with layers of flavor and a velvety finish.
Widely accepted as the finest wine of its appellation, this red drinks as forcefully as the domaine's name ("blood of the stones") suggests. Rife with aromas of roasted meats, espresso, and dark-and-sensuous cassis syrup, it seems almost

made-to-order for fatty birds with crispy skin and a good dollop of hot Dijon mustard. $30–35
Rhône, France
Imported by Kermit Lynch

Laderas de Pinoso
ALICANTE "El Sequé"
Very full-bodied.
Sheer power and class, with an incredibly lengthy finish.
This old-vines Grenache, from an estate owned by the legendary Artadi family of Rioja, is similar to Priorat but seems drier and more Rhônelike. An impressive wine, it sports bacony, leathery, and complex iron-and-mineral aromas. Cellar it or serve with a rack of lamb or roasted meats of any kind—the more garlicky, the better. Also look for **Laderas de El Sequé** ($12–14), the estate's superb second label. $35–40
Valencia, Spain
Imported by European Cellars

Charles Melton
NINE POPES
Very full-bodied. What Australians do best: huge power wedded to thick, delicious fruit.
A 70% Grenache from ancient vines blended with Shiraz and Mourvèdre and aged fifteen months in French and American oak. The finished wine's nuances of pepper, chocolate, and leather are very attractive, but it's mostly the mouth-flooding fruit you're paying for. You could cellar this wine, but we like drinking it young with delectables like sauce-slathered baby back ribs. $35–40
Barossa Valley, South Australia
Imported by Commonwealth

Over $40

Le Bosquet des Papes
CHÂTEAUNEUF-DU-PAPE
Medium- to full-bodied.
A plush, cellarable wine.
This definitive Châteauneuf, from the husband-and-wife winemakers the Boirons, has enormous appeal, with liqueurlike richness and Sunday-breakfast aromas of strong coffee, mixed-berry jam, and sizzling bacon. It's a strong choice for grilled and smoked meats, hard cheeses, and good old-fashioned beef Stroganoff. Some tasters prefer **"Cuvée Grenache"** ($26–28), the 100% Grenache release. $40–45
Rhône, France
Imported by Alain Junguenet

Rotllan Torra
PRIORAT "Amadís"
Very full-bodied.
Dark, sensuous, and tannic.
This is the flagship cuvée of a young winery housed in an ancient monastery. Winemakers Jordy and Albert Rotllan make wine from 100% Grenache and age it in barrel and bottle for several years. The result is a powerful mingling of raisins, chocolate, coffee, smoked meat, and sensuous black cherries at the finish. It goes best with the richest fare: game birds, sausages, winter stews, or chateaubriand with Béarnaise sauce. Don't overlook their juicy, vigorous second label wine, **Selleccio**—at $15, a true bargain! $50–60
Catalonia, Spain
Imported by De Maison

Merlot

In California, this European blending grape came on like gangbusters in the 1980s. Today it's the basis for one of America's best-selling wines.

F AMERICANS were waiting for a red counterpart to Chardonnay—the gentle-natured white of low acidity, soft structure, and responsiveness to oak treatment—they found it in Merlot. "Smooth" is the adjective most often used to encapsulate Merlot's appeal, and a less complex wine such as this has its place as a nice 'n' easy sipper. With food, however, it often falls short because of its low acidity and invariably heavy oak treatment.

Merlot's runaway success has much to do with timing. It came along just as Americans were becoming more interested in red wine, then rapidly became so popular that American producers could barely keep up with the demand.

Across the Atlantic, Merlot is Cabernet Sauvignon's partner in the traditional blends of Bordeaux, where it lends softness and, in some cases, additional fruit (it ripens sooner in the vineyard than Cabernet). Where Cabernet likes rocky soils with good drainage and warm weather, Merlot prefers clay soils and cooler weather—at least in Pomerol and St. Émilion, where many of the world's best Merlot-dominant wines are produced. There's also plenty of Merlot coming from Italy, although some American palates find it a little too earthy and herby. No such reservations are likely to apply to the Merlots of South America—particularly those from Chile, which offers rich, simple versions at bargain prices.

In this country, states north, south, east, and west have joined California in the rush to produce Merlot, with Washington and New York leading the pack. As a result, many valuable old vines of heirloom varieties—Zinfandel chief among them—have been ripped out. As Merlot's popularity wanes, it will be interesting to see what will happen to all these newly planted vines. Will they, too, be replaced? Or will American vintners, faced with economic need, return to Merlot for its original use—as the perfect blending grape?

Note: A second or third wine rarely crops up in the following recommendations because Merlot makers usually stick to the basic varietal.

Under $12

Reserve St. Martin
MERLOT
**Light- to medium-bodied.
A juicy red with a smooth,
easy-sipping character.**
This French Merlot has a touch
of spice and lots of fruit—mostly
plums and fresh figs. A fine
cocktail-party wine or picnic
partner. $6–7
Languedoc, France
Imported by Pasternak

Pierre Jean
MERLOT
**Light- to medium-bodied.
Simple and fruity.**
Red berries are the theme of this
pleasing cocktail-style Merlot.
Have a glass when you get home
late from a hard day at the office
and a second glass with the pizza
you order later. $6–7
Languedoc, France
Imported by House of Fine Wines

Aresti
MERLOT "Montemar"
Medium-bodied. Big, bold style.
A surprisingly inexpensive Merlot
from the heart of Chilean wine
country—the Curico Valley in
Maule. Its bargain price, plus the
intriguing flavors of cocoa and
roasted coffee, make this wine a
winner. It's terrific for all things
grilled—especially burgers loaded
with cheese and bacon. $7–8
Maule, Chile
Imported by Broadbent

Domaine de la Patience
MERLOT "Cuvée St. Guilhem"
**Medium-bodied. Surprising heft
at a low price.**
A rustic, satisfying red table wine
from vineyards on the Gard River
between the French cities of
Nîmes and Avignon. Flavors of
black fruits and earth seem
highly concentrated, and the
winemaker goes easy on the oak.
Good just on its own, this wine is
also rich enough for meats. $8–10
Languedoc, France
Imported by World Wide Wine

McGuigan Brothers
MERLOT "Black Label"
**Medium-bodied. A quaffing wine
with plenty of fruit and no oak.**
This Aussie Merlot is the kind of
wine you pray they're pouring by
the glass at your corner bar and
grill. Easy to drink, no hard edges,
and blissfully unoaked—just pure,
honest cherry fruit. A versatile
wine with pub grub, and fruity
enough for even the spiciest
Buffalo chicken wings. $7–9
Hunter Valley, New South Wales
Imported by Winebow

AN AMAZING CHILEAN BARGAIN
How and why the Carta Vieja estate turns out such delicious wines selling
for as little as $4 remains a mystery. Then again, maybe it's because this
winery in Chile's Maule Valley has been owned and operated by the del
Pedregal family for seven generations. A textbook case of practice makes
perfect? Easily the peer of any $10–15 Bordeaux, the medium-bodied **Carta
Vieja Merlot** ($4–5) has cherries and plums to spare. It's a Merlot that's
plump, smooth, and perfectly balanced—and with terrific mouthfeel in the
bargain. Serve it at your next party, either with the appetizers or as a base
for sangria. *Imported by Frederick Wildman*

Petit Chapeau
MERLOT
Medium-bodied.
Soft and round in the mouth, with ripe fruit in good vintages.
Selected and "made to spec" for New York's celebrity sommelier Daniel Johnnes, this Merlot hits the bull's-eye with its spiced red cherry fruit and food-friendly balance. Pour it at your next pizza party or backyard barbecue. $9–10
Languedoc, France
Imported by Daniel Johnnes

Château Les Tuileries
BORDEAUX
Light- to medium-bodied. A zesty, bright-fruited cocktail red.
This Bordeaux hits the shelves early each year and is often gone by the end of summer. Ripe, soft, and easy to drink, it's good served as a predinner apéritif, alongside cold cuts and grilled meats, or with game hens stuffed with herby wild rice. $9–10
Bordeaux
Imported by International Gourmet

Hahn Estates
MERLOT
Medium-bodied. Supple, fruity, and noticeably oaked.
It's easy to see why this cool climate Merlot, with its simple, pleasing palate of red berries and wood, is so popular. It's as good for sipping as it is alongside the likes of fried chicken or spicy catfish fillets. $10–12
Monterey, California

Bogle Vineyards
MERLOT
Medium-bodied. A good, fleshy style that's smooth and satisfying.
After twenty years in California, the reliable Bogle winery produces one of the smoothest and tastiest Merlots out there. Burgers and fried chicken are pleasant partners, but any Merlot lover could enjoy this wine on its own. $10–12
Monterey, California

Guilhem Durand
MERLOT
Medium- to full-bodied.
A gutsy red with smooth balance and concentration.
For fans of big French reds who don't want to pay a big price. Dark chocolate, smoke, and black currant rule the palate in a wine with an emphasis on ripeness and a pleasantly strong aftertaste. Great with lamb couscous, chops, cheeses, cold cuts, and sausage. $11–13
Languedoc, France
Imported by Weygandt/Metzler

Waterstone
MERLOT
Medium-bodied. Medium fruit, medium tannins, medium price.
This California Merlot is one of the surest red wine values around. Hints of spiciness and malt nicely complement the very soft core of fruit. Sip it on its own, with takeout chicken, or with simple luncheon fare. $11–13
California

$12 to $20

Cartlidge & Browne
MERLOT
Medium-bodied. Classic California Merlot—only better and bigger than most.
Tony Cartlidge has long been a reliable source for value wines (his Manzanita Canyon line is a hit with supermarket shoppers,

CALIFORNIAN AND KOSHER

The Baron Herzog Winery makes some of the most consistently high-quality bargain reds and whites in the world—and kosher in every sense of the word. The fruit for **Baron Herzog Merlot** ($11–13) is sometimes sourced from Bordeaux, sometimes from California. Either way, the finished wine is easy to enjoy, with a lush taste of red fruits and modest hints of sweet tobacco. At the table, it's a classic chicken casserole and pot roast partner.

Headed by master winemaker Peter Stern, the winery combines a forward-looking California attitude with the strict kosher supervision accorded its Merlots, Chardonnays, Cabs, and other California varietals.

and rightly so). We like his premium Merlot, which features figs and cherries and an aftertaste of vanilla oak. It's an honest, no-nonsense red with a burger. $12–14
California

Ternhaven Cellars
MERLOT
Medium-bodied. Smooth, fruit-forward, and even chillable.
Here's an artfully made New York State Merlot from the Wesley Hall vineyard in Cutchogue, Long Island. Its refreshing cranberry/cherry style of fruit and modest alcohol lend it a summertime feel, so pack it in your picnic basket or quaff it at your next barbecue. $12–14
North Fork of Long Island, New York

Scarbolo
MERLOT
Medium- to full-bodied. Strong, savory, and dry.
Italy's interpretation of Merlot tends to be earthier and a little edgier than the oaky American version—so, while this is an absolutely elegant, well-turned wine from an esteemed estate, it's not for everyone. In any case, it definitely wants food. Think baked pastas, roast chicken, and prosciutto. $12–14
Friuli, Italy
Imported by Domaine Select

Señorio de Sarria
MERLOT "Viñedo No. 4"
Medium-bodied. Silky-soft and incredibly fruity—an atypical Spanish red.
Cherries, cherries, cherries! The sweetness, succulence, and powerful

fruit of this Spanish wine are the perfect foil for salty Smithfield ham and dishes peppered with chilies. $13–15
Navarra, Spain
Imported by Spain Wine Collection

Château Penin
BORDEAUX SUPÉRIEUR
**Medium-bodied.
Soft and seductive.**
No secret recipe here: just a mouthful of cherryish, satiny-textured Merlot beefed up with a little Cabernet in a perfectly balanced composition. What's not to like? Superb with *steak frites* (garlicky hanger steak with shoestring fries) or a savory mushroom tart. $13–14
Bordeaux
Imported by Bayfield

Coturri
MERLOT "Workingman's"
Full-bodied. An organic
red-cherry mélange.
Crafted by one of California's
best winemakers, this rigorously
organic, turbo-driven Merlot is
halfway to kirsch yet has an
almost completely dry finish. At
the table, it goes well with fall
and winter dishes like roast
turkey and acorn squash.
Occasionally, the estate also
releases pricier Merlots from
neighboring vineyards—**Maclise**
($25–28) and **Feingold** ($50+),
hedonistic wines with Portlike
finishes. $16–18
California

Château La Fleur Plaisance
ST. ÉMILION Grand Cru
Medium-bodied. A gentle wine
that lingers on the palate.
This is an extremely elegant and
refined Bordeaux, showing
textbook aromatics; think black
cherries dusted with cocoa. Early
twentieth-century wine writers
(and the French) would call it
"feminine." Surprisingly, the
estate's second label from
Montagne–St. Émilion ($10–12)
is often the heartier wine, but
coarser. Pair both with London
broil smothered in mushrooms.
$18–20
Bordeaux
Imported by Bayfield

Château Grand Pey Lescours
ST. ÉMILION Grand Cru
Medium-bodied.
A traditional Bordeaux—
very dry and succulent.
The aromas of this
wine suggest a
comforting,
congenial
gentlemen's club:
Cigar box, wood
smoke, and soft

leather accent a basic palate of
sun-dried cherries. Better still, all
of an excellent wine's building
blocks are firmly in place. Enjoy
it with a steak with Bordelaise
sauce and quietly contemplate
the lost pleasures of the Gilded
Age. $18–20
Bordeaux
Imported by Bayfield

Clos La Chance
MERLOT
Medium- to full-bodied.
A sleek, graceful style with
multidimensional flavors.
Excellent acidity propels the
flavors in this California blend
(85% Merlot and a little Cabernet
Franc, Petite Sirah, and Cabernet
Sauvignon) which range from
cherry, mulberry, and plum to a
whiff of graham cracker. Our
choice for chicken potpie,
double-crème cheeses, and
burgers with the works. $18–20
Central Coast, California

Casa Lapostolle
MERLOT "Cuvée Alexandre"
Medium- to full-bodied.
A deep, sensuously textured
wine with a powerful finish.
From a Chilean estate renowned
for both value and quality. With
help from Bordeaux oenologist
Michel Rolland and a fine
selection of fifty-year-old vines,
Lapostolle produces a modern
Merlot that delivers nice black
cherry fruit backed by secondary
flavors of coffee and soil that
remain recognizably Chilean.
Serve it with marinated flank
steaks or broiled portobello
mushrooms. $18–21
Colchagua, Chile
Imported by Moët Hennessy

$20 to $40

Montes
MERLOT "Alpha"
Full-bodied. A powerful Chilean red that responds well to cellaring.
Somewhere between the lean French Merlots and the fat, oaky American ones stands this "gaucho wine" redolent of beef, tar, campfire smoke, and coffee. Montes Alpha, as it's known, will impress anyone who likes big reds. (In fact, we prefer it to the "Alpha M," which is three times the price.) Have it as the cattle barons do, with barbecued brisket and links with red beans on the side. $20–23
Santa Cruz, Chile
Imported by TGIC

Château Garraud
LALANDE DE POMEROL
Medium-bodied.
Well concentrated and silky.
Here's a Merlot-filled Bordeaux graced with a dollop of Cabernet Franc. Hand-harvesting, small yields, and precise attention to detail  make this wine impressive—yet it remains largely unknown. It's a perfectly balanced pleasure as cherry, berry, and sweet tobacco flavors come to the fore. Try it with savory foods like pâté, hard cheeses, oniony bean dishes, and herb-dusted roasted root vegetables. $20–25
Bordeaux
Imported by Bayfield

Clos Pegase
MERLOT
"Mitsuko's Vineyard"
Medium-bodied. Creamy and lavish in the mouth, with judicious oaking.
This wine from cool clay vineyards is aged twenty months in new French barrels. The owner was apprently trained in Bordeaux—but if the definitive premium California Merlot were picked out, this would probably be it. Suave, forward, and driven by the butterscotch and vanilla flavors of oak, it's a rich drink to enjoy with chops or Wisconsin cheddar. $23–25
Carneros, California

Katnook Estate
MERLOT
Medium-bodied. A subtle, expertly balanced wine.
This small Australian producer makes a complex, sophisticated wine expressive of the rich red soils of Coonawarra. It's also aromatically assertive, with scents of red plums, mushrooms, and mocha. Fine older vintages like '98 and '99 are still on the market. A special wine for a Sunday roast with mushroom gravy. $24–28
Coonawarra, South Australia
Imported by Wingara

Penley Estate
MERLOT
Medium- to full-bodied.
Suave and deeply sensuous.
Australian Kym Tolley's midsize winery in Coonawarra makes terrific wines across the board, with extravagantly ripe fruit and the judicious use of French oak in the Merlot. Serve alongside barbecued beef or pulled pork. $28–30
Coonawarra, South Australia
Imported by Old Bridge Cellars

GRADE-A WINE FROM WALLA WALLA

The benchmark Washington red may be **L'Ecole No. 41 Merlot** ($33–35). The family-owned winery that makes this full-bodied, dense, thick-textured (and cellarable) wine is housed in a turn-of-the-century schoolhouse in the village of Frenchtown, in District No. 41.

Deeply extracted, barrel-aged for a year and a half, and sourced from fruit purchased across the Yakima and Columbia valleys, this Merlot is clearly an effort to cram as much black cherry flavor as possible into a bottle. Serve it with grilled red meats or duck in cherry sauce.

Mietz
MERLOT
Medium- to full-bodied. Plush and sumptuous in the mouth, with sweet fruit that lasts.
Keith and Nancy Mietz source amazing Merlots every year from a little vineyard they planted in the Russian River valley near Chalk Hill in 1981. They emphasize fruit over oak and manage to capture plenty of fresh blueberries and black cherries in a sensuous style. Veal, pork, and baby back ribs all excel, as do foods with sweet sauces; this Merlot is also a tried-and-true Thanksgiving wine. $28–30
Sonoma

Havens
MERLOT "Reserve"
Medium- to full-bodied. A big, barrel-influenced, well-muscled style.
Some of the best Merlot in California is made by Michael Havens. His '97 and '99 were stellar, but any vintage is worth tasting. Intelligently blended with about 6% Cabernet Franc and packed with meaty roasted fruit, sweet herbs, and oak, this is a red-meat wine par excellence. Try it with a beef stew or whole duck stuffed with wild rice and prunes. Havens also makes a hearty Syrah and an interesting Albariño. $30–35
Carneros, California

Over $40

Newton
MERLOT "Epic"
Full-bodied. This behemoth in a bottle has ample oak and an intoxicating texture.
Since the early '90s, proprietor Peter Newton and his wife Su Hua have made some of the most sought-after Merlots in California. The wines are fermented with natural yeasts and bottled unfiltered and unfined. Flavors of jet-black espresso and kirsch emerge with lots of swirling, so allow for plenty of breathing time. Some suggest cellaring, but we prefer this wine when it's young— especially if there's a nicely marbled roast beef or mustardy leg of lamb waiting. $50–65
Napa

Pepper Bridge
MERLOT
Medium- to full-bodied. Bordeaux-like, with spicy, savory character.
This phenomenal Merlot is made by the former winemaker at Heitz Cellars in Napa. The wine is earthy, herbal, and eucalyptus-scented, with sweet red currant and plum fruit and the smoky/roasted finish typical of Washington *terroir*. A Merlot for foodies, it's great served

---

A FRENCH HIGH–FLIER

In France's Bordeaux region, the Pomerol appellation's 1,900 acres are planted mostly with Merlot, which adores the gravelly clay soils. The medium- to full-bodied **Château Petit Village** ($70–120) reflects the appellation's high elevation with extra helpings of sun-ripened fruit and firm tannins. Traditionally, this blend (80% Merlot, 10% Cabernet Sauvignon, 10% Cab Franc) is fairly austere, and those used to fruit-forward American reds may not like it. But if you crave minerality in your wines and enjoy the more high-toned flavors detected in Pomerol—tobacco, cedar, red currant, and licorice—then you'll make room for this Bordeaux in your cellar. Serve with a roasted game bird like quail, lean cuts of beef, or that funky English classic, steak–and–kidney pie. *Imported by Diageo*

---

with minted lamb, stuffed peppers, or a salad of sliced flank steak and mixed greens.
$50–60
Walla Walla, Washington

Le Petit Cheval
ST. ÉMILION **Grand Cru**
Medium- to full-bodied. Supple and often luxuriant in texture, with tremendous, vibrant fruit.
This Merlot/Cabernet Franc second label of famed Cheval Blanc unfolds like a Japanese fan with flavors of dried cherries, caramel, cocoa, violets, and sweet pipe tobacco. One gets the idea that no corners are cut at this estate, even for the second-label wine. Serve with rare roast beef or a rack of lamb.
$85–90
Bordeaux
Imported by Diageo

Clos l'Église
POMEROL
Medium- to full-bodied. Creamy, almost liqueurlike in good vintages, and cellarable.
This is one of the jewels of the Pomerol appellation, with sweet tobacco and soft mocha/ chocolate nuances in evidence. Strangely, prices are all over the map. The recently released 2000 commands an untenable $300, so look instead for the perfectly good '99 (around $100) or the superb '95 and '96 vintages— inexplicably still available at $30–40. Slow-roasted meats and hearty beef or lamb casseroles are great with this wine, but short ribs would be perfection.
$30–300
Bordeaux
Imported by Diageo

Nebbiolo

Grown almost exclusively on the slopes of the Piedmont region of Italy, this storied black grape gave the world the powerful wines of Barolo and Barbaresco.

*N*EBBIOLO is to Italy what Cabernet Sauvignon is to France: the noblest grape. Its realm is the Piedmont, literally the "foothills" of the Alps, where *nebbia* (Italian for fog) floats over the vineyards. There the grape is known by various regional names, among them Spanna, Gattinara, Ghemme, and Carema—all yielding rustic wines of wildly varying quality—and the finer Nebbiolo d'Alba, capable of gorgeous fragrance and elegance. But it is in the steep Langhe hills of southwestern Piedmont that Nebbiolo's most renowned (and expensive) wines are produced: Barolo, from the village for which it is named and ten nearby small towns; and Barbaresco, from Barbaresco and two other tiny villages.

Both of these wines are 100% Nebbiolo and offer complex, alluring aromas and flavors often described as tar, roses, licorice, prunes, figs, chocolate, truffles, leather, and espresso—the last with its distinctive hint of bitterness. High-alcohol, high-acid Barolo and Barbaresco, extremely tannic when young, are wines that need serious cellaring.

What's the difference between the two? Conventional wisdom calls Barolo more powerful and long-lived, Barbaresco a bit more approachable. But the debate that rages is not between regions but between styles. The "traditionalists," led by vintners like Bruno Giacosa and Giuseppe Mascarello, choose to make tannic, long-lived wines that often require up to twenty years in bottle. "Modernists" like Aldo Conterno, Piero Busso, and Barbaresco's legendary Angelo Gaja use shorter fermentations, new French oak, and other methods to make deeper, fruit-driven, earlier-maturing wines. Both styles can succeed, and which style one prefers is strictly a matter of taste.

Few growers outside the Piedmont grow Nebbiolo, and then mostly for using in blends. California growers have experimented with Nebbiolo-based wines, but with mixed results at best. It seems that this ancient grape is one that prefers to stick close to home.

$12 to $20

Ferrando
CAVANESE ROSSO
Medium-bodied. A vigorous Piedmontese cocktail.
Half Nebbiolo and half Barbera, this quirky wine is hard to stop sipping—especially with food. We love its cherry-berry fragrance and succulent acidity with red sauces, sun-dried tomatoes, grilled fare, or even a whole stuffed fish.
$13–14
Piedmont, Italy
Imported by Rosenthal

Rainoldi
ROSSO DI VALTELLINA
Medium-bodied. Vividly fruity and juicy—almost sweet.
With all that lively blackberry fruit and the magenta-purple gleam in the glass, you'd think this wine was Barbera or Zinfandel, not Nebbiolo. And, like Barbera, it's versatile with food—especially spicy tomato sauces.
$14–16
Lombardy, Italy
Imported by Opici

Antichi Vigneti di Cantalupo
COLLINE NOVARESE
"Agamium"
Medium-bodied. Aromatically complex, with juicy acidity and a long finish.
From the northernmost vineyards in the Piedmont, this pretty wine eschews the hard, vigorous style of Barolo, focusing instead on lush red fruits capped by scents of roses and leather. It's a deluxe choice for pizza with black olives or pasta puttanesca. Also try the single-vineyard **Ghemme** ($40–50), for which this producer is famed.
$17–20
Piedmont, Italy
Imported by Polaner

$20 to $40

Marziano & Enrico Abbona
NEBBIOLO D'ALBA
Medium- to full-bodied. Unusually ripe-fruited for Nebbiolo, with incredibly forceful aromatics.
This wine easily beats half the Barolos out there for sheer flavor and enjoyment. The elusive tar, spice, and dried flower notes of the Nebbiolo grape come through in spades, but the chunk of fruit at the wine's core makes it downright sexy. Hovering around 14% alcohol, yet never out of balance, it's perfect drunk young with rich polentas, pork medallions, or a mushroom risotto.
$20–25
Piedmont, Italy
Imported by Polaner

Valdinera
NEBBIOLO D'ALBA "Sontuoso"
Medium- to full-bodied. This deep, sleek wine lives up to its name—"sumptuous."
Only about 1,600 cases of this gorgeous wine are made each year, sourced from the sunniest part of the Careglio family vineyards in Alba. Sweet for Nebbiolo, cherryish, leathery in scent, and deeply satisfying, it outdoes  itself with osso buco and other slowly braised meats. $20–25
Piedmont, Italy
Imported by John Given

Antoniolo
NEBBIOLO "Juvenia"
Full-bodied. Plush and velvety with opulent aromas.
What's not to like in this wine? It's fresher tasting than Barolo,

cheaper than Barbaresco, and fruitier than Spanna. Serve with steak or lamb. $20–22
Piedmont, Italy
Imported by Marc de Grazia

Aurelio Settimo
NEBBIOLO LANGHE
Medium-bodied. Ripe and earthy, with a succulent finish.
Tiziana Settimo, daughter of Aurelio, makes a superb, highly traditional **Rocche Barolo** ($50–55), but she also puts aside a small amount of Nebbiolo juice from Langhe each year for earlier release. Her Nebbiolo Langhe is aged for a year, then bottled for drinking in the near term. This earthy, berryish, super value is perfect for slow-cooked meats or polenta with mushrooms. $21–23
Piedmont, Italy
Imported by Verdoni

Antario
BAROLO "Vignetto Castelleto"
Medium-bodied. Particularly supple for Barolo.
Easy on the palate and pocketbook alike, this gentle, pleasing Barolo has a sexy floral nose and a faint licoricey note in the back. Enjoy it with white meats or stuffed cannelloni. $30–32
Piedmont, Italy
Imported by House of Burgundy

$40 to $60

Piero Busso
BARBARESCO "Vigna Borgese"
Medium- to full-bodied. Needs breathing, but comes around with a wallop of fruit.
Barbaresco can sometimes be harsh, but not Busso's. Pure blackberries dominate the palate, augmented by the classic violety, earthy aromas of Nebbiolo. This suave, "modern" style from

organically grown fruit is quite versatile with red meats, baked pastas, grilled kebabs, and roasted winter vegetables. $40–48
Piedmont, Italy
Imported by Vias

Monchiero Carbone
BAROLO "Montanello"
Medium-bodied. Exotically fragrant, forward, and richly layered.
Marco Monchiero makes several exciting Nebbiolos, including a bargain **Roero Superiore** ($20), but the vineyard-designated Montanello is his flagship wine. An hour's breathing time will release its entrancing violet and lavender aromas. Serve with well-marbled beef or lamb—and if you can find truffle-infused olive oil at your market, use it! $40–50
Piedmont, Italy
Imported by Matt Brothers

Roagna
BARBARESCO
Medium- to full-bodied. Seductively fragrant, lasting, and balanced.
Father-and-son winemakers Giovanni and Alfredo Roagna own twelve of the fourteen acres of I Paglieri, one of the Piedmont's blue-chip vineyards. From here they make a wonderful tar- and violet-scented Barbaresco that continuously evolves on the palate. Serve with braised beef shanks or a chunk of good Parmesan cheese. The Roagnas' more opulent "Pajé" ($50) is excellent with game meats like venison and smoked duck breast. $40–42
Piedmont, Italy
Imported by Summa Vitis

Schiavenza
BAROLO
Medium- to full-bodied. Traditional, artisanal, and utterly satisfying.
This wine, which was sold from the cellar door until the 1999 made it to

America, is pure *terroir* wedded to delicious, suave red fruit. A fragrant wine for fragrant, savory cuisine like game birds and osso buco Milanese. The single vineyard **"Vigneto Prapo"** ($65–75) is magnificent but needs time. $50–60
Piedmont, Italy
Imported by Weygandt/Metzler

Over $60

Aldo Conterno
BAROLO "Colonnello"
Full-bodied. Strong in every aspect, from tannin to alcohol to flavor intensity—the Barolo *ne plus ultra.*
The legendary Aldo Conterno isn't averse to experimentation, but his Barolos remain among the most consistently opulent wines made in Italy. His crown jewel, the Riserva **Granbussia** ($120–700), is mostly seen at auctions—but the more approachable Colonnello is the one we know best. Aged three years in oak casks and one in the bottle, it is typically grand: deeply saturated in color, hugely tannic, and replete with scents of tar, tea

rose, leather, and dark chocolate. Cellar this and all of Conterno's Barolos patiently and unveil them with game meats or rare roasted lamb. $100–150
Piedmont, Italy
Imported by Vias

Bruno Giacosa
BAROLO "Falletto"
Medium- to full-bodied. Lengthily aged, concentrated, and capped by lasting tannins.
Founded in 1890, Giacosa is on everybody's shortlist of Piedmont's finest and most traditional estates. Their Falletto is highly scented with baked earth, truffles, and tar (there's even a hint of saltiness in some vintages), and the tannins are unapologetically hard. It needs some time: The '95 and '96 (two great Barolo vintages of the '90s) are still slow to come around. Give it ten years or so in a cool cellar, then decant and serve with thinly sliced rare beef, braciola, and the freshest Parmigiano-Reggiano you can find. $150–200+
Piedmont, Italy
Imported by Winebow/ Leonardo LoCascio

Pinot Noir

*Though notoriously pricey and vintage-sensitive,
Pinot Noir remains the wine most prized by chefs and collectors,
especially in the great growths of Burgundy.*

*T*HEY CALL IT the "heartbreak grape," and for good reason. Pinot Noir is prone to disease and mutation in the vineyard while demanding a lengthy, cool growing season. It's picky about its soils, terribly susceptible to vintage variation, and because of its high acidity, it makes particularly thin, tart wines when poorly handled. Worse, as the wine matures, it's sheer luck whether it turns out magnificent or falls to pieces. As a result, this prima donna is expensive—and if it isn't, it's usually because the wine has been blended with other grapes or chemically altered. Yet the grape still manages to give the world one of its greatest wines: Burgundy.

In the Grand Cru vineyards of Burgundy's Côte d'Or (Golden Slope), a thirty-mile strip of hills south of Dijon, Pinot yields its riches. Its wines turn silken and deep, behaving, in the best examples, like a liquid distillate of the landscape. The large, balloonlike Burgundy wineglass was designed to capture as much of the bewitching bouquet as possible. Burgundies from the northern part of the region tend to taste and smell of black fruits, while Southern Burgundies and most American Pinots tend toward red ones like strawberry and cranberry. With age, earthy, gamey, and woodsy flavors crop up. Specific flavors and aromas detected by tasters could fill a small book, with truffles, perfume, mushrooms, cedar, cigar, and worn leather often noted.

The coupling of complexity and good acidity makes Pinot Noir one of the most versatile food wines in the world. It spans the divide between vegetables, meat, and fish, encouraging the diner to explore one wine throughout multiple courses of a meal.

Where, beyond Burgundy, is Pinot grown? In Europe, close by in the Loire and in northern Italy, Germany, Austria, and Switzerland. In America, Oregon's Willamette Valley and California's Russian River, Carneros, and Central Coast are the major growing areas, with wines from New York State offering noteworthy variations in style. Some nice Pinots also come from the Southern Hemisphere, though, like elsewhere, getting the best out of the grape is touch and go.

Under $12

HRM Rex Goliath
PINOT NOIR "Free Range"
Light- to medium-bodied. Graceful, varietally true Pinot that costs less than ten bucks.

This soft, velvety, cherryish wine is easy to spot, thanks to the forty-seven-pound rooster on the label. A fine intro to Pinot, it's tasty with sandwiches, salty snacks, and picnic fare. $7–9
Central Coast, California

William Cole
PINOT NOIR
Light-bodied. Bright and simple— a sipping wine with a juicy edge.

Sometimes you have to go below the equator to find tasty, affordable Pinot Noir. This Chilean version has a straightforward red berry character tinged with earth, plus lovely balance for a meal centered on veggies or quiche. $10–12
Casablanca, Chile
Imported by Metropolis

Wyatt
PINOT NOIR
Light- to medium-bodied. A wonderful sipping wine with a gentle, juicy finish.

This wine is "made to order" for a New York importer but is available nationally. Sourced mainly from the Carneros appellation, it is not only well balanced but has delicious cherry pie flavors and a touch of earth. It's a choice bargain red for vegetarian dishes and chicken dishes alike. $11–13
California

$12 to $20

Carneros Creek
PINOT NOIR
"Fleur de Carneros"
Light-bodied. Delicate, yet very fruity.

We feel this inexpensive bottling from Carneros Creek is their best wine—maybe the reason it sells out every year. The wine's flavors of tea roses and strawberries seem to float across the palate, leaving a sense of refreshment. A perfect red for light fish or paella. $12–15
Carneros, California

Avila
PINOT NOIR
Medium-bodied. Hearty style with dark fruit and plentiful oak.

This rich, sappy, earth- and plum-scented Pinot from warmer climes has something almost Zinfandel-like about it. An attractive red for hearty fare like roast chicken, charcuterie, and bean dishes. $14–16
San Luis Obispo, California

Bouchaine
PINOT NOIR
"Buchli Station"
Medium-bodied. Plump, fleshy, soft, and mouthwatering— hard not to like.

A lovely red, dripping with cherries and pomegranate, Buchli Station made its debut in 2002, perhaps as a casual, less-expensive alternative to this winery's premium offerings. Thanks to its lack of earthiness or heaviness, it's a jubilant match for trendy pan-Asian and pan-Latino dishes. Its colorful Americana label also makes it a

fitting Thanksgiving wine. $14–16
Napa

Ramsay
PINOT NOIR
Medium-bodied. Soft and easy to drink and persistent in the finish.
Vintage after vintage, Kent Rasmussen's second label is an elegant, high-quality Pinot. Caramelly oak is balanced nicely with the wine's floral aromas and ripe cherry and cranberry flavors. Delicious with vegetables au gratin, just fruity enough for spicy Chinese and Thai, yummy with fried chicken, and fun to drink in general. $15–17
California

Zenith Vineyards
PINOT NOIR
Light- to medium-bodied. A juicy, jazzy, winningly sweet Pinot.
This delightful sipping wine (name your red fruit and it's here) hails from the north half of New Zealand's South Island. On the culinary front, the terrific acidity that's making your mouth water turns this Pinot into a fantastic seafood and vegetable partner. A dish like poached salmon on a bed of braised leeks in cream is the perfect match. Need we say more? Yes: Give it a bit of a chill. $15–17
Marlborough, New Zealand
Imported by Southern Starz

Guy Chaumont
CÔTE CHALONNAISE
Light-bodied. A delicate Pinot that's organically grown and vinted.
Pure, sweet strawberries on the nose and featherweight character will make this wine appealing to anyone who likes light reds. It chills well and is a delicate adornment to fish, vegetables, and pasta primavera. $15–17
Burgundy
Imported by Organic Vintages

Warwick Valley Winery
PINOT NOIR
Light-bodied. A dry, graceful, slightly earthy wine for foodies.
Amidst the apple trees and old windmills of upstate New York, the father-son team at Warwick crafts a tasty, pale-hued Pinot whose blanched cherry fruit and fine balance will enhance all kinds of food. Pour it slightly chilled with hors d'oeuvres, pasta with mushrooms, light white meats, fish steaks, rice pilaf, or even sushi. $15–18
Hudson Valley, New York

Henri Bourgeois
SANCERRE ROUGE
"Le Porte de Cailloux"
Light-bodied. A tad deeper than rosé, high in natural acidity, and beautifully delicate.
We call this slender willow of a wine the Gwyneth Paltrow of Pinots. While it's highly vintage-sensitive (like all Sancerre reds), the quality-conscious co-op that makes it does admirably well each year and excels in good vintages such as 1997 and 2002. Cranberries and watermelon are the dominant flavors. A lithe choice for sushi and ceviche. $15–17
Loire Valley, France
Imported by Monsieur Touton

Willamette Valley Vineyards
PINOT NOIR "Whole Cluster"
Light-bodied. Ebulliently fruity, bordering on sweet.
This distinctive Pinot is fruitier than the norm because its whole berry fermentation method emulates that of Beaujolais winemakers. In some vintages it's like biting into fresh strawberries. Great for spicy fare, sausages, saucy Caribbean/Indian/Mexican, or a Cantonese sweet 'n' sour fish. $15–18
Oregon

Nicolas Potel
BOURGOGNE "Vielles Vignes"
Light- to medium-bodied.
Fabulously perfumed, silky,
and easy to sip.
Although famed *négociant* Nicolas
Potel makes great Pommards and
Clos Vougeots, we're frankly most
excited about his least-expensive
wine—the basic, everyday
Bourgogne. Its gentle cherry-
and tobacco-scented palate makes
it an amicable predinner sipper,
great with creamy soups,
appetizers, or light poultry. $16–18
Burgundy
Imported by Frederick Wildman

Piper's Brook
PINOT NOIR "Ninth Island"
Light- to medium-bodied.
A sassy, fun style with cleanly
expressed fruit.
Tasmanian Pinot Noir? It turns out
that Australia's island state has a
cool, hilly, wet climate at its north
end, perfect for growing the
world's most fickle grape. Piper's
Brook is one of the "big three"
wineries in what's called Tassie.
Enjoy this rosy, berryish, balanced
Pinot with all kinds of vegetarian
dishes, omelets, and fish. $16–19
Tasmania, Australia
Imported by Lauber

Saint Clair
PINOT NOIR "Doctor's Creek"
Medium-bodied. Fruity, plump
and pleasing.
This is a red wine from New
Zealand's white wine country, so
it's no surprise to find juiciness
and the kind of pure, clean fruit
that cool-climate winemaking
engenders. A touch of oak adds
depth and a sweet vanilla note.
Try it with all manner of grilled fare
or mild meat dishes like pot roast.
$18–20
Marlborough, New Zealand
Imported by Lauber

Domaine Joseph Voillot
BOURGOGNE
Medium-bodied. Salaciously ripe
and tempting.
This fabulous hillside Pinot from
seventy-year-old vines is nurtured
by Jean-Pierre Charlot, who
taught viticulture at Beaune's
Lycée Viticole. (Profound Volnays
and Pommards emanate from this
domaine, too.) Start a leisurely
lunch with the pungent, berryish
Bourgogne and a slab of pâté.
$18–20
Burgundy
Imported by Vintage '59

Marc Brocot
MARSANNAY "Les Échezeaux"
Light- to medium-bodied.
Ripe, flavorsome Pinot with
gentle, pleasing mouthfeel.
This is a bargain Burgundy—
lighter in some years, richer in
others, but always fragrant and
abundantly fruity. At its best,
Asian spices, licorice, and hints
of real Burgundian *goût de terroir*
(taste of the earth) come
through. It pairs gracefully
with salmon, swordfish, and
light poultry.
$18–20
Burgundy
Imported by V.O.S.

Didier Fornerol
CÔTE DE NUITS-VILLAGES
Light- to medium-bodied.
Delicate, piquant Pinot with
an elegantly balanced finish.
Here's a pleasing café wine
with a black fruit theme nicely
nuanced by mineral traces, olives,
and black pepper. Serve it with
smoked cold cuts, cheese toast,
or grilled vegetables.
$18–22
Burgundy
Imported by Daniel Johnnes

Claude Maréchal
BOURGOGNE "Cuvée Gravel"
Medium-bodied. Pure, plush
fruit all the way. Fun!
A very pure Pinot for pleasure-seekers—very strawberryish,
with terrific
staying power.
Drink it young
with vividly
flavored fare
like pineapple
ham, Hunan dishes, and Cajun/
Creole. The more structured
Savigny-Les-Beaune "Vielles
Vignes" ($30+) is also superb,
but works better with subtler
savory fare like stuffed mush-rooms and garlicky hanger steak.
$18–22
Burgundy
Imported by Louis/Dressner

Millbrook
PINOT NOIR
Light- to medium-bodied.
A fruit-driven, pleasing Pinot
with a juicy finish.
This is probably the best-known
Pinot from the East Coast, made
under the sure hand of wine-maker John Graziano since 1985.
Briefly aged in French oak, it's a
tasty mouthful of cherries, cocoa,
and strawberries that wants a
little food. Try it with grilled or
broiled fish steaks. $19–22
Hudson Valley, New York

$20 to $40

Ransom
PINOT NOIR "Barrel Select"
Medium-bodied. Earthy and dry,
with honest Pinot character.
Tad Seestadt is a one-man show
in Willamette, doing great work
with Pinot Noir and Pinot Gris.
His red is definitively Oregonian
in style, with spice, earth, and
leathery scents at the forefront.
The Barrel Select is his premier
wine, worthy of roasted pork
and veal. His second label, called
Jigsaw ($16–18), is lighter and
fruitier, making it a proper
regional match for grilled
Copper River salmon.
$20–23
Oregon

AN AMERICAN IN BEAUNE

Alex Gambal is that rarest of birds: an American making wine in Burgundy.
What's more, he's making splendid wines from several top appellations. He
moved his family to the Burgundy wine center of Beaune on a whim in
1993, started winemaking in 1996, and came to our attention (and many
others') with his superb 1999 vintage. When asked how he got access to
Burgundy's hallowed vineyards, Gambal said modestly, "I joined the PTA at
my kids' school, chatted with the other parents at soccer games, made some
winemaker friends. . . ."

Gambal's **Bourgogne Pinot Noir "Cuvée Les Deux Papis"** ($16–19)
reveals the most about Gambal's winemaking style: It is strawberryish and
friendly, yet aptly expresses the earthy, salty *terroir* of Burgundy. As a com-plement for food, it's versatile and delicious with stuffed chickens, pastas
with sausage, mustardy medallions of pork, or an assortment of soft French
cheeses. The estate also makes a fantastic **Chambolle–Musigny** ($40–45),
which is satiny, fruity, and serious all at once—a sensuous wine that will
benefit from cellaring. *Both wines imported by House of Burgundy*

Calera
PINOT NOIR
Medium-bodied. A drier, earthier style results in a more "Burgundian" California Pinot.
Winemaker Josh Jensen is considered a benchmark producer of California Pinot. With the exception of the new value-priced "El Niño" line ($13–15), we find Jensen's wines less about pure fruit than about spice, minerality, and dry earth tones—hardly typical of Pinot grown in California but very interesting. His exceedingly rare single-vineyard bottlings of "Mt. Harlan" ($25–55) receive 30% new oak, while his Central Coast wine sees half that. Cellar the Mt. Harlan and drink the regular Pinot with chops or chicken. $20–25
Central Coast, California

François Raquillet
MERCUREY
"Vielles Vignes"
Medium-bodied. Great texture and rich in fruit.
Mercurey lies in the "sweet spot" of the Côte Chalonaise in southern Burgundy, and Raquillet is regularly the top producer there. Exuberant and fruity (think cherries and boysenberries), the Vielles Vignes is drinkable right from the get-go. Try it with a holiday turkey or ham, with blackened redfish or other Cajun/Creole specialties, or dine Burgundian style with charcuterie and pungent cheeses. For a few dollars more, Raquillet's single-vineyard selections "Les Chazeaux" and "Les Veleys" ($30–34) are definitely worth seeking out. $24–26
Burgundy
Imported by Bayfield

Domaine Vincent Girardin
SANTENAY 1er Cru
"La Maladière"
Medium-bodied. Fruit-forward, quintessential modern Burgundy.
Not everyone likes Burgundy that's funky and stubborn to "come around." To that end, super-*négociant* Girardin deftly mixes sweet oak, oodles of ripe fruit from naturally maintained vineyards, and meticulous craftsmanship to make a slew of sumptuous Burgundies that drink great young. From his home in Santenay comes this plummy, supple offering, which is versatile with chicken and fish. His Premier Crus and Grand Crus from Volnay ($50+) and Chambertin ($80+) are ravishing. $25–30
Burgundy
Imported by Vineyard Brands

David Bruce
PINOT NOIR
"Vintner's Select"
Medium-bodied. Saturated in color, with smooth, mouthfilling texture.
Bruce is a forty-year veteran winemaker in Santa Cruz who makes a Pinot striking for its concentrated black fruit, sweet vanilla oak, and heady alcohol. While he does several bottlings, including two from the Central Coast, we prefer the fruitiness of the Sonoma. A fine match for grilled chops or steaks. $26–28
Sonoma

Adelsheim Vineyard
PINOT NOIR
Light- to medium-bodied. Silky, delicate, easy on the oak, and drinkable now.
As so often happens in wine, this is a case when a winery's most basic bottling is its best. Wine pioneers David and Ginny Adelsheim craft their Oregon

Pinot from ten different sites in the Willamette Valley. Its intricately lacy, strawberry-scented character makes it pair beautifully with fish and vegetable dishes.
$27–30
Oregon

Lane Tanner
PINOT NOIR "Bien Nacido"
Medium-bodied. Subtle and sophisticated, with a dry palate and lip-smacking acidity.
Ms. Tanner works with small parcels of superb fruit in central California and quietly makes some of America's most renowned Pinots. This carefully crafted example is appealing for its baked cherry/cranberry fruit and the elusive milk chocolate in its finish. It really comes alive when paired with grilled fish steaks, turkey, or roasted root vegetables. $28–32
Santa Barbara, California

Gary Farrell
PINOT NOIR "Russian River"
Light- to medium-bodied. Pale and pretty, very succulent, and a classy style overall.
Gary Farrell, who has one of the most beautiful wineries in the Russian River, painstakingly makes a lithe, lissome Pinot with a complex red fruit profile, hints of new French oak, and high-toned herbal flavors like mint and sage. This is a complex food wine that can stand up to calf's liver, sweetbreads, and other organ meats. And it's amazing with coastal California's specialty: barbecued oysters!
$30–33
Russian River, California

Domaine Jean-Marc Millot
SAVIGNY-LES-BEAUNE
Medium-bodied. A stylish red Burgundy with robust fruit and terrific mouthfeel.
Jean-Marc Millot is one of the most stubborn traditionalists in all of Burgundy. His wines are organically grown, hand-harvested at very low yields, and see little new oak. We consistently enjoy the lively Savigny-les-Beaune with rich fish steaks of salmon or tuna.
$30–35
Burgundy
Imported by New Castle

Capiaux
PINOT NOIR
"Widdoes Vineyard"
Medium- to full-bodied. Exotic aromas, very rich mouthfeel, and a deep finish that lasts and lasts.
After winemaking stints in Napa and Sonoma, Sean Capiaux has mastered Pinot Noir in the Russian River valley. His Widdoes Vineyard Pinot, with fewer than five hundred cases produced annually, is about as close to a great Nuits-St.-Georges (Burgundy) as we've tasted in California. Explosively aromatic, earthy, chocolatey, and long and liqueurlike on the palate, it's great teamed with duck, game birds, or braised short ribs. A little breathing in a decanter is advisable. $32–40
Russian River, California

Coturri
PINOT NOIR "Jewell Vineyard"
Full-bodied. Dazzling fruit and over-the-top ripeness—more like Pinot liqueur.
In this surreal cocktail of perfume, pomegranate, and cherry Kool-Aid, heightened acidity and extravagant alcohol remain tenuously in balance with the wine's sweetness—which makes the dry finish something of a

shock. If you're feeling adventurous, explore this organic über-Pinot with such sweet-and-sour edibles as Carolina barbecue. It's also good with aged semi-soft cheeses. $35–40
Sonoma

Domaine Philippe Charlopin-Parizot
CHAMBOLLE-MUSIGNY
Medium-bodied. Graceful, lush, and enticing.
Ambitious, skilled, and rising to prominence in Burgundy, Philippe Charlopin-Parizot is known as a vintner to watch. His Chambolle-Musigny, with its concentrated black currant fruit, feels "slurpy," and the ripe-but-soft tannins allow it to be drunk right away. Serve this amiable Pinot with roasted poultry, slow-cooked meats, and grilled fare of all kinds. Look also for the estate's well-priced, cherryish **Marsannay** ($25), recognizable by its amusingly generic-looking plain brown labels. $35–40
Burgundy
Imported by House of Fine Wines

Domaine Jean-Luc Joillot
POMMARD "Les Noizons"
Medium-bodied. A wonderfully old-fashioned Burgundy, rustic and hearty as they come.
This Pinot combines the classic funkiness of Pommard with oriental spice reminiscent of jasmine tea. With bottle age, the wine becomes satiny-smooth, floral, spicy, minerally, and very complex. Try it with short ribs or pork chops. $35–40
Burgundy
Imported by Bayfield

Domaine Hervé Sigaut
CHAMBOLLE-MUSIGNY 1er Cru "Les Chatelots"
Medium-bodied. A complex Pinot with mild tannin and lots of character.
When young, this enchanting wine from traditionalist Hervé Sigaut shows pure cherry fruit with peppery notes; it then becomes spicier as it ages. What doesn't change is its clear expression of Chambolle *terroir*, succulent mouthfeel, and gentle, lingering finish. Relish it with small birds, wild mushrooms, or terrines of pork or veal. For a bargain, try the Bourgogne

"HIS AND HERS" PINOTS

Husband-and-wife winemakers Jim and Morgan Clendenen enjoy a friendly rivalry. They each make delicious world-renowned Pinot Noirs in Santa Barbara, yet in wildly different styles. Jim's Au Bon Climat wines are vibrant and strongly fruit-driven—clearly Californian in their sunny sensuality. His **Au Bon Climat Pinot Noir "Santa Barbara"** ($18–20) is always good value and a hit with grills and stir-fries, while the resplendent **Barham-Mendelsohn Pinot Noir** ($45) from the Russian River and his many single vineyard cuvées from Santa Maria make gorgeous duck and game partners.

Morgan, meanwhile, makes only one Pinot under her Cold Heaven label: **Cold Heaven Pinot Noir "Le Bon Climat"** ($32–35), a labor of love from a tiny parcel of Le Bon Climat, a 40-acre vineyard she co-owns with Jim. Purely crafted, unfiltered, and redolent of earth, baked cherries, and tea roses, this is Pinot à la Burgundy, best served with roasted white meats and your favorite pungent cheeses.

"Les Hattets" ($18–20), the winning kid sister of this wine at half the price. $35–40
Burgundy
Imported by Bayfield

Argyle
PINOT NOIR **"Nuthouse"**
Medium-bodied. Silky and layered, with flavors that recur persistently in the finish.
Like many of Argyle's Pinots, this wine demands the taster's attention—flavors of strawberry, cranberry, fresh flowers, and earth are there, but they're subtle. Yet they seem to spring to life when this Pinot is paired with salty and savory fare. A fine pick for baked ham with a mustard glaze. $38–40
Willamette Valley, Oregon

$40 to $60

François Buffet
VOLNAY 1er Cru
"Les Champans"
Medium-bodied. Sensuous, silken, and tender. The appealing creaminess is typical of Volnay.
Fun to drink when it's young—all sweet red fruit splashing brightly on the palate. That quality recedes as the wine ages into warm Asian spices and a subtler palate overall. Les Champans will pair beautifully with any game bird or poultry dish. Also look for Buffet's basic **Volnay** ($30) which, while lighter, is made in the same style. $40–45
Burgundy
Imported by Bayfield

Domaine Henri Gouges
NUITS-ST. GEORGES 1er Cru
"Les Chênes Carteaux"
Medium- to full-bodied. The new oak is evident, but so is the dense fruit that absorbs it.

Christian Gouges makes wines that are collectibles for detail-oriented Burgundy lovers, including Les Chênes Carteaux. one of the heartier Burgundies we know of. The black fruit is buried beneath aromas of bittersweet chocolate and tar, meaning this wine needs five or so years in the cellar—and then some charred red meat or game to tame it. $40–50
Burgundy
Imported by Vineyard Brands

Domaine Chandon de Briailles
PERNAND-VERGELESSES 1er Cru
"Ile des Vergelesses"
Light- to medium-bodied. A charming and delicate Burgundy
with flavors that linger.
This is the finest wine of its appellation, tended

DOMAINE CHANDON DE BRIAILLES
PERNAND-VERGELESSES
PREMIER CRU
ILE DES VERGELESSES
APPELLATION CONTROLEE
DOMAINE CHANDON DE BRIAILLES
VITICULTEUR A SAVIGNY-LES-BEAUNE, COTE D'OR, FRANCE

biodynamically by a mother and daughter who put passion into their work. The fruit is almost ethereal on the palate, hinting at blanched cherries, strawberries, minerals, and potpourri. There's hardly a better seafood red in the world. $45–50
Burgundy
Imported by Daniel Johnnes

Domaine Joblot
GIVRY 1er Cru
"Clos du Cellier aux Moines"
Medium-bodied. A paradox of delicacy and strength.
Easily the finest vintner in Givry, Jean-Marc Joblot makes exquisite Pinots with an almost bewildering textural quality. Is it light or rich? Pretty or profound? Cellarable or drinkable now? The answer is "all of the above." Ripe, satiny tannins and terrific concentration belie a light-handedness in the wine

that just feels great, while cassis and potpourri flavors keep going on and on . . . It's a perfect fish red but offers a refreshing contrast for filet mignon as well. $45–50
Burgundy
Imported by Robert Kacher

Vincent Dancer
POMMARD 1er Cru
"Les Pézerolles"
Medium-bodied. Fresh-tasting, lively in the mouth, and enjoyable when young.

This recent import into the U.S. is slick, modern wine-making in the

best sense. Dancer crafts a seductive "drink-me-now" Pinot Noir with cranberries, raspberries, and apricots running riot. ("**Les Perrières**" is, at $40–45, a few dollars less and easier to find, but it's not a Premier Cru.) Serve with rich fish steaks or dishes flavored with Middle Eastern spices. $50–60
Burgundy
Imported by Martin Scott

Domaine Drouhin
PINOT NOIR "Laurène"
Medium-bodied. A rich, sculpted Pinot that often needs cellaring.
Winemaker Veronique Drouhin is the daughter of famed Burgundy *négociant* Robert Drouhin. Her Laurène bottling (named for her daughter) is her best, consistently offering compact black cherry,

blackberry, and oaky chocolate flavors. The wines aren't

flashy—just elegant. Decant and serve with oily broiled fish like tuna, salmon, mako, and bluefish. $50–60
Oregon

Over $60

Domaine François Lamarche
VOSNE-ROMANÉE 1er Cru
"La Croix Rameau"
Medium-bodied. Surprisingly mellow for cellarable Burgundy.
A once-famed domaine now in rebirth, Lamarche makes a wide range of classy, understated Premier Cru and Grand Cru wines. Their monopole **La Grand Rue Grand Cru** ($75) is justly famed, but we love the La Croix Rameau Premier Cru for its finesse, suave fruit, and sheer drinkability. Decant it and enjoy with Cornish hens in a reduction of wine and mushrooms. $60–70
Burgundy
Imported by House of Fine Wines

Domaine de la Pousse d'Or
VOLNAY 1er Cru
"Clos des 60 Ouvrées"
Medium- to full-bodied. Fabulously ripe, sensuous, and satiny, with a profound finish.
Organically vinted and aged in old and new oak, this Volnay is a glorious portrait of great Burgundy. The fruit is intense, like molten cherries. Roasted nuts and coffee play through the finish, and the mineral complexity amazes. More famed, but not as hedonistic, is the **Volnay 1er Cru "Clos de la Bousse d'Or"** ($120–160). Both wines are cellarable for twenty-plus years in vintages like '96, '99, and '02. Serve with decadent dishes such as *boeuf bourguignonne*. $80–150
Burgundy
Imported by Langdon Shiverick

Domaine Drouhin–Laroze
CLOS DE VOUGEOT Grand Cru
Medium- to full-bodied. Deep in
color, powerful, penetrating,
and in need of cellaring.
Produced by Bernard Drouhin
and his son Philippe from a tiny
parcel of vines, this big, classically
proportioned Burgundy is a
satisfying splurge. Front-loaded
with cherries, berries, cinnamon
spice, and sweet cocoa, it's a
special partner for slow-cooked
beef, duck confit, or grilled organ
meats like sweetbreads.
$95–100
Burgundy
Imported by Bayfield

Domaine René Engel
CLOS DE VOUGEOT Grand Cru
Medium- to full-bodied.
Authoritatively rich and meaty,
with excellent complexity.
Philippe Engel owns, among
several splendid sites, a minuscule
plot of Clos de Vougeot composed mostly of vines planted in
1922. The wine he makes from
there is firm, ruddy, and redolent
of roasted black fruits, soy, and
Asian spice. Cellar it and serve
with stuffed Cornish hens or
peppered filets of beef.
$90–115
Burgundy
Imported by House of Burgundy

A SECRET ADDITIVE

Before spilling the beans, let's clear up the confusion over Burgundy and
Bordeaux of times past and the nature of these two wines today. Burgundy
was once the bigger wine, Bordeaux the more delicate (the word *claret* for
Bordeaux referred to its pale color). Today, the opposite is true.

Why the reversal? Because Burgundy used to be regularly adulterated
with wines from other areas to give it color and strength. Much Rhône
Syrah and god-knows-what from Morocco and Algeria were spilled into
Burgundy tanks to beef it up and darken it to the level customers expected.
Today's Burgundy is not only lighter but better regulated and purer than
its antecedents. The worst malfeasance currently occurring is the constant,
little-talked-about addition of beet sugar to many of the wines (even
famous ones)—a practice that boosts alcohol levels and overall weight.

Short of spying on the winemaker, there is no prepurchase way to
detect a surreptitious dose of beet sugar. The clues come only when 1) you
taste the wine and it seems thin but very high in alcohol or 2) when a
Burgundy that has been cellared doesn't last as long as it should.

Sangiovese

With its myriad subvarieties, the dominant grape in Chianti is also the most widely planted in Italy. The reds it yields are generally high in acid, tannins, and spiciness.

HIANTI—Tuscany's most important winegrowing region—may have put Sangiovese on the map, but this grape grows all over central Italy, appearing on its own or more frequently in blends from Umbria, Emilia-Romagna, Molise, and Abruzzi.

Several other important clones of Sangiovese have made their mark. Prugnolo Gentile, a dark, thick-skinned variation, is the grape of the robust, highly prized, and cellar-worthy Vino Nobile di Montepulciano. Wines made from the clone Brunello are traditionally tannic, quite dry, and matured at length in wooden barrels (large and old), while the modern style is more fruit-driven and sweetened and softened by new oak, often French.

Then there's Chianti, the version of Sangiovese most of us know best. Traditionally a blend of four grapes (Sangiovese, Canaiolo, Trebbiano, Malvasia), Chianti can be a light, quaffable little cocktail or a rich, oak-aged powerhouse, especially in its most "serious" form: Chianti Classico Riserva. "Super Tuscans" are wines that ignore the rules of the Chianti appellation, often by using nontraditional grapes (Merlot, Cabernet) or aging in new oak; many are rare and expensive.

Sangioveses are usually red-fruit driven (think cherries, raspberries, and strawberries), though in warmer climes they occasionally taste of blackberry and black cherry (see Morellino di Scansano, page 62). All, however, are fairly high in acidity, savor, and spice, which makes them uniquely appropriate partners for Italian food, especially red sauces.

Until recently, Sangiovese was part of the "Cal-Ital" boom in bottlings of Sangiovese, Barbera, and Nebbiolo from coastal and northern California. Though the boom fizzled, a few delicious Sangiovese-based wines resulted and are found in these pages.

Under $12

Farnese
**SANGIOVESE DAUNIA
"Farneto Valley"**
**Light-bodied. A simple, rustic
"spaghetti red."**
This is a tasty, chillable red with
no pretensions but great flavor.
Strawberryish, bright, and
quaffable, it's a choice pizza/
party/picnic wine. $5–7
Abruzzi, Italy
Imported by Farnese/Americal

Villa Diana
SANGIOVESE
**Light-bodied. A fun, casual
sipping red—nice and juicy.**
This wine is probably made by
the tankerful, but we can't
complain. Bright berries and
spice move zestily along your
palate, washing down pizza,
pasta, and burgers with ease.
$5–7
Abruzzi, Italy
*Imported by Winebow/
Leonardo LoCascio*

Di Majo Norante
SANGIOVESE "San Giorgio"
**Light- to medium-bodied.
A bright, juicy, very food-
friendly style.**
From Molise, a little-known
Italian province down the
Adriatic coast from Abruzzi.

Consistent on the palate with soft
cherry, strawberry, and fig flavors,
this Sangiovese has a pleasingly
tart twist and surprising length.
Good with light and salty foods
like chips, dips, and antipasti.
$6–8
Molise, Italy
*Imported by Winebow/
Leonardo LoCascio*

Il Bastardo
SANGIOVESE DI TOSCANA
**Light- to medium-bodied.
A darkly fruity wine with a
cedar-spice aroma.**
Given this
Sangiovese's
adorable label by
Botero, naughty
name, and great
price, its goodness is
icing on the cake. Drink it from
jelly jars with heaping mounds
of spaghetti or baked ziti.
$7–10
Tuscany
Imported by House of Burgundy

Badia a Coltibuono
CHIANTI "Cetamura"
**Medium-bodied. Good balance
and a sweetish finish make this
pleasing to a wide audience.**
The wine we now know as Chianti
was purportedly invented at the
abbey at this estate, and its pricier
Chianti Classicos reflect more of
that tradition. This little guy,

"MR. TOMATO MAN"
That's what we call **Due Tigli Maestro del Pomidoro**
("Master of the Tomato"), Sangiovese di Romagna ($7–9) from
Emilia–Romagna, the Italian winegrowing region north of
Tuscany and south of Veneto and Lombardy. We like this
light- to medium–bodied wine's juicy fruit, its good texture,
and touch of friendly "funk." A great bargain, it's Chianti-
esque, full of cherries and spice, and just the wine to have
when you're dining on—you guessed it—anything with
tomato sauce. *Imported by Wines for Food*

Maestro del Pomidoro

however, is a simple, modern pleasure with mac 'n' cheese, tomato-sauced dishes, and kebabs. $8–10
Tuscany
Imported by Dalla Terra

Renzo Masi
CHIANTI RUFINA
Light- to medium-bodied. Lively and flavorful.
Grapes for this rather berryish style of Chianti come from the highest elevation area in the region. We love it with pizza and spicy chicken wings. The estate's fuller-bodied "Riserva" ($12–13) is aged three years in oak and offers amazing value. $8–10
Tuscany
Imported by Lauber

$12 to $20

Baroncini
MORELLINO DI SCANSANO "Le Mandorlae"
Medium-bodied. Dark and musky with deep fruit and a very dry finish.
Morellino is the local name for Sangiovese grown in the village of Scansano in the southeast corner of Tuscany. It's got sappy, blackberry/black cherry fruit (perhaps a little licorice, too) and an honesty we admire. A beautiful wine for roasted hens and a reasonable lasagna choice as well. $12–14
Tuscany
Imported by OmniWines

Terra Nostra
CHIANTI RISERVA
Medium-bodied. Rich with excellent ripeness—and surprising complexity at this price.
Made from 90% Sangiovese, 5% Canaiolo, 5% white grapes, and aged one year in barrel, this

wine is smooth and seductive in the mouth. Earth, strawberry, and violet notes abound. A good-value choice for roasted poultry and veal Parmigiano. $13–15
Tuscany
Imported by Verdoni

Zerbina
SANGIOVESE DI ROMAGNA "Ceregio"
Light- to medium-bodied. A vivacious, fruity style with no oak.
This cherry-berry cocktail red (100% Sangiovese aged in stainless steel tanks) can go places woody Chianti can't—like alongside grilled fish and vegetables, mild cheeses, and spicy fare. $14–16
Emilia-Romagna
Imported by Europvin

La Braccesca
ROSSO DI MONTEPULCIANO "Sabazio"
Medium-bodied.
A savory, hearty wine with traditional Tuscan character.
Here's a big-boned blend of Sangiovese (or its Prugnolo Gentile clone) and 20% black-cherryish Canaiolo—like a Chianti but with hair on its chest. Great with meaty red sauces, steak with Italian seasonings, or Cornish hens stuffed with porcini and sun-dried tomatoes. $14–17
Tuscany
Imported by Winebow/ Leonardo LoCascio

Monti Verdi
CHIANTI CLASSICO
Medium-bodied. Friendly and easy, lush and long.
A year in Slavonian oak and six months in bottle yields a balanced, silky Chianti that's delicious right

out of the gate. Made from 90% Sangiovese and 10% Canaiolo from thirty-year-old vines, it offers a palate of fresh and dried cherries and is tasty on its own or with a platter of focaccia, olives, and *salumi* (Italian cold cuts). The **Riserva** ($35–40), oak-aged three years, is black, velvety, and a burly red for lamb. $15–17
Tuscany
Imported by Verdoni

Ca' del Solo
SANGIOVESE "Il Fiasco"
Medium-bodied.
A fruit bomb—definitely more Californian than Tuscan.
This 100% Sangiovese from Santa Cruz's philosopher-cum-wine guru Randall Grahm is altogether pleasing: the essence of raspberry preserves and just the right balance for copious swigging. It's magnificent with barbecued chicken or stuffed veggies with tomato sauce. $16–18
California

Coturri
SANGIOVESE "Weiss Vineyard"
Medium- to full-bodied.
Modest in alcohol and dry—yet an explosively flavorful red.

California vintner Tony Coturri's usual extremity of style is curbed here to fine effect. His West Coast organic take on Sangiovese is fragrant with sweet berries, leather, and allspice but remains expertly balanced—not to mention versatile at the table. Enjoy with rotisserie chickens or braised lamb shanks. $16–18
Napa

Moris Farms
MORELLINO DI SCANSANO
Medium- to full-bodied.
A bold, dark, expansive wine with abundant flavor.
Deepening as it breathes, this luxurious wine lures you in with a host of black cherry and roasted-coffee aromas. Enjoy the seduction with a chunk of fresh Parmesan cheese, a pork loin wrapped in pancetta, or roast duck. The estate's **Riserva** ($30–35) is for folks who want all of the sensual qualities above plus lots of oak. $16–18
Tuscany
Imported by Polaner

Fattoria Le Pupille
MORELLINO DI SCANSANO
Medium-bodied.
Rich with fruit and texture.
Le Pupille, made by Elisabetta Geppetti, is perhaps the best-

---

CHIANTI TO CROW ABOUT

Wines from Chianti Classico, the historical heart of the Chianti growing region, are recognizable by the black rooster that usually appears on the label. They're also said to be a cut above wines from Chianti's subzones. An archetype is the medium-bodied **Rodano Chianti Classico** ($15–17), whose makers don't fool around with new oak or any tricks of the modern wine trade; this Chianti is picked ripe at low yields, aged in giant, neutral wood casks, and perfumed with rose, incense, and sour cherries. Firm and juicy, it's great with savory Italian fare like veal or chicken scallopine, eggplant Parmigiano, and spaghetti Bolognese. Rodano's fine, powerful "super-Tuscan" **Monna Claudia** ($35–40) is 50/50 Cabernet and Sangiovese.
Imported by Polaner

known Morellino, the local variant of Sangiovese from southeast Tuscany. Its complexity and depth, with scents of wild cherry, plum, and leather, plus a palate hinting at black olives and iron, make it a gutsy choice for game meats. $16–18
Tuscany
Imported by Domaine Select

Caparzo
ROSSO DI MONTALCINO
Medium-bodied. Suave and comfortable on the palate.
Here's a textbook Rosso di Montalcino. Crafted from the young Brunello vines of this famous estate, it's a mouthful of cherry fruit and sandalwood, balanced for early drinking. Serve it tonight with hearty lasagnas and manicotti, carpaccio with pepper and olive oil, or an Italian veal dish of your choice. $18–20
Tuscany
Imported by Vineyard Brands

Piancornello
ROSSO TOSCANA
"Poggio dei Lecci"
Light- to medium-bodied. Gentle, understated red with class.
A Tuscan Sangiovese from an ICT (*Indicazione Geografica Tipica*), a category of wines roughly equivalent to the French *vin de pays*. Limpid, pale, and graced with a soft spiced-cherry palate, this wine is just right for penne with vodka sauce. Piancornello also makes a finely detailed **Brunello de Montalcino** ($55–75), as superb as the price suggests. $18–20
Tuscany
Imported by Domaine Select

Corte Pavone
ROSSO DI MONTALCINO
Medium-bodied. As complex and delicious as these wines get.
Call this 100% organic Rosso di Montalcino, made from the young vines of Brunello, a "baby Brunello" if you wish—but it is inarguably serious wine. Toast, leather, and spiced-wood notes surf a rippling wave of red fruit. Classy and ebullient, it deserves a major-league Tuscan feast of balsamic-marinated hens, steak Fiorentina, or rabbit with white beans. $20–22
Tuscany
Imported by Wines We Are

Fanti
ROSSO DI MONTALCINO
Medium- to full-bodied.
An especially big wine that's spicy with rich tannins.
This is a traditionalist Rosso built for the long haul, so don't expect a fun 'n' fruity wine. It's replete with earth, dried red fruits, and the pepper-spice aromatics and tannins that come with two years aging in new and used oak. It's a great match for braised meats and pungent cheeses. FYI, Fanti's **Brunello** ($60–90) is impressive but often overpriced. $22–25
Tuscany
*Imported by Winebow/
Leonardo LoCascio*

Valdipiatta
VINO NOBILE DI MONTEPULCIANO
Medium- to full-bodied. As sexy as Sangiovese gets, with tons of fruit and deep, inky color.
All Vino Nobiles need time, and this one—made from 80% Prugnolo Gentile (a Sangiovese clone) and 20% Canaiolo and boasting a scrumptious palate of black bramble fruits—wants four or five

years to shed its battery of tannins. Serve this big luscious beast with steaks, lamb, or spit-roasted hens.
$22–25
Tuscany
Imported by John Given

Castello di Bossi
CHIANTI CLASSICO
Medium-bodied. More about spice and earth than fruit— and very dry at the finish.
This is Chianti the old-fashioned way: old-wood flavors, firm mouthfeel, and spicy, delicious figs and dates all the way through. There's also no shortage of tannins, so this wine begs for rich food. Have it with mushroom dishes, sheep's milk cheeses, and hearty stews of beans, pancetta, and Italian herbs. $25–27
Tuscany
Imported by Winebow/ Leonardo LoCascio

Over $40

Pertimali
BRUNELLO DI MONTALCINO
Medium- to full-bodied.
A mouthfilling, multilayered, rounded style.  Livio Sassetti's Brunello shows deeper fruit than most. Aromas of black cherry, leather, and moist earth are underpinned by velvety tannins. Enjoy a bottle with sliced rare duck breast, carpaccio, truffled hens, or a variety of firm, salty cheeses. Your steak wine is Sassetti's **Vigna dei Fili di Seta** ($60+), a blend of Cabernet and Sangiovese—a satiny "super Tuscan" that's judiciously oaked

and delivers tremendously concentrated flavor. $45–50
Tuscany
Imported by Marc de Grazia

Ciacci Piccolomini d'Aragona
BRUNELLO DI MONTALCINO
Medium- to full-bodied.
A lavishly built, hearty wine that needs time.
This superstar traditionalist, a darling of ours since 1993, is revered on both sides of the Atlantic. The smoky, pruney wine is saturated in color and scented heavily with minerals and moist earth. It's also a red meat wine to be sure, for garlicky leg of lamb, standing rib roasts, and so on. The estate's **Rosso di Montalcino "Vigna della Fonte"** ($22–25) is also sensational, and richer than many pricier Brunellos. We'd drink it with a T-bone any night. Both wines are cellar-worthy.
$50–60
Tuscany
Imported by Marc de Grazia

Antinori
BRUNELLO DI MONTALCINO
"Pian delle Vigne"
Medium- to full-bodied.
Very traditional-tasting, with plush texture and lots of spice.
Aged two to three years in small barrels, this 100% Sangiovese from twenty-year-old vines isn't released until five years after the vintage. The '97 got incredible press, but we like the '98 as well; its warm cherry pie, plum, and cinnamon character is wide-open and enticing, which is unusual for young Brunello. Decant and serve with racks of lamb or beef.
$60–75
Tuscany
Imported by Rémy Amerique

Syrah/Shiraz

*In the wine stakes, this grape with two names
truly excels in only three parts of the world—
the Rhône, Australia, and California—
yet it's giving "King Cab" a run for its money.*

*S*YRAH, a sturdy black grape variety, is responsible for some of the world's most "serious" red wines—and some of its most delightfully "unserious" ones as well. In France, the minerally, tannic Syrahs from the northern Rhône Valley taste of pepper, tar, and blackberries and often benefit from cellaring. The lush Australian Shirazes, most for immediate drinking, are thick, fruity, and chocolatey. California, where vintners usually call their wine Syrah, produces rich, ripe wines that fall somewhere in the middle ground.

Regardless of origin, these wines are enjoying a surge in popularity. One reason is their relatively reasonable price, with Rhône Syrahs usually costing much less than their counterparts in Bordeaux and Burgundy, and New World examples priced under $25.

Why the two names? Long ago Syrah was also called Scyras, a name preferred by James Busby, the Scottish viniculturist who took the grape from the Rhône to Australia in 1832. The similarity to "Shiraz," the Persian city, may explain the gradual shift to the latter name. The "Persian connection" also has fed speculation that the grape was brought to France by a Crusader. More likely, it is indigenous to France, where the vines have been grown since the time of the Romans.

Though Syrah is often used in southern France for blending, the northern Rhône is the place for 100% Syrah. The main communes are St. Joseph, where fruity wines are typical; tiny Cornas, home to bold, rustic wines; Côte Rôtie, where powerful, fragrant wines often include Viognier in the blend; the Hermitage, the rock-strewn hillside that makes the world's most renowned Syrah; and Crozes-Hermitage, the vast wine-producing acreage that surrounds it.

Most Aussie Shirazes originate in South Eastern Australia, though some from Western Australia are superb. California Syrah/Shiraz grows statewide, with the central coast producing much of the best.

Outside of the "big three" growing areas, Syrah blends are produced throughout southern France, in a few places in Italy, in South Africa (as Shiraz)—and, on these shores, in Washington State.

Under $20

Barefoot Cellars
SYRAH
Medium-bodied.
A deep-purple fruit bomb.
Nothing fancy here: just a plump, purple party wine at a great price. It's great with burgers, burritos, chicken fingers, and other microwaveable treats. $6–8
California

Les Hautes Blaches
CROZES HERMITAGE
Light- to medium-bodied.
**Gentle, savory Syrah in a
bistro style.**

Looking for a good Crozes that won't break the bank? This one is mild but has true Crozes Hermitage character—smoke, herbs, baked black fruit, and a dry finish. Its excellent balance makes it a hit on its own or with cheese assortments and cold cuts. $10–12
Rhône, France
Imported by Baron François

McManis
SYRAH
Light- to medium-bodied.
A soft, easy-drinking Syrah.
Made just south of Lodi, California, by a fourth-generation wine-making family, this wine has a whiff of smoke and spice to keep things interesting. Try it with summertime burgers and franks. $10–12
California

Cartlidge & Browne
SYRAH
Medium-bodied. Sturdy and bold.
This surprisingly Rhône-like Syrah from the West Coast has smoky, lasting black fruit and a shot of espresso in the finish. Pair it with burgers, lean steaks, and roasted poultry. Great value! $10–12
California

Fess Parker
FRONTIER RED
**Medium-bodied.
Rich, strong, and
pleasantly funky.**

The nonvintage blend (70% Syrah, 12% Grenache, 6% Mourvèdre,

DEALS FROM DOWN UNDER

Over the past decade, the North American market has been flooded with millions of gallons of inexpensive Australian Shiraz, a welcome trend in the wake of higher prices for European and California wines. Much of this Aussie juice is delicious, although little of it shows any notable regional or individual character. It's just good, sippin' fun—and for certain parties, picnics, and casual meals at home, that's just what the doctor ordered.

When searching out a good Australian Shiraz costing twelve bucks or less, you won't go wrong with one of these: **Jindalee** ($6–8; *imported by Frederick Wildman*); **Miranda "Firefly" Shiraz** ($6–8; *imported by F & F Fine Wines*); **Alice White Shiraz** ($7–9; *imported by Old Bridge Cellars*); **McGuigan Shiraz "Black Label"** ($7–9; *imported by Winebow*); **Ghost Gum Shiraz** ($8–10; *imported by Importicos*); and **Nugan Shiraz** ($10–12, *imported by Southern Starz*).

5% Cinsault, 4% Cab Franc, 3% Counoise) has hints of earth, black pepper, and prune. It pairs handily with burgers, chops, and take-out chicken. $10–12
California

Teal Lake
SHIRAZ
Medium-bodied. A lush, silky-soft, and extremely ripe kosher wine.
You don't drink this kosher wine for its complexity. You drink it because it's basically a caramel-drizzled bowlful of cherries and raspberries that goes down like butter. It's a great foil for sweet, saucy meats like barbecued chicken or short ribs. $11–13
South Eastern Australia
Imported by Royal Wine

Guilhem Durand
SYRAH "Vielles Vignes"
Medium- to full-bodied. Deeply flavored and thrillingly rich.
An incredible value, this unfiltered Syrah made from thirty- to fifty-year-old vines is blessed with those great smoky, brambly, leather-scented wafts that you usually get only from the northern Rhône. Serve it with stews and red meats.
$11–13
Languedoc, France
Imported by Weygandt/Metzler

Chateau Mourgues de Gres
COSTIÈRES DE NIMES
"Les Galets Rouges"
Medium- to full-bodied. Deep purple, lavish, and mouthfilling.
This knockout Syrah, brimming with black cherries and pepper, is perfect for hearty fare like rotisserie chickens, fried chops, Cuban *ropa vieja,* and anything grilled. The *galets* of the name

are round, flat stones prevalent in southern French vineyards, where they do winemakers a favor by absorbing heat by day and then warming the vines by night. $12–14
Rhône, France
Imported by Weygandt/Metzler

Domaine d'Andézon
CÔTES DU RHÔNE
Medium- to full-bodied.
An especially saturated,
aggressive style.
Always a deeply flavored and structured wine, this 100% Syrah from sixty- to ninety-year-old vines is worth trying in any year. Laced with dried cherries and licorice, it's great with steaks, Chinese duck, and hard cheeses. We also find it delightful with veal Parmigiano. $12–14
Rhône, France
Imported by European Cellars

Cave de Tain l'Hermitage
CROZES HERMITAGE
"Les Hauts du Fief"
Medium-bodied. Seems restrained at first, but swiftly expands into something rich and savory.
Made by one of the best growers' co-ops in France, this Crozes has a character that's roasty and pepper-scented, with black fruit that grows with airing in the glass. Marvelous for game and French bistro fare—mushroom tarts, pâté, and baked Brie. $12–14
Rhône, France
Imported by Diageo

Simon Hackett
SHIRAZ "The Gatekeeper"
Medium- to full-bodied. Aussie Shiraz with a French accent.
A heady brew of McLaren Vale and Riverland fruit, this Shiraz is

really Syrah on a beach vacation. The Aussie chocolatey sweetness peeks out from behind a Rhône-like array of complex smoke, spice, and sun-roasted flavors. Awesome with smoked Texas brisket or a roast beef sandwich slathered with horseradish. $13–15
McLaren Vale, South Australia
Imported by Weygandt/Metzler

Mas des Chimères
COTEAUX DU LANGUEDOC
Medium- to full-bodied.
Wonderful ripeness and balance.
Guilhem Dardé blends 70% Syrah, 20% Grenache, and 10% Cabernet into his wine, which he ages in *barriques* and bottles unfined and unfiltered. (*Barriques* is the Burgundian word for small oak barrels, and an "unfined" wine is one that hasn't undergone the clarification process known as fining.) An array of brown spices and rustic, "peasanty" character make this plump little red very appealing. Drink it with chicken Provençal or pack it in the picnic basket with pâté, olives, and farmhouse cheeses.
$13–15
Languedoc, France
Imported by Louis/Dressner

Abbaye de Tholomies
MINERVOIS
Medium- to full-bodied.
Full-flavored and spicy,
with a sun-baked feel.
Here's a peppery organic blend (60% Syrah, 30% Grenache, 10% Mourvèdre) that's jammed with fruit and has a lingering baked-berry finish. It is only 12.5% alcohol, which is modest for a wine this rich-tasting. It goes particularly well with beef stew, roasted vegetables, and Caribbean and other slightly spicy dishes. "**The Sanctus**" ($13–15) is

bigger, and a real teeth-stainer—funny, given the winemaker's former profession: dentistry.
$14–17
Languedoc, France
Imported by International Gourmet

Plunkett
SHIRAZ "Blackwood Ridge"
Medium-bodied. Juicy, elegant,
and dry—a subtler style of Shiraz.
With its leather-and-spice complexity and rather dry finish, this Shiraz seems more like a Rhône wine than the typical Australian jam-juice. That's why it pairs nicely with more savory fare like smoked meats and root vegetables.
$14–16
Goulburn Valley, Victoria
Imported by Wines We Are

Coturri
SYRAH "Workingman's"
Full-bodied. Vibrant, mouth-watering texture and a dry finish.
Like all his other wines, Tony Coturri's Sonoma Syrah is best described as dramatic. This one's a bit drier, stronger, and juicier, offering smoky, tarry, roasted black fruit flavors with just a touch of pink grapefruit around the edges.

In terms of power for the dollar, this may be one of the best buys in California. Brilliant served alongside black beans, roast duck, fried foods, and pasta with hearty tomato sauce. $16–18
Sonoma

Marquis Philips
SHIRAZ
Medium- to full-bodied.
Very high in everything—alcohol, fruit extract, and oak.
Based in Padthaway (a South Australian wine center whose name is derived from the Aboriginal word

---

TWO OF A KIND

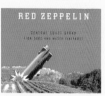

Vintners Dan Lewis and Stillman Brown pull no punches—neither in their wines nor in life, as their marvelously eccentric Web site attests (address on page 224). Their buoyant **Jory Winery "Red Zeppelin"** ($18–20) is just one of the wines they became famous for after they founded the winery—now in Paso Robles, California—in 1986.

As fun as its label, this medium–bodied, easy-to-drink wine is a raucous blend of old–vine Syrah and Barbera. The predominant flavors? Mixed red fruits and cinnamon. The vintners' motto is "You be the judge; we'll be the Jory"—so we hereby rule "Red Zeppelin" a killer barbecue wine. Another good bet is the winery's harder-to-find **Black Hand Syrah** ($18–20).

---

for "good water"), winemakers Sarah and Sparky Marquis make a red that delivers a truckload of blackberries and almost confectionery sweetness from oak. The perfect barbecue wine. $17–20
South Eastern Australia
Imported by Grateful Palate

Bleasdale
SHIRAZ "Mulberry Tree"
Medium-bodied. A silky, textured, non-tannic, sweetly fruity sipping wine.
This Australian Shiraz tastes like plum compote with a couple of chocolate mints thrown in. Serve it young with saucy Chinese and Indian dishes or pepper jack cheese. Bleasdale's lighter-styled **Shiraz/Cabernet Sauvignon** ($14–16) is a surefire crowd pleaser. $18–20
Langhorne Creek, South Australia
Imported by Southern Starz

Domaine l'Aiguelière
MONTPEYROUX
Full-bodied. Black and thick and memorable.
You can taste the soil in this wine (and maybe, some say, even the feet of the grape stompers!). It is undeniably intense—a rustic, full-throttle southern French blend

of Syrah, Grenache, Mourvèdre, and local grape varieties. The Syrah seems to dominate, offering telltale peppery, floral nuances. Serve with game meats or sausage-stuffed peppers. $18–20
Coteaux de Languedoc
Imported by North Berkeley

Pascal Jamet
ST. JOSEPH
Medium-bodied.
Purple, grapey, and fun.
This is Syrah's fruitier side, with red cherry-berry flavors with an olivey note. Serve it with sweeter, flavorful foods like pork stuffed with prunes, glazed ham, or grilled fish wrapped in bacon. For a bargain, try the estate's **Syrah** ($10–12), a winner with peppered cold cuts, cheeses, and spicy fare. $18–20
Rhône, France
Imported by Village Wines

Shottesbrooke
SHIRAZ
Medium- to full-bodied. A wine with a very seductive and carefully crafted style.
It can be bolder in some vintages and subtler in others, but this Aussie Shiraz boasts a flood of spearmint, cloves, vanilla, and rich

blueberry and cherry flavor that's consistent from year to year—and for that we have winemaker Nick Holmes to thank. Fantastic with minted lamb or pork chops with a sagey dressing.
$18–20
McLaren Vale, South Australia
Imported by Ravensvale

Domaine Olivier Dumaine
CROZES HERMITAGE
Medium to full-bodied. Extremely dry and highly complex.
This Crozes Hermitage is highly traditional—like a cup of black coffee, very dark and roasted-tasting. Avoid it with sweet sauces and enjoy instead with smoked meats, sausages, and country pâtés. $18–20
Rhône, France
Imported by Daniel Johnnes

Clos Mimi
SYRAH "Petite Rousse"
Full-bodied. Thick, smooth, and very compelling.
The California vineyard Clos Mimi makes Syrah exclusively. Three thousand cases of Petite Rousse were bottled, as the label says, "unfined and unfiltered, under the new moon in August 2003." The wine is thick and velvety, tasting of raspberry, dark chocolate, and almond—smooth as you please and incredibly tasty with red meats and blue cheeses.
$18–22
Paso Robles, California

$20 to $40

Lake Breeze
BERNOOTA
Full-bodied. A big, fat, yummy red wine.
From the heart of wine country in South Australia, Greg Follett's Rubenesque blend of Shiraz and

Cabernet Sauvignon is turbo-driven by 15% alcohol—but with that amazing fruit, you don't really feel it (until later, that is). Chocolatey and straightforward, it's a wine you drink for loud hedonic pleasure, not quiet contemplation. Enjoy it with anything on the grill or your Thanksgiving turkey.
$20–25
Langhorne Creek, South Australia
Imported by American Estate

Domaine Gilles Robin
CROZES HERMITAGE
"Cuvée Albéric Bouvet"
Medium-bodied. Strikes the perfect balance between power and finesse.
Delicate scents of lilies, violets, and lavender invite you into this haunting wine as its extreme minerality gives you much to contemplate. Just slice up some London broil with a white wine-and-mushroom sauce and prepare to enjoy one of winedom's perfect pairings.
$20–25
Rhône, France
Imported by Daniel Johnnes

Mount Langi Ghiran
SHIRAZ
Full-bodied. Concentrated and flavorful in the grand style.
This Australian wine, picked late and aged in French and American oak, offers Shiraz fanatics ample black pepper and super-ripe blackberry and blueberry fruit. The same estate also makes a more savory, juicier wine for Rhône lovers called **"Cliff Edge"** ($20–25). Both wines can be cellared, but there's no reason not to grill some lamb chops and drink one or the other tonight.
$21–23
Victoria, Australia
Imported by Epic Wines

Beckett's Flat
SHIRAZ
Full-bodied. A richly textured kosher wine with plenty of ripe fruit.

No one will believe it's kosher when you serve this flamboyantly deep, chocolatey, blackberry-scented Shiraz from Western Australia. Great with red meat, magnificent with barbecue, and capable of impressing the pickiest wine snobs on your holiday guest list. $22–25
Margaret River, Western Australia
Imported by Abarbanel

Alain Graillot
CROZES HERMITAGE
Full-bodied. Jammier in some years, sterner in others—but always striking.

A *terroir*-driven, sought-after "star" of the northern Rhône that is sometimes hard to find. Suave tannins and excellent acidity give a lift to this beautifully extracted Crozes, which you can either cellar for a moderate period or serve up now with the likes of short ribs, shanks, and other fatty meats. $24–30
Rhône, France
Imported by Europvin

Thierry Allemand
CORNAS "Chaillot"
Full-bodied. A sense of "orderly opulence" pervades this fabulous, age-worthy Syrah.

In Cornas (the smallest of the key appellations in the northern Rhône), Allemand is lately considered one of the best estates. Chaillot is dense, meaty, and packed with sweet black fruit, roastiness, and peppers of every color. No new oak is used. The '97 drank quite well young, but heftier vintages like 2000 and '01 need much more time. Serve it over the holidays with duck, goose, or game hens in a red wine sauce. $35–50
Rhône, France
Imported by Kermit Lynch

$40 to $60

Bremerton
SHIRAZ "Old Adam"
Full-bodied. Tremendous power and intensity of flavor.

Australian winemaker Rebecca Wilson selects her best Shiraz for the Old Adam and ages it twenty months in American oak and ten months in bottle. This powerful glass of black fruits is ripe and

---

CALIFORNIA MEETS THE RHÔNE

California's pioneering "Rhône Ranger" Steve Edmunds is an eloquent defender of sustainable agriculture. He uses indigenous yeasts, absolutely no new oak, and fruit purchased from a network of small garden vineyards running from Paso Robles to northern Sonoma. His curranty, European-style **Edmunds St. John Syrah** ($20–24) is made from grapes sourced from several sites—a medium- to full-bodied wine offering big, savory Syrah flavor at a reasonable price. Serve it with meaty fare. Edmunds's **"Rocks and Gravel"** ($20–24) is riper and gentler, while the vineyard-designated **"Wylie/Fenaughty"** ($35–38) and new **"Bassetti"** ($45–50) are extraordinarily deep and earthy; these last two are capable of cellaring.

sweet, with surprising viscosity. Save it for your richest barbecue, duck, and roast lamb—but buy it fast, since only five hundred cases are made each year. Easier to find, and impressive for its price, is **Tamblyn** ($20–25), a Shiraz/Cab/Merlot blend. $40–45
Langhorne Creek, South Australia
Imported by Ravensvale

Fife Vineyards
MAX CUVÉE
Full-bodied. Concentrated like Syrahs of the northern Rhône but unmistakably Californian in style. With its opaque purple color and deliciously ripe black cherry and cassis, Max Cuvée pays homage to the blends of California's early winegrowers. Pair this heavy, powerful wine with classic Texas barbecue. $42–45
Napa

Patrick Jasmin
CÔTE RÔTIE
Medium-bodied. An abundantly fragrant, succulent Syrah.

Jasmin owns just under ten acres in the Côte-Brune and Côte-Blonde, steep-terraced slopes that must be tended by hand. He uses no new oak, preferring two- and three-year-old Burgundy barrels *(barriques)*, and the wine's time in wood is minimal. The result is a surprisingly fresh, floral bouquet that darkens swiftly into black currant on the palate. Red meat and mushrooms excel. $45–50
Rhône, France
Imported by Kermit Lynch

Alban Vineyards
SYRAH "Reva"
Full-bodied. Strong and thick, and perhaps America's finest Syrah. Somehow, John Alban maximizes the luscious fruit typical of

California and compounds it with the complexity and earth-driven character of such Rhône Syrahs as Cornas and Côte Rôtie. The high alcohol of Reva is masked by the rolling flavor of cassis and black fig, with results that would impress any lover of red wine. A wine that can be cellared for a decade or more, it's decadent with slow-cooked meats. $50–60
Edna Valley, California

Over $60

Marie–Claude Lafoy et Vincent Gasse
CÔTE RÔTIE "Vielles Vignes"
Medium- to full-bodied. Perfumed and impressive from the first sip. Vincent Gasse grows vines biodynamically—no pesticides, minimal sulfites, and plantings scheduled to astrological phases and rhythms. Sourced from

sixty-plus-year-old vines on the Côte Rôtie ("roasted slope"), this elegant wine releases its violety, country hillside fragrance after extensive breathing. With some cellaring, it's a perfect match for roast lamb or osso buco. $60–70
Rhône, France
Imported by Weygandt/Metzler

René Rostaing
CÔTE RÔTIE
Medium-bodied. Luscious and very seductive for a Côte Rôtie. Rostaing is a forward-thinking winemaker who makes very ripe Syrahs with a lot of new oak and clean, deep fruit. (The wines have been so successful

73

HERMITAGE WINES

*T*HE **HERMITAGE APPELLATION,** in the northern Rhône just south of Lyon, has produced some of France's greatest wines since the reign of Louis XIV. The Hermitage itself—a rocky, domed hill topped by a humble thirteenth-century chapel—has an intriguing, if hazy, history. Legend has it that Henri-Gaspard de Sterimburg, a knight, returned from the Crusades wounded and in need of seclusion. He retreated to the hilltop, planted vines, and lived as a hermit. Whether he built the chapel is open to question, but man and edifice are of such a piece that the truth is of little import.

Today, father-and-son team Gerard and Jean-Louis Chave craft their **J. L. Chave Hermitage** ($100–200) and other wines much as their family has for over five hundred years. Hand-plowing the fields using no chemicals and fermenting in open wood vats with native yeasts, they make separate wines from their nine *climats* (vine parcels) on the Hermitage hill and blend them for the final bottling. Given a year to eighteen months in old and new oak for finishing, the resulting elegant, full-bodied wine has fine tannins, perfectly ripened fruit, and a savoriness that showcases its complexity. The classic smoke, blackberry, licorice, leather, flint, and flowers of Syrah are all here, but so is the almost "sweaty" pungency of the Hermitage *terroir.* We'd open a bottle with a simple roast duckling and savor the last of it with a plate of sheep's milk cheese and Roquefort or Danish Blue. *Imported by Willette Wines*

Another jewel is **Paul Jaboulet Aine Hermitage "La Chapelle"** ($100–200). Muted on the palate when young, it's a very beefy, dry, complex wine built to last. Let it breathe and look for black pepper, wood smoke, green herbs, leather, and intense minerality. Cellar and serve with grilled lamb or duck with wild mushrooms. *Imported by Frederick Wildman*

they're now hard to come by.)
His basic Côte Rôtie offers a
lengthy mouthful of black fruit,
earth, soy, and pepper. Ideally,
drink it two to four years after
the vintage, serving it with
marbled beef. Collectors prize the
fulsome **Côte Blonde** ($100–120)
and **La Landonne** ($95–105),
both exceedingly rare. $60–80
Rhône, France
Imported by Rare Wine

Sean H. Thackrey
ORION
"Rossi Vineyard–Old Vines"
Medium- to full-bodied.
Maybe the most cellarable
Syrah in California.
With each vintage, Sean Thackrey
ekes out fewer than eight
hundred cases of this wine from
century-old Syrah vines.
Surprisingly grapey when
young, the Orion keeps its fruit
as it ages, adding complexity and
spicy anise, tar, pepper, and violet
flavors with time. Serve with a
well-marbled roast encrusted
with herbs. Also seek out the
non-vintage **Pleiades** ($25–30)
a blend of Syrah, Grenache,
Barbera, and Carignan; it's
fantastic with grilled bluefish.
$75–100
California

M. Chapoutier
ERMITAGE "Le Pavillon"
Medium- to full-bodied.
A biodynamic beauty.
Michel Chapoutier has been the
lead flag-waver of biodynamic
viticulture in
the Rhône
since 1988,
taking his cues
from the stars.
A lovely touch

is the planting of rose bushes at
the bottom of each vine row
(roses, subject to many of the
same pests as grapes, act as a
bellwether for trouble).
He is the largest vineyard owner
in the Hermitage (*Ermitage* in
French), and his hard-to-find
wines from there are his best.
All are vibrantly acidic and
minerally when young and are
focused on elegance and
complexity, not power. Le
Pavillon may be the most prized,
with black depths, powerful
tannins, and roasty aromas
accented by black pepper. The
much less costly **"La Sizeranne"**
($50–70) is a virtuosic expression
of its vineyard but rather dry and
stubborn until it's had some years
of cellaring. Both wines are a
food lover's fantasy when served
with the likes of spit-roasted
lamb and olives, sheep's milk
cheese, and roasted potatoes.
$250–400
Rhône, France
Imported by Paterno

Tempranillo

The pride of Spain is the main grape in user-friendly Rioja and aristocratic Ribera del Duero. Reflecting Tempranillo's easy adaptability is its multiplicity of regional names.

TEMPRANILLO has much in common with its Italian neighbor Sangiovese: a love of warm weather, lively acidity, and the ability to take oak gracefully and yield a range of light to heavy wines. Both also taste of red fruits—Tempranillo of cherry in particular—and go by different names. In Spain, Tempranillo is called, among other things, Ojo de Libre (eye of the hare) in the Penèdes region and Tinto Fino (fine red wine) in Ribera del Duero.

Tempranillo is also known for having a spicy quality, but that may have as much to do with its oak treatment as inherent flavor. The wines of Rioja and Navarra are traditionally aged in American oak, a coarser-grained wood that imparts a malty or chocolatey flavor. In Ribera del Duero, wines are often aged in French oak and tend to be darker, firmer, and more Bordeaux-like in style.

Tempranillo's adaptability extends to blending in a big way. While it is frequently blended with Grenache (known as Garnacha in Spain), the "better" Spanish wines contain more Tempranillo and less (or no) Grenache. By definition, Rioja wines are a blend of up to five grapes: Tempranillo, Grenache, Mazuela (the Spanish name for Carignan), Graciano, and the Spanish white grape known as Viura or Macabeo.

With the exception of Portugal, where the grape is named Tinta Cao, and Argentina, where it's called Tinta Roriz, Tempranillo is rarely grown outside Spain. Some serious wine lovers wonder why the grape isn't grown more in Australia and California, where conditions are in place to produce outstanding Tempranillo-based wines. Time (or a heroic vintner!) will provide an answer.

Under $20

Dominio de Eguren
PROTOCOLO RED
**Light- to medium-bodied.
A simple and fresh-tasting
cocktail red.**
So many Spanish
bargains, so little
time to enjoy
them! This
cherry-berry
pleasure is a
perfect party and
pizza wine. Serve
it lightly chilled. $5–6
*Tierra de Manchuela, Spain
Imported by Tempranillo*

Vicente Gandia
HOYA DE CADEÑAS Reserva
**Light- to medium-bodied.
Smooth as silk and surprisingly
fruity for its age.**
Released late (the current
vintage is '97), this inexpensive
mature Tempranillo, with its
spiced-cherry and cocoa finish,
is an amazing bargain. It takes
especially well to rice 'n' beans
and party snacks like olives and
mild cheeses. $7–9
*Utiel-Requena, Levante, Spain
Imported by Tri-Vin*

Pinord
PENÈDES Clos Torribas
**Light- to medium-bodied.
A bright everyday sipper.**
Easygoing cherry and straw-
berry flavors make this a treat
with Spanish/Latino soul food
like empanadas, sliced ham, and
plantains. It's a fine cocktail red,
too. Serve lightly chilled.
$7–9
*Penèdes, Spain
Imported by Pleasant*

Ramblilla
TEMPRANILLO
**Medium-bodied. Bold-textured
and bursting with fruit.**
The newest appellation in Spain,
Ribera del Jucar (in the north,
near Galicia), has yet to make
the textbooks. Still, this
promising Tempranillo is dark
and exciting, dense with fruit,
and accented with a whiff of
oregano; it's also free of tannins.
Great for drinking with roast
pork, black olives, and Middle
Eastern kebabs and curries.
For just a little more, enjoy
Ramblilla's **Crianza** ($12–14),
which is oak-aged and spicier.
$8–10
*Ribera del Jucar, Spain
Imported by Frontier*

Palacios Remondo
RIOJA "La Vendimmia"
**Medium-bodied. A taste of
succulent, vibrant fruit.**
A blend of 70% Tempranillo,
20% Garnacha, and doses of
Fraciano and Mazuela, this
ultramodern Rioja is made partly
by whole berry fermentation
(which makes the wine fruitier)
and then given a quick nap in
new French oak. We love it with
burgers of beef, lamb, turkey, or
even buffalo and with Middle
Eastern specialties like falafel,
kebabs, and merguez sausage.
Wine lovers seeking more serious
Rioja from famed winemaker
Alvaro Palacios should taste the
Rioja Crianza "La Montesa
($17–20), named for the
vineyard planted by Alvaro's
father, Remondo. Aged a year in
oak—and beautifully balanced,
layered, and lasting—this is the
new face of Rioja, and happily so.
$11–13
*Rioja, Spain
Imported by Rare Wine*

ALL IN THE FAMILY:
TWO RIOJA GRAN RESERVAS

The 120-year-old bodega of R. Lopez de Heredia Viña Tondonia in Rioja Alta brooks no compromise. The two sisters who run it are steeped in their family tradition, creating singular artisanal wines that fly in the face of the modern "international" style. While they make numerous wines, it is the Gran Reservas for which the bodega is justly famed.

Lopez de Heredia Gran Reserva "Viña Bosconia", ($32–34) spends six years in barrel and six more in bottle before public release. It tends

to be the Lopez de Heredias' burliest wine, in contrast to the graceful **Gran Reserva Viña Tondonia**, ($38–40) which drinks very much like prized Premier Cru Volnay Burgundy.

All the wines are consistent within the house style, each rather like a perfectly aged little plum cake from a different recipe, variously accented by strawberries, salty minerals, spicy oak, potpourri, and varying degrees of "sherried" character. Many current vintages on the market are twenty years old or more—and at $50 to $250 depending on their age, they are considered bargains. *Imported by Think Global*

Antonio Barcelo
RIBERA DEL DUERO Crianza
"Viña Mayor"
Medium-bodied. Plump, fruity, and a lot of wine for its price. From rugged mountain climes, this popular red really satisfies. Nice with pork chops, fried foods, and sandwiches. Also try the non-oaked **Viña Mayor Tinto** ($8–10) for even fruitier sipping. $12–14
Ribera del Duero, Spain
Imported by Rémy Amerique

Abadia Retuerta
SARDON DEL DUERO **"Rivola"**
Medium-bodied. A rich, barrel-aged, fragrant blend. This blend (60% Tempranillo, 40% Cabernet Sauvignon) is warm and smoky. Enjoy it

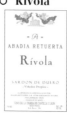

with ketchupy burgers, bistro steaks, and hearty stews of all kinds. $14–16
Castilla y Léon, Spain
Imported by Tempranillo

Gorri Biurko
RIOJA **"Los Valles"**
Medium-bodied. A modern Rioja with the rich depths of a Reserva, minus the oak. This 100% organic wine is stuffed with ripe blackberry and black plum fruit, soft tannins, and a load of spicy cocoa flavor. A cool steak wine, extra-cool lamb wine, and an intriguing partner to spicy chicken dishes like the Peruvian *pollo a la brasa*. $14–16
Rioja, Spain
Imported by De Maison

Pagor
TEMPRANILLO
Medium-bodied. Tender, sweetly ripe, ready to drink, and totally delicious.
The grape of Rioja—Spain's noble, historic red—with a California twist. It's alive with aromas of maraschino cherries and pomegranate and forgoes new oak—a gutsy choice on the part of the winemaker. Enjoy it on its own or with white meats, paella, or fish dishes richly sauced.
$16–18
California

Over $20

Pesquera
RIBERA DEL DUERO
"Condado de Haza"
Medium- to full-bodied. Seemingly a nod to Bordeaux, but with rich Spanish roastiness.
The Pesquera wines from Alejandro Fernandez remain the touchstones for the appellation. Condado de Haza is his second-label wine, which we prefer because it's less oaked, less expensive, and food-friendlier than the main release. Dusty black cherries, cola, and coffee flavors surge through it, especially in older vintages. Serve with garlicky steaks, roasts, and firm Spanish cheese like Manchego and Garrotxa.
$20–23
Ribera del Duero, Spain
Imported by Classical Wines

Bodegas Garanz
TORO Crianza "Cyan"
Medium- to full-bodied.
Rich and bold.
This resplendent Toro, made from the local clone of Tempranillo called Tinta de Toro, is like Rioja on steroids: a deep, beefy, and wonderfully satisfying red with firm finishing tannins. It's a born partner for the spit-roasted sheep and swine of classic Spanish cuisine.
$20–23
Toro, Spain
Imported by Vinos and Gourmet

Dominio de Atauta
RIBERA DEL DUERO
Full-bodied. Bordeaux-like in many ways, with good depth and length.
The vineyard where this wine is made escaped Spain's phylloxera louse plague in the 1800s, so the hundred-plus-year-old vines are on original, ungrafted rootstock—each a precious piece of natural history. The wine is dry and full, with bold black raspberry fruit and bittersweet cocoa making a direct hit on the palate. It's also got nice potential for aging. An extraordinary lamb and roast beef partner. $35–40
Ribera del Duero, Spain
Imported by Rare Wine

Zinfandel

Zinfandel—also known as Zin—is thought of as "America's red wine" because it is grown almost exclusively in California.

THE FORTY-NINERS who flooded California in the Gold Rush of 1849 may have given a push to the wine that today has a huge following. A good percentage of the prospectors took up agriculture, which depended in part on plant material shipped from back east. Among the goodies in the huge shipment of 1852 was Zinfandal [sic], a grape vine that had taken hold in the Northeast after its importation from Europe in 1829. Within a decade, vineyards in both Napa and Sonoma were growing this newcomer. Dozens of those early plantings still thrive and are considered treasures—the reason so many wines on the next three pages are noted as having been made from grapes grown from hundred-year-old (or thereabouts) vines.

Zinfandel is a late-ripener, which makes it sweet yet relatively high in acid. It tends toward high alcohol, the result of high sugar levels at harvest. Zin is also a hard grape to pick: Most bunches have green fruit and red fruit on the same cluster, meaning pickers have to go more than once through the vineyard to harvest enough ripe grapes.

When it comes to aging, American oak is the traditional medium for Zinfandel. The flavor of the finished product is usually described, in order of frequency, as raspberry or blackberry (often paired as "bramble fruits"), black pepper, and spice. For food, Zin is barbecue wine, plain and simple. In fact, there's hardly a better wine-food combo around.

White Zinfandel, the craze that swamped America with sweetish pink wine in the 1980s, grew out of the surplus of Zinfandel California growers found on their hands. In a stroke of marketing genius, Sutter Home turned the surplus to good use, employing the method for making rosé: removing the skin from the grapes just after they are crushed so that just a touch of color remains. (It's the pigment in grape skins that gives red wine its color.) The result was a soft, pink wine sweetened further with a little added sugar. And that's how "blush wine" was born.

Under $20

Cartlidge & Browne
ZINFANDEL
Light- to medium-bodied. Easy-drinking Zinfandel for casual sipping.
Seeking bargain Zin with a bright, berryish character for warm-weather sipping? This is it. A spiced bouquet with a hint of anise is the prelude to plummy, brambly flavors. Burgers, kebabs, Tex-Mex, fried chicken, and party snacks find it friendly. $11–13
California

Benson Ferry
ZINFANDEL
Medium-bodied. Supple, satiny, and gloriously fruity.
Take a sip and feel cherries and boysenberries bounce across your palate like ping-pong balls. Surprisingly, this Zin's daunting 15% alcohol is overwhelmed by the bright flavors—a miraculous feat of balance. You'll enjoy this wine with foods as dissimilar as Chinese takeout and creamy blue cheeses, but it's also great on its own. $13–15
Lodi, California

Easton
ZINFANDEL
Full-bodied. A fruity, food-friendly Zin with terrific length.

Smartly tended very old vines make an old-fashioned Zinfandel that delivers tasty, sun-roasted blackberry fruit with little tannic distraction. Drink this with charcoal-grilled fish or chicken, black bean dishes, and stews. $13–16
Amador, California

Blockheadia Winery
ZINFANDEL
"Blockheadia Ringnosii"
Medium- to full-bodied. A plump, pleasing Zin with a gentle finish.
The Blockheadia winery is so named because its owners use very specific "blocks" of vineyards to create their blends. The ripeness, richness, and tempting red fruit of their Blockheadia Ringnosii (92% Zinfandel, 8% Carignan), graced with a little black peppercorn, is perfectly balanced for white meats like poultry and pork. Blockheadia's **Napa** Zinfandel ($28–30), with 10% Petite Sirah, is better suited to red meats. $16–18
California

Rancho Zabaco
ZINFANDEL **"Dry Creek"**
Full-bodied. Grand-scale Zinfandel with intense alcohol and fruit.
A powerful American red wine, this Zin is unfiltered and rapturously deep, with black raspberry and dried fruit flavors. A shot of Petite Sirah adds extra depth and flavor. It's a perfect pairing with grilled rib-eye steak. Also recommended is **"Chiotti Vineyard"** ($20–22)—darker and even heftier. $16–18
Dry Creek, California

Seghesio
ZINFANDEL **"Sonoma"**
Medium- to full-bodied. Spicy, succulent, and splendid— a perfect introduction to Zin.
Made at a century-old estate from a blend of new and old vineyards in

the Alexander and Dry Creek valleys. Cracked black pepper and a filmy haze of juicy blackberry/ raspberry fruit linger in this delicious wine. Serve it with

THE ZIN OF ZINS?

The third generation at H. Coturri & Sons—namely, Tony the winemaker and Phil the grape grower—are so committed to the cause of great wines made by traditional, sustainable, organic viticulture that it is second nature to them to work as they do. Age–old farming practices that protect and nourish the ecology of their vineyards produce eye–popping wines distinct from any grown in California. The vineyards themselves are like primeval gardens, overgrown with clover, bell beans, mustard flowers, and rye that serve as cover crops during the winter. The wines are made in a converted garage, where all work is painstakingly carried out by hand. Used oak barrels are reconditioned by scraping out their insides to get at the "new" wood beneath, and fermentations proceed naturally until rambunctious levels of alcohol and sweetness are achieved.

While the wines made by the Coturris are among the most opulently sweet, texturally intense wines commercially available, they don't appeal to every palate. Portlike is the typical descriptor, but that doesn't do justice to the wines' remarkable balance. The alcohol is masked by breathtaking layers of black currant, boysenberry, pomegranate, wild strawberry, chocolate, and plum pudding.

A good introduction to the house style is **"Workingman's" Zinfandel** ($16–18), great with most food (the richer the better). Both the single–vineyard **"Forsythe"** and **"Freiberg" Zins** ($25–30) call up liqueur (cassis and framboise, respectively), while the **"Chauvet" Zin** ($22–25), from ancient, gnarled vines, is a hedonistic bowl of fruit compote. These heavenly three beg for fois gras and smoky barbecued ribs.

sausage-flecked red sauces or a pork tenderloin rubbed with mustard. $17–19
Sonoma

Marietta Cellars
ZINFANDEL
Very full-bodied. Super ripe, with no holds barred.
Black currant-scented and nice 'n' thick. Sourced from very old vines in the Dry Creek and Alexander valleys, this Zin has power and sweetness that make it the ultimate challenge for roast duck or a Texas-style brisket. $17–19
Sonoma

Midnight Cellars
ZINFANDEL
Medium-bodied. Drier and more savory than many Zins, and especially good with food.
This is harvested from low-yielding vines, then aged for a year and a half in French oak—an unusual method that yields an unusual Zin. Savory, plummy, and slightly herbal, it has beautiful concentration and a warm accent that seems as much Tuscan as Californian. Try it with rich red sauces, polenta, pork loin, and baked ziti. $18–20
Paso Robles, California

$20 to $40

Saucelito Canyon
ZINFANDEL
Full-bodied. Basically a pot of jam with the added bonus of alcohol.
Here's surreally ripe Zinfandel in practically every vintage, sourced from carefully tended hundred-year-old rootstock planted near San Luis Obispo. In spite of its richness, it remains graceful, with a nice "lift" to its raspberry-bramble finish. A gorgeous grilling mate and especially winning in combo with Carolina pulled pork. $20–24
Arroyo Grande, California

Cosentino
ZINFANDEL "The Zin"
Medium- to full-bodied. Powerful and seductive in good vintages.
A spicy, black-fruited Zin that's made about 75% from old vines and blended with small portions of Syrah and Carignan. We've passed up some of the oakier vintages, but in years like '00 and '01 the wines show tremendous fruit that would please the most serious Zin-head. A nicely charred T-bone is a fine partner.
$23–25
Lodi, California

Summers
ZINFANDEL "Villa Andriana"
Full-bodied. Ravishing, creamy, seductive.
This Zinfandel, grown in the volcanic, hot springs–studded soils of Calistoga, is an immensely pleasurable wine. Incredibly textured and long lasting on the palate, it has remarkably modest alcohol yet tastes of intense mixed berry fruit with a vanilla background. It is also hard to find. We like it with maple-glazed medallions of pork or veal.
$22–24
Napa

Edmeades
ZINFANDEL "Alden Vineyard"
Full-bodied.
WOW, that's sweet!
Here's a wonderful, late-harvested Zin. All our favorite methods are used: native yeasts, no fining, no filtering, minimal handling, and shameless pursuit of excess. Port, baked cherries, and pomegranate fill the mouth and blow the mind. Drink this one with triple-crème and blue cheeses after a meal. $25–30
Mendocino, California

Spelletich Cellars
ZINFANDEL "Tim and Edie"
Full-bodied. The high alcohol content isn't for everyone, but the flavors are gorgeous.
Barbara and Timothy Spelletich make just one thousand cases of this Zin, whose rampant alcohol is tempered by vibrant flavors of plum, strawberry, cinnamon, vanilla, and cherry liqueur. (It's also packaged in a bottle that must weigh at least five pounds.) Challenging yet appealing, it's a winter warmer worthy of game meats and slow-cooked shanks of lamb or beef.
$23–25
Shenandoah, California

THE FUN OF TASTING

*A*T A WINE CLASS you sip a featured Syrah, and the instructor waits for impressions. One classmate announces "prunes" and another pipes up with "ash." Still another ventures "plums." You taste none of the above, but do sense something flowery.

Wine tasting is more science than art. That's because everyone's taste buds are the same, contrary to what many early wine writers believed. The buds on the tongue's surface differ only in which of the four basic flavors they register. Sweetness is registered at the tongue's tip, sourness at its sides, and bitterness at the back. Saltiness registers over the whole surface.

But that's where the commonality ends. Which descriptors pop into your head as the wine washes over your tongue—cherries, herbs, or even leather or wet stones—may be yours and yours alone. In other words, there's hardly ever a "correct" answer to the question of a wine's taste. This doesn't mean that versions of some wines don't have unmistakable flavors (grapefruit in Sauvignon Blanc, black currants in Cabernet), but whatever you think "correct" for your enjoyment is ultimately all that matters.

The Procedure

The first step in tasting is to swirl the wine in the glass to release its aromas. Then raise it to your nose and take a good sniff. Aroma and flavor are inextricably intertwined, and smell alone is often enough to tell you not only what's in store but whether a wine's gone bad. (We find wine a great way to get in touch with one's sense of smell.)

Now take a sip and swish it around to saturate your tongue. After swallowing, smack your lips once or twice to bring air into your retronasal passages and intensify the flavors and aromas. Does the wine taste clean and fresh? Does it have one dominant aroma (say, citrus) or many? Is it lively on the tongue, or does it just sit there? Do the flavors linger in a nice finish?

Above all, look for balance—the relationship between a wine's acids (see Glossary, page 217), sweetness (page 221), and tannins (page 217), if any, and body

(page 217). This sweet white needs acidity to keep from becoming cloying. That red is light and juicy but flavorless because it lacks ripe fruit. A balanced wine just feels right in the mouth.

The reward of paying such close attention to your first sip is the confirmation that no two wines are alike—one reason why appreciating the fruit of the vine is so interesting and downright fun.

CHAPTER TWO

Other Choice Reds

Lacrima di Morro. Abouriou. Malvasia Nera. While you may not be even remotely acquainted with these and other secondary grapes, most are certainly worth getting to know, whether in blends or on their own. In this chapter the wines they yield earn our respect alongside old friends like Barbera, Malbec, and Petite Sirah.

Interestingly, today's obscure also-ran could well become tomorrow's phenomenon. Case in point: Winegrowers never gave much thought to Merlot as anything but a blending grape until the 1980s. So, of the thousands of grape varieties out there, which might be the "next big thing"?

Other Choice Reds

So much red wine, so little time. Surveys show that Americans prefer reds over whites almost three to one— explained, most likely, by the wines' bolder flavors.

ALL IT WHAT YOU WILL—*rouge* (French), *rosso* (Italian), *tinto* (Spanish, Portuguese), or *rot* (German)—red wine is vinted and treasured the world over. Almost anywhere there's a pocket of warmth and arable soil, vines will be planted, grapes will be crushed, vinification will take place, and the bottled product will find its way to a wine store's shelves.

One of the aims of this guide is to introduce you to some choice reds from far and wide, most not as famous as the Cabernets, Pinots, and Merlots (nor in many cases as easy to find). But isn't the discovery of something new one of the most exciting things about wine?

Your search will be abetted by remembering something very basic: Old World wines (i.e., European) tend to be named by their region, while New World wines (those from the Americas and the antipodes) are named by grape. Another word to the wise: Appreciate the beauty of blended wines. Some of the best wines the world has to offer are blends—Bordeaux and Chianti, to name two. Above all, get to know your wines in the company of different foods. That big chewy red that tasted so awful with last night's chicken enchilada may rock your world with tonight's steak Diane. So spread your wings and *explore!*

Still, the territory is sometimes difficult to navigate, especially since wines and their names are anything but cut and dried. Grapevines mutate readily, resulting in numerous subvarieties known as clones. Clonal selection then makes it possible for winegrowers to propagate new strains. Add to this the cloudy history of which grape was imported from where (often centuries and centuries ago), and the branches of the family tree of *Vitis vinifera* and the few other species that provide us with our favorite potable are more than a little tangled.

For example, the Italian grapes Brunello and Prugnolo Gentile fall under the parental umbrella of Sangiovese. Petite Sirah may be either a clone of Syrah or an extinct Rhône variety called Dourif. But in the end, who but a botanist or a winegrower cares? Your focus should be on what you're enjoying at the moment, then expanding your horizons by trying something new, whether a nice sipper or a dinner wine.

Under $10

Casa di Pescatori
SICILIAN RED
Light-bodied. A fun, fruity rosso to drink from carafes.
This bright red is made from Barbera, which juices it up, and Nero d'Avola, which gives it more depth. It's great with lighter Mediterranean foods: pastas, focaccia, olives, cheeses, and *pissaladière*, Nice's pizzalike tart. $5–6
Sicily
Imported by William Grant

Villa Diana
MONTEPULCIANO D'ABRUZZO
Light- to medium-bodied. Perfectly ripe and balanced, and food-versatile.
A steal if there ever was one! This unbelievably underpriced red from the sweet, dark Montepulciano grape goes with any Mediterranean fare you care to throw at it. Ruby red, fragrant, and dry and mellow in taste, it's meant to be enjoyed right away. $5–7
Abruzzi, Italy
Imported by Winebow/ Leonardo LoCascio

Quinta dos Carvalhais
GRAO VASCO
Light- to medium-bodied. A jammy, ripe, cheerfully rustic Portuguese wine.
A tasty blend of Portuguese grapes, this red brings you the pleasure of rich cherry fruit, a shot of café au lait, and the earthiness typical of Portuguese wines. Versatile with food, it's a traditional match for *bacalao,* Portugal's famous dried salt cod. $5–7
Dão, Portugal
Imported by Tri-Vin

Farnese
MONTEPULCIANO D'ABRUZZO "Farneto Valley"
Light- to medium-bodied. An easygoing, fun-to-drink party red.
Here's a fruity *vino di tavola* (Italian table wine) from Montepulciano grapes. Its taste? Berries with a hint of vanilla and smoke. Pure pleasure in a glass at spaghetti dinners and casual get-togethers. $6–8
Abruzzi, Italy
Imported by Farnese/Americal

Cataldo
NERO D'AVOLA
Medium-bodied. A whopping mouthful of fruit for its price.
Dark, earth-and-chocolate-scented fruit from the sun-baked hillsides of Sicily is the signature of this red, which has just enough edge to keep it interesting. If it doesn't put you in the mood for a pizza with the works, nothing will. $6–8
Sicily
Imported by Tri-Vin

Villa Fanelli
PRIMITIVO
Medium-bodied. Delicious fruit at a miraculous price.

Serve this to unsuspecting Italian wine lovers and let them think it's a $20 wine. We love its leathery red fruit and wild, woodsy character with dishes like sausage-and-peppers or polenta with a dollop of red sauce. $6–8
Apulia, Italy
Imported by Verdoni

Domaine de la Chanade
CÔTES DU TARN "Les Rials"
Light-bodied. A delicate wine with a firm touch at the finish.
The grape is Malbec, though the label specifies Braucol—Malbec's

name in the local dialect of the commune of Gaillac in south-western France. This red is floral and wispy, with subtle black fruit. It makes a good conversation-starter at cocktail parties, so put a bottle next to the bean dip. $7–9

Southwest France
Imported by Monsieur Touton

Feudo Monaci
SALICE SALENTINO
Medium-bodied. A bargain bottling of southern Italian richness, rusticity, and flair.
This blend of 80% Negroamaro and 20% Malvasia Nera is scented with dried cherries, spices, and sunbaked earth. It's also the wine for a plateful of sausage and peppers. The grape Negroamaro (in Italian, a merging of "black" and "bitter") is traditionally used for blending. Malvasia Nera is the red subvariety of the white grape Malvasia, which is thought to be native to Turkey and Greece. $7–9

Apulia, Italy
Imported by Frederick Wildman

Château d'Oupia
VIN DE PAYS L'HEURAULT
"Les Hérétiques"
Light- to medium-bodied. A picture-perfect bistro red.
From André Iché's gnarly old vines of Carignan (60%), Syrah (30%), and Grenache (10%) comes a dark, fruity, gulpable *vin de table* for some serious French snacking on baguettes and cheese. $7–9

Languedoc, France
Imported by Louis/Dressner

L. A. Cetto
PETITE SIRAH
Medium-bodied. Sweetly ripe, with a satiny sheen.
Mexican wine? You've gotta try this one. Grown in coastal Baja at high elevation under a hot sun and cool ocean breezes, it's a chocolatey, basso profundo wine for red meats, chipotle chili, and fajitas *al carbon*. The winery's **Cabernet Sauvignon Vino Tinto** ($7–9) is good too, but the Petite Sirah is A+ casual fun. $7–9

Baja, Mexico
Imported by International Importers

Château Aiguilloux
CORBIÈRES
Medium-bodied. Full of fruit and complex earthiness, it tastes much more expensive than it is.
A blend of mostly Carignan and Grenache vinified in the method of Beaujolais, this jumble of cherries, spiced plums, earth, lavender, and leather is a good match for most cheeses, grilled meats, broiled salmon, and bowlfuls of chili or Szechuan noodles. At this price, it's also a great wedding wine. $7–9
Languedoc, France
Imported by Monsieur Touton

Colosi
ROSSO
Medium-bodied. Ruddy, sweet, and remarkably smooth.
This old brand drinks like a concocted brew of raisins, cherry compote, and campfire smoke. It's got also that "peasanty" some-thing that makes you want to drink it from tumblers in the Sicilian sunshine. Enjoy it with deep-dish pizza or spaghetti puttanesca, or veer toward Texas and dig into a platter of nachos loaded with cheese. $7–10
Sicily
Imported by Vias

BARBERA:
BEST RED FOR FOOD?

*W*HILE YET TO BECOME one of the world's widely recognized grapes, Barbera—with its pure cherry bouquet and excellent levels of natural acidity—may be one of wine's best food partners. It is native to Piedmont, where the locals drink it young as they wait for their Barolos and Barbarescos to mature. Happily, that hardly means Barbera's usefulness at the table is limited to Italian cuisine.

Light versions work gracefully with many kinds of seafood and spicy fare, behaving much as white wines do but with the added dimension of red fruit. They take a chill nicely, too. Fuller versions, often aged in *barriques* (small, new, French oak barrels), offer lush ripeness wedded to power and complexity—the holy trinity of great winemaking.

Anyone partial to dishes with fruit or honey and to slow-cooked meats (with a special kind of sweetness all their own) would do well to complement them with Barbera. But above all, this wine almost seems created for tomato sauce (lighter Barberas for light and spicy red sauces, richer ones for meaty red sauces).

For a pure and fruity Barbera to serve with pizza or any other relatively light, tomatoey fare, try **Gallino Barbera d'Alba** ($13–15, *imported by Villa Italia/Lorenzo Scarpone*). For a full-bodied example with ripe tannins and a finish that stands up to meaty lasagna, duck, or a pork roast, an excellent choice is **Bruno Giacosa Barbera d'Alba** ($20–25). It's a regal wine, barrel-aged and built to last. (*Imported by Winebow/Leonardo LoCascio*)

COUNTRY WINES FROM PORTUGAL

Estremadura is a *vinho regional*, a Portuguese wine designation similar to that of the French *vin de pays*. But the two examples cited here are no bumpkins. The ripe, medium–bodied **Quinta de Bons–Ventos Estremadura** ($6–7), made from the local grapes Periquita, Camarate, Tinta Miuda, and Touriga Nacional, offers ample black fruit and a bit of sweet cocoa. It's good with any Mexican dish with "mole" in the name, and we've used it as a sangria base with tremendous results. The lighter **Aveleda Estremadura** ($6–8) is made solely from Periquita, Portugal's "parakeet grape." Cherryish and mild–ly spicy, this nice foil for hard sausages and a bowl of chili is also a good addition to the picnic basket. *Both wines imported by Tri-Vin*

Navarro Correas
MALBEC
Medium-bodied. An attractive luncheon partner with lots of fruit and spice.
This is a great example of the everyday wines from Argentina, made by one of the largest estates there. Enjoy its dusty raspberries and earthy savor with herby bean stews, burgers, and meaty wraps or sandwiches. $7–10
Mendoza, Argentina
Imported by Palm Bay

Feudo Monaci
PRIMITIVO
Medium-bodied. A smooth red with nice depth and juicy fruit that lasts.
You no longer have to travel to southern Italy to enjoy wines like this. The grape many call Italian Zinfandel is here rendered in a dark, brash style loaded with roasted fruit and black olives. (By the way, Primitivo is almost identical to Zinfandel, as DNA testing proved a decade or so ago.) Serve it with grilled fare, fried pork chops, and southern Italian meats and pastas. $8–10
Apulia, Italy
Imported by Frederick Wildman

Viñedos Agapito Rico
CARCHELO
Medium-bodied.
A hearty, sun-warmed red.
Southern Spain is hot, both climatically and metaphorically. This ruddy blend of 50% Mourvèdre (or Monastrell as it's known in Spain), 20% Merlot, 10% Tempranillo, 10% Syrah, and 10% Cabernet Sauvignon is one of our favorites from that sunstruck clime. Simultaneously gutsy and grapey, it's a fine choice for fatty meats and all sorts of bean dishes and cheeses. $8–10
Jumilla, Spain
Imported by Classical Wines

Caves Alianca
ALENTEJO "Alabastro"
Medium-bodied.
Softly rich and warming.
A cherryish Portuguese wine with a sensuous oak-chocolatey finish, this blend of Periquita, Trincadeira, and Cabernet Sauvignon handles the sausages, olives, and rich brown stews of its native cuisine. For something lighter, try the fruity "Tagra" ($7–8), a 100% Periquita grown in Terras do Sado. $8–10
Alentejo, Portugal
Imported by Tri-Vin

Graffigna
MALBEC
"Seleccion Especial"
Medium-bodied. Smooth, sensuous, and sweetly oaked.
Made at a 130-year-old estate in Argentina and redolent of mocha and warm black fruits, this *vino latino* is more than a little enticing. At a casual lunch, it's a fitting empanadas or steak sandwich choice.
$8–10
Tulum, Argentina
Imported by Lauber

Château La Baronne
CORBIÈRES
"Montagne d'Alaric"
Medium-bodied. Great mouthfeel and sun-baked, sweetly ripe fruit.
This consistently lavish blend of old-vine Carignan with doses of Grenache, Mourvèdre, and Syrah is organically cultivated and hand-harvested. It offers licoricey, peppery dark

fruit and *terroir*-oriented complexity for the likes of spicy tagines and chicken mole poblano. How could a wine so good possibly stay at this price?
$8–10
Languedoc, France
Imported by Polaner

Charles Back
GOATS DO ROAM
Medium-bodied.
A plump 'n' hearty mouthful of everyday red (shameless pun notwithstanding).
Côtes du Rhônish? Not really, but a tempting blend of Pinotage,

Shiraz, Cinsault, Grenache, and Carignan. The smoky nose is followed by a rush of plum, black cherry, mocha, and cloves. This hearty red is also versatile with food, so don't limit it to hot dogs and hamburgers. $8–10
Paarl, South Africa
Imported by Vineyard Brands

ONE FROM ONTARIO

If you thought Canadians couldn't produce a decent red wine, Henry of Pelham will set you straight. And who, pray tell, is the man who sounds like an obscure heir to the British throne? He's Henry Smith, born in the early 1700s and the namesake of a Niagara, Ontario, vineyard that puts the Baco Noir grape—developed in a French nursery in 1894—to excellent use.

The brothers Speck (Paul, Matt, and Daniel) run the Henry of Pelham Family Vineyard on land that was deeded to their great, great, great grandfather (Nicholas Smith, father of Henry) in 1794. But their approach to winemaking is thoroughly modern, as evidenced by **Henry of Pelham Baco Noir** ($8–10)—spiritually similar to Zinfandel but more untamed; it suggests a fistful of unwashed late summer

blackberries. Deploy its high acidity with sweet 'n' sour dishes, liver-and-onions, or hot, sizzling sausages. *Imported by Bayfield*

Two notes of interest: 1) The Henry Smith Tavern, built on the family's land by Smith in the mid-1800s, is still in use today as the winery boutique and tour center. 2) One could say the Speck brothers produce a "thinking man's wine," considering all three were philosophy majors in college.

Colonnara
ROSSO PICENO
"Lyricus"
Medium-bodied. Full of flavor, masterfully balanced, and impressive for its price.
Just uncork the bottle, cook up your best pasta marinara, and quaff this peppery, fruity Montepulciano Italian-style from small tumblers all night long. If you're not in the mood to cook, this rosso will make your take-out pizza taste even better. $8–10
Marches, Italy
Imported by Winebow/ Leonardo LoCascio

Sogrape
VINHA DO MONTE
Medium-bodied. Well-built, with a dry oak finish.
From the same folks who brought you . . . Mateus! Be that as it may, this impressive dry red is densely layered with black cherry, cola, and smoke, then capped by a substantial finish and ripe tannins. It's a red-meat wine for sure, especially when the meat is stewed or braised. $8–11
Dão, Portugal
Imported by Evaton

Warwick Valley Winery
BLACK DIRT RED
Medium-bodied.
Wild, grapey, and tingly.
Made from the century-old French hybrid grape Baco Noir, this delicious red tastes like what your great-grandpa might have brewed in the backyard during Prohibition. Pleasingly tart and perfumed with bramble berries, it's wicked fun with shish kebabs and pizza. $9–11
New York State

Apollonio
COPERTINO ROSSO
Medium-bodied.
A big, fat, concentrated wine with a smooth finish.
This red is 88% Negroamaro, with Malvasia Nera, Sangiovese, and Montepulciano accounting for the rest. Unfiltered, unfined, and scented with roasted fruit and a touch of tar and unsweetened chocolate, this ain't kid stuff. Think baked pastas like manicotti, ziti, and cannelloni. $9–11
Apulia, Italy
Imported by Vin Divino

Monte del Fra
BARDOLINO
"Sorelle"
Light-bodied. Fruity and lively, with pleasing astringency.
Corvina is the dominant grape of the Bardolinos and Valpolicellas from Veneto; here, it shared the vat with Sangiovese, Barbera, Molinara, and Rondinella. One of the café sippers of Lake Garda and its environs in the north of Italy, it may be the most refreshing red wine anywhere. Have it with antipasti or delicate fare: seafood, pastas, fresh vegetables. Serve lightly chilled. $9–11
Veneto, Italy
Imported by Wines for Food

$10 to $20

Ars Poetica
VULCANO
Medium-bodied. A rustic, funky, gorgeous table red.
Grown on the volcanic hills of southwestern Italy, the Aglianico grape can make deep, cellarable powerhouse wines or spicy, brick-colored, clay-scented little

---

CAL-I-FORNIA DRINKIN'

If the hippy-dippy Mamas & Papas of *California Dreamin'* fame were still together, they'd probably be singing this wine's praises. The super-ripe, grapey **Belvedere Vineyards Jest Red** ($10–12) is Bob Berteau's labor of love—and a place to use all the delicious grapes he has on his hands but can't always use in his "formal" wines: Petite Sirah, Zinfandel, Pinot Noir, and a hodgepodge of others. With its Portlike nose and whirling vortex of blackberry, raspberry, black currant, and licorice, the medium- to full-bodied Jest Red is as fun as they come. Fire up the grill for this one.

---

quaffers for the local sausages and cheeses. Guess which one this is.
$10–12
Basilicata, Italy
Imported by Verdoni

Poggio Bidini
NERO D'AVOLA
Light- to medium-bodied. Miraculously full-flavored.
With its aromas of dried black fruits and tar, this soft, ruddy wine evokes the "old country"—to be precise, Sicily. We find it perfect with polentas, calzones, sweet sausages, and, of course, spaghetti with gigantic Sicilian meatballs.
$10–12
Sicily
Imported by Panebianco

Taurino
SALICE SALENTINO
Medium-bodied. Quite rich and satisfying—the safest choice on most Italian restaurant lists.
A rustic, popular red blend of Negroamaro and Malvasia Nera that wafts out of the bottle and brings to mind the roasted fruits and warm earth of southern Italy. It's a great pick for pasta and pizza. The heartier, more complex "Notarpanaro" ($14–16) is an Apulian classic. Paired with lamb ragout or a sausage-stuffed green pepper, it's *la dolce vita* in a glass.
$10–12
Apulia, Italy
Imported by Winebow/ Leonardo LoCascio

Les Vignerons d'Estézargues
CÔTES DU RHÔNE
"Les Grandes Vignes"
Medium-bodied. Sleek and satiny, with fascinating, vibrant flavor.
High-acid, low-tannin Cinsault is a French grape that's very rarely seen unblended. Yet here we have a 100% Cinsault—organically made, dripping with ripe red fruit, and as smooth as you please. Better still, it's rich enough for red meats, soft enough for chicken and other white meats, and terrific with Kung Pao chicken. $10–12
Rhône, France
Imported by World Wide Wine

Villa Giada
BARBERA D'ASTI **"Suri Russ"**
Medium-bodied. A juicy, jazzy Barbera with a super-fruity finish.
This chunk of pure cherry fruit seems genetically designed to go with tomato sauce. So why resist the inevitable? Sip it as you dig into old-fashioned spaghetti and meatballs or a sauce-doused veal Parmigiana. It's also great with a mound of crispy onion rings or grilled veggies.
$10–12
Piedmont, Italy
Imported by Vin Divino

BIERZO'S COMEBACK

In ancient times, the steep hillsides of El Bierzo—a small corner of Spain's Castilla y León region—were planted with vines of the grape Mencía, now known to be closely related to Cabernet Franc. But not until the late 1990s did Bierzo vineyards yield anything other than cheap wines enjoyed by the locals. That was when famed Priorat vintner Alvaro Palacios and his nephew, Ricardo Perez, purchased what they saw as Bierzo's best vineyards, situated in and around the small town of Corullón, where old Mencía vines rooted in chalk and schist yield wines of silken texture and sensuous red fruit. Their first vintage, in 1999, bore the label Decendientes de José Palacios in honor of their father and uncle.

Other producers soon followed, and most pursue Mencía's fine potential for lighter, food-friendly wines. The bright, berryish **Bodegas Pucho Bierzo** ($11–$13; *imported by De Maison*) is a fun example, especially well suited to paella, jambalaya, and other spicy rice dishes. **Tilenus Bierzo Roble** ($15–17; *imported by European Cellars*) is a mouthwatering, complex Mencía shot through with rivulets of succulent raspberry; it's a natural with tapas classics like olives and paper-thin slices of Spanish ham. The wine that started it all is much pricier: **Decendientes Corullón** ($60–90; *imported by Rare Wine*), which is atypically powerful for Bierzo; enjoy it with more opulent, meatier fare like leg of lamb.

Terranoble
CARMENÈRE Reserva
Medium- to full-bodied.
A brash red with ample oak
and intense tannins.
Popular in Bordeaux before the
phylloxera louse wreaked havoc
on the vines, Carmenère took
root in South America and
became the main red grape of
Chile even as it became extinct
in France. The Terranoble
Reserva, a blend of 85%
Carmenère and 15% Cabernet
Sauvignon, is built like a tank,
with cocoa, coffee, and black
fruit dominant. Serve it to your
carnivorous friends with a
mixed grill. The usual remarkably
low Chilean pricing is another
plus.
$10–12
Maule, Chile
*Imported by Winebow/
Leonard LoCascio*

Ars Poetica
AGLIANICO DEL VULTURE
Medium-bodied. A ruddy and
rustic country red.
"Grown under the volcano," one
might say, since this dusty, brick-
scented Negroamaro hails from
sun-baked volcanic hillsides.
Enjoy it with earthy stuff:
polenta, baked pastas, and
olivey dishes. $10–12
Basilicata, Italy
Imported by Verdoni

Beni di Batasiolo
BARBERA D'ALBA
Light- to medium-bodied.
A plump, pleasing Barbera in
an especially smooth style.
A nice glass of red plums and
gently spiced cherries that's
lovely paired with pasta in red
sauce, bruschetta, or simple
regional cheeses like Paglia and
Toma. Batasiolo also makes a
much fuller, gamier, *barrique*-
aged Barbera they've christened

"**Sovrana**" ($20–22). It's magnificent with slow-cooked shanks of veal or lamb. $10–12
Piedmont, Italy
Imported by Boisset America

Kasnove
MASIA "M"
Medium-bodied. Rich and rustic, with a spiciness that lasts.
You'll feel the heat (read alcohol) in this 100% old-vine Carignan, grown by a dedicated French perfectionist near the Spanish border—but it's countered by a great burst of brick-scented black fruit flavor. Try it with sausages, beef stew, or a skirt steak with plenty of garlic. $10–12
Roussillon, France
Imported by Sussex

Cantine del Locorotondo
PUGLIA ROSSO "Sfida"
Medium-bodied.
Warm, ruddy, and rustic.
Three grapes achieve a wonderful synergy in this rosso—a blend of 40% Negroamaro (meaning "black and bitter"), 30% Primitivo (jammy and fruity), and 30% Aglianico (subtly clay-scented and lightly tannic). The result is sinfully rich and flavorsome. Fabulous with smoked sausages, pasta with puttanesca sauce, and stinky cheeses. $10–12
Apulia, Italy
Imported by Matt Brothers

Beni di Batasiolo
DOLCETTO D'ALBA
Light- to medium-bodied.
A bistro-style Dolcetto—grapey, soft textured, easy to enjoy.
This wine's rather autumnal palate of black plums and earth best complements antipasti on the order of Italian sausages, sheep cheeses, olives, peppers, and fresh figs. It's also a nice thin-crust pizza choice. Or just sip it on the porch while watching the leaves fall. $10–12
Piedmont, Italy
Imported by Boisset America

Teal Lake
PETIT-VERDOT/ CABERNET SAUVIGNON
Medium-bodied. An intense kosher wine, dark and satisfying.
The unusual addition of Verdot (the "fifth grape" of Bordeaux) adds a lush, berryish quality to this kosher wine, but what you feel at the finish is the oaky tannin. Clearly primed for grill-marked burgers and steaks. $11–13
South Eastern Australia
Imported by Royal Wine

Domaine Saint Antonin
FAUGÈRES
Medium-bodied. A dry, fragrant country red with hearty tannins.
At its best, Faugères should smell intensely of raspberries, with varying degrees of the uniquely French earth-and-heather scent called *garrigue*—and this friendly, delicious example (unfiltered and blended from old vine Grenache, Carignan, and Mourvèdre) rises to the challenge. We find it a good match for herby sausages, root vegetables, and pâté. $11–13
Languedoc, France
Imported by European Cellars

Coop. Del Masroig
MONTSANT
Negre Jove "Les Sorts"
Light- to medium-bodied. Juicy-fruity and buoyant on the palate.
Spain's answer to Beaujolais, this delightful Spanish blend of Garnacha (Grenache) and Cariñena (Carignan) is made in the *negre jove,* or "fresh red" style, meaning whole berry fermentation and light, cherry and vanilla character. It's very appealing on its own or served

with salty or spicy foods.
Give it a little chill. $11–13
Montsant, Spain
Imported by Distinct Expressions

Palama
ROSSO DEL SALENTO "Metiusco"
Medium-bodied. Raisiny and enticingly sweet on the palate.
This blend of 50% Negroamaro, 25% Montepulciano, 20% Malvasia Nera, and 5% Primitivo evokes the rugged, sun-roasted hills of Apulia. The wine is rich with ripe black fruit and aromas of dry earth, musk, and cappuccino. Hearty Italian fare is its ideal partner, with an emphasis on mushrooms, olives, sausages, and game meats. Palama's lighter **Salice Salentino** ($8–10) makes a nice sipper. $12–14
Apulia, Italy
Imported by John Given

Avide
CERASUOLO DI VITTORIA
Medium-bodied.
A seemingly modern style from an ancient place.
The chief appeal of this blend of Nero d'Avola and the Sicilian blending grape Frappato is its creamy, sensuous smoothness and straightforward cherry aromatics. Ideal for roast pork (especially stuffed and sauced), salty cheeses, or flaky fish fillets grilled with fresh herbs. $12–14
Sicily
Imported by Supreme

Shooting Star
BLUE FRANC
Medium-bodied. A sassy, fruity, palate-awakener.
Made from Lemberger, the grape known as Blaufrankish in Austria. Winemaker Jed Steele, of Kendall-Jackson fame, discovered it growing in Washington's Yakima Valley, anglicized it to Blue Franc, added a touch of oak, and in the process crafted a blueberry-and-plum-scented marvel. Fun with fried foods, pizza, roasted veggies, and picnic fare. $12–14
Washington

Convento di Cappuccini
BARBERA D'ASTI
Medium-bodied. A classic Barbera—savory-sweet and elegantly balanced.
A plump, ripe red with a black cherry theme. Use it to complement dishes with northern Italian sauces like Bolognese and the spicy Fra Diavola. It also excels with grilled foods and blunts the bitterness of braised radicchio and similar chicories. $12–14
Piedmont, Italy
Imported by Supreme

Marietta Cellars
OLD VINE RED
Medium- to full-bodied.
Ripe and enticing, with a thick fruit palate.
A nonvintage blend of practically everything but the kitchen sink: Zinfandel, Petite Sirah, Carignan, Gamay, and whatever other grapes the old-timers planted in Sonoma. This delicious mother lode of berries, milk chocolate, and sweet pipe tobacco suggests what Sonoma could do best if vintners would stop yanking out the old vines to plant Merlot. A magnificent soul food choice and a fitting partner for any gutsy, saucy cuisine. $12–14
Sonoma

Domaine Mouréou
MADIRAN
Medium- to full-bodied.
A rock-solid, meat-eater's red.
Here's a ripe, rustic blend of Cabernet and Tannat, the

indigenous grape of Madiran in southwestern France. The blackest of black fruits (blackberry, black currant) are accompanied by strong tannins—the reason Madiran is best served with something fatty or fleshy, including smoked cheeses and thick, meaty stews.
$12–14
Southwest France
Imported by Wines for Food

Boccadigabbia
ROSSO PICENO
Medium- to full-bodied. A sturdy, modern Adriatic red.
This Montepulciano drinks like good Bordeaux. Gratifyingly dark, robust, and firm-textured, it's graced with a smoky element as well. Great with a grilled rib eye or firm grana cheeses. $12–14
Marches, Italy
Imported by Marc de Grazia

Cosse Maisonneuve
CAHORS "Les Laquets"
Medium- to full-bodied. Effortlessly combines richness, length of flavor, and enormous power.
This is the legendary "black wine of Cahors," made from Malbec and boasting striking aromas of fresh soil, black pepper, and violets. Not your simple sipper by any

means, it begs for fatty fare and smoked sausages and meaty stews. As it matures, its oak becomes more apparent.
$12–14
Southwest France
Imported by European Cellars

Olivares
MONASTRELL
"Altos de la Hoya"
Medium- to full-bodied. Full of power and good concentration.
Made from 100% Monastrell (Mourvèdre in France), a red grape capable of yielding big, black-hued wines. This version adds a lovely Spanish earthiness and strong espresso flavors to the finished product. A superb red meat mate at a bargain price!
$12–15
Jumilla, Spain
Imported by Polaner

Château La Caminade
CAHORS "La Commandery"
Medium-bodied. Very dry, savory, and about as elegant as rustic Cahors can get.
La Caminade makes classic Cahors, with its Malbec varietal scents of dried black fruit, lavender, and leather. This example also has great balance, thanks to the beneficial addition of a little Merlot. Excellent with

ARGENTINA'S MAINSTAY GRAPE

Malbec is the mainstay grape of Argentine reds, and here are two attractive examples. **Altos Las Hormigas Malbec** ($10–12) is a firm, rich, dry red with an enticing fragrance. Lovers of California wine won't be disappointed by this mouthful of coffee, cocoa, black fruits, and something faintly floral. (Merlot lovers will flip for it!) While steak is its natural partner, it's fruity enough for pork chops with red beans and rice. *Imported by Marc de Grazia*

Giaquinta Malbec "Cavas del Valle" ($13–15) is fruitier and more vivacious than many Malbecs, reminiscent of a full-bodied Dolcetto. Though plump and loaded with blackberry fruit, it's what might be called "Malbec Lite." Still, like all Malbecs, it's Grade A steak wine, especially with the garlicky steak chimichurri. *Imported by Bayfield*

A LITTLE SWEETIE?

While its name translates as "little sweet one," the Dolcetto grape isn't so much sweet as grapey and spicey, making the light wines it yields very easy to drink. The small Piedmont village of Dogliani claims to be the birthplace of the grape, but the wines of Dolcetto d'Alba appellation, home to more high-quality producers, are better known. Still, that doesn't keep Dolcetto di Dogliani from turning out some real winners.

Here are two worth trying. **Francesco Boschis Dolcetto di Dogliani "Pianezzo"** ($13–15) is fragrant, nicely concentrated, and piquant. Its berry aromas and lavender notes make it a good fit for focaccia, pizza, baked chicken, and rich pastas. A bolder Dolcetto from the same vineyard is **Dolcetto di Dogliani "Sori San Martino"** ($15–18), a strong, deep purple, a carnivore's wine that is said to improve with age. *Imported by Marc de Grazia*

---

cold cuts, firm cheeses, and duck confit. $12–15
Southwest France
Imported by Bayfield

Bogle Vineyards
PETITE SIRAH
Medium- to full-bodied.
Simply put, a big black wine.
With plenty of fruit and tannins, this is a dense, chocolatey red. What is still California's best deal in Petite Sirah will make you sing hallelujah when you pair it with grilled steaks, burgers, fried pork chops, or pizza with the works. $12–15
California

Hauner
SALINA ROSSO
Medium-bodied. Very earthy and savory, with a finish full of spice.
This super-ripe Sicilian rosso is made from 100% Nerello Moscalese, a grape with a wildly perfumed mix of earth, dried fruit, and the scent that can only be described as cigar box. Try it with ripe cheeses or meaty potpie. $13–15
Sicily
Imported by Bacchanal

Felline
PRIMITIVO DI MANDURIA
Medium- to full-bodied.
A big, suavely textured, "modern" Primitivo.
Creamy black-raspberry fruit and notable oak styling result in a half-Californian, half-Italian variation on traditional Primitivo—one that's irresistible to most folks. Ideal partners are rich, doughy pastas and deep-dish pizza. $13–15
Apulia, Italy
Imported by Domaine Select

Mayol
BONARDA "Vista Flores"
Medium-bodied.
Fresh and invigorating, with a long and sassy fruit finish.
An Italian grape now thriving in Argentina, Bonarda has a piquancy that's exceptionally appealing when the grape is properly ripened. Mayol's bright magenta wine offers blackberry and vanilla flavors that seem to glow from somewhere in its depths. Intriguing with Asian dishes, and a regional match with spicy steak chimichurri. $13–15
Mendoza, Argentina
Imported by OmniWines

Battistotti
MARZEMINO
Light- to medium-bodied. Fruity, with a pleasing astringency.
From an Italian appellation far north in the Italian Alps comes this pale, dry Marzemino, which is berryish and flowery up front, then earthier and dry at the finish. It needs food, but what Italian wine doesn't? Star pairings include sausages, antipasti, roasted red peppers with anchovies, pasta carbonara, and light dishes with herby red sauces. $13–15
Trentino, Italy
Imported by Vias

La Ghersa
MONFERRATO "Piage"
**Medium-bodied.
Dark and vigorous, with ample fruit and a meaty finish.**
Barbera, Syrah, and Merlot—a weird combination that really works here! While the ripe, juicy, cherry fruitiness of Barbera stands out, the other grapes tone this wine down to something more serious. Good matches at the table include hearty baked pastas and gravied dishes like veal Marsala. $13–15
Piedmont
Imported by Epic Wines

Montes
CABERNET SAUVIGNON/ CARMENÈRE "Apalta Vineyard"
**Medium- to full-bodied.
Darker, a tad sweeter, and more exotic than straight Cabernet.**
From Montes's "Limited Selection" series, this is a single-vineyard wine made from 70% Cabernet and 30% Carmenère, the grape dubbed Chile's "great red hope." Reminiscent of a roasty, tarry Haut-Médoc from

Bordeaux, the blend is a bold companion to garlicky steaks and lamb. $13–15
Santa Cruz, Chile
Imported by TGIC

Tasca d'Almerita
REGALEALI ROSSO
Medium-bodied. A gentle, juicy, and ultratraditional Sicilian red.
Perhaps the best-known wine of Sicily, this attractively plump blend of native grapes (90% Nero d'Avola and 10% Perricone) sings with red cherry and fig notes. Match it with pasta puttanesca and similarly piquant dishes. Collectors prize the **"Rosso del Conte"** ($42–45), a reserve bottling of the same blend; this one's enormously rich and matured in new French oak. $14–16
Sicily
Imported by Winebow/ Leonard LoCascio

Vinum Cellars
PETITE SIRAH "Pets"
Full-bodied. Smooth and sun-roasted, with a soft, opulent finish.
Here's a sultry, full-blooded entry from that uniquely Californian grape, Petite Sirah. It floods the mouth  with blackberries. Ready for action with grilled red meats, turkey, and the heartiest black bean soups. That's Tanker the dog on the label. Woof! $14–16
Clarksburg, California

Monte Schiavo
LACRIMA DI MORRO D'ALBA
Light- to medium-bodied. Tender and gentle, with a haunting floral fragrance.
A terrific wine, buoyant with a nose like fresh roses, texture like

99

MONTEPULCIANO:
NOT TO BE CONFUSED WITH. . .

A BRIEF LESSON on the Italian grape Montepulciano is a favor to wine lovers. Main point one: The grape is grown primarily in the region of Abruzzi, wherein lies the Montepulciano d'Abruzzo appellation, the varietal wines of which range from ordinary to sublime. Main point two: The treasured wines of the Vino Nobile di Montepulciano appellation, to the northwest in central Tuscany, are made from Sangiovese and various blending grapes—none of which is Montepulciano.

To sum up: Montepulician d'Abruzzo wines take their name from the grape, while the more coveted Vino Nobile di Montepulciano is named for a tiny town in the Tuscan hills southeast of Florence.

Now it's time to doff your thinking cap and enjoy what the Abruzzi wines have to offer, starting with **Cantina Zaccagnini Montepulciano d'Abruzzo** ($14–16). This wine comes with a little vine cutting tied to the bottleneck—a cute rustic touch hinting at the raucous, wood-spiced pleasures within. Full-bodied and flavorful, it's an unbridled pleasure with Italian food of all sorts, including steaks, chops, hearty lasagnas, and grills. *Imported by Viva Vino*

Way up the price scale is **Emidio Pepe Montepulciano d'Abruzzo** ($70–125, more for older vintages). This full-bodied beauty is late-released, meaning any vintage will be mature and extremely complex. In fact, this wine is incredible—a jet-black, endlessly aromatic red teeming with nuts, dried black currants, and earthy varietal character (the grapes are actually stomped on). Serve with steaks and game, or contemplate it on its own as a throwback to a bygone era. A footnote: Winemaker Emidio Pepe has a collection of available vintages from the '70s and '80s awaiting intrepid collectors who want something spectacular and different for their cellars—and the pricing is surprisingly low. *Imported by Cadet*

Church of San Biagio, in the town of Montepulciano—the "other" appellation

sheer silk, and a very cherryish finish. Excellent with fish, it's also great to sip with a homey tuna noodle casserole or similar creamy dishes. $14–16
Marches, Italy
Imported by Verdoni

Giuseppe Mascarello
FREISA "Toetto"
Medium-bodied.
An electrifying shot of zippy, jamlike fruit and spice.
An obscure but wonderful entry from Mascarello, our favorite Piedmont estate. Strawberry-scented, super-juicy Freisa is a little-known Piedmontese specialty, great for peppery dishes, salty sausages, and antipasti. It drinks best with a slight chill. $14–16
Piedmont, Italy
Imported by Polaner

Cataldi Madonna
MONTEPULCIANO D'ABRUZZO
Medium-bodied. Opulent texture and good, strong flavors—compelling overall.
Vintage after vintage, this one's always a hit. Its burst of black cherries and cocoa makes for satisfying drinking with meaty Italian victuals like veal Marsala and Tuscan steak. The Cabernet-Montepulciano blend called **Malandrino** ($18–21) is also quite nice but oakier. $14–16
Abruzzi, Italy
Imported by Vias

Trentadue
OLD PATCH RED
Medium-bodied. Deeply fruity.
This old-vines California blend (Zinfandel, Carignan, Petite Sirah) sports chocolate-dipped cherries, boysenberries, and red currants from start to finish.

A great spring and summer cookout wine, it's also delicious with a range of Tex-Mex or Latino dishes from your local takeout. $15–17
Sonoma

La Vis
LAGREIN "I Baldazzini"
Medium-bodied. Complex, subtle, and fascinating with food.
Lagrein is an indigenous black grape of Alpine Italy—now very rare (it's confined to a few hundred acres) and beloved by Italian wine fanatics. The La Vis cooperative's wines have an especially appealing style, yet they're atypical: soft, subtle, and extraordinarily complex for a wine not usually known for being so. Aromas of meat, mushrooms, black currants, and coffee are woven into the bouquet in ways that become more fascinating as you sip. Enjoy this red alongside slow-cooked meats, jambalaya, aromatic cheeses, or anything with mushrooms. $15–17
Trentino, Italy
Imported by OmniWines

Tommaso Bussola
VALPOLICELLA Classico "bg"
Medium-bodied. A special rendition of its type—extremely rich, ripe and lasting.
This is a grapefest in a bottle, with 20% Rondinella, 65% Corvina, and varying doses of Cabernet Franc, Cabernet Sauvignon, Dindarella, and Pindara—all from low-yielding old vines. The wine sees modest amounts of new oak and is thick with sweet plum, vanilla, and cherry fruit. The "bg" is the standard line and the best price/quality ratio; some prefer the higher-end "tb" ($38–40),

which is a deeper, more structured wine. Serve with glazed ham, calves-liver or other organ meats, or game birds such as quail or partridge. $15–17
Veneto, Italy
Imported by Polaner

Clay Station
PETITE SIRAH
Medium-bodied.
Surprisingly mild for such a dark, concentrated wine.
From the Indelicato family, an old winemaking dynasty in Lodi. Only 1,250 cases are produced of this blackish California specialty. A year in American and French oak adds some weight, but it's the rich blueberry fruit that shines. An all-American red for all-American favorites like hot dogs, barbecue, chili. $15–17
Lodi, California

Giuseppe Mascarello
DOLCETTO D'ALBA
"Santo Stefano di Perno"
Medium-bodied. Complex and forceful, with a touch of sweetness and coarse tannins. The real deal!
Get ready for a gorgeously rustic, leathery-scented red that's redolent of the vineyard soil. Let it breathe a little, then enjoy it with venison, Italian sausage, or mushroom dishes. $15–17
Piedmont, Italy
Imported by Polaner

José Maria da Fonseca
PRIMUM
Medium- to full-bodied.
One of Portugal's more elegant wines, barrel-aged and rich.
The deluxe offering from a huge family-owned Portuguese estate, made from Touriga Nacional and Touriga Francesca, indigenous grapes used in Port. Think of it as a modest Bordeaux that's

been super-ripened. You'll find it ravishing with a glazed roast loin of pork with herb-flecked new potatoes on the side. $15–18
Terras do Sado, Portugal
Imported by Tri-Vin

San Rustico
VALPOLICELLA
Classico Superiore "Gaso"
Medium- to full-bodied. Ripe, deeply layered, and juicy.
This single-vineyard boutique bottling is blended from the traditional Veronese troika of Corvina, Molinara, and Rondinella. A portion of the fruit is air-dried, resulting in a wine with raisiny, concentrated flavors that make it a velvety partner for carbonara and sweetly sauced poultry or pork. The estate also produces a consistently fine **Amarone della Valpolicella "Gaso"** ($38–40), a strong, flamboyant red that's a beautiful after-dinner choice with salty cheeses like Parmesan, Grana Padano, and Gorgonzola. $16–18
Veneto, Italy
Imported by John Given

Elian Daros
CÔTES DU MARMANDAIS
"Chante Coucou"
Medium-bodied. A dark purple wine with a bold personality.
Elian Daros's organic, hand-harvested wines are the best in this tiny region just southeast of Bordeaux on the Garonne River. The chief grape is Abouriou—about as obscure as a grape can be. But who cares once you taste this juicy mouthful of mulberries and Concord grape jam? The wine's assertiveness conquers foods many other wines can't handle, like greasy fried chicken and vinegary dishes. $16–18
Southwest France
Imported by European Cellars

Muri-Gries
LAGREIN Dunkel
**Medium- to full-bodied.
This dark (dunkel) red is
lavish and beefy.**
Made according to strict
tradition by the brothers of the
Benedictine order of the Muri-
Gries, this wine has deeply
ensconced layers of black fruit,
smoke, and freshly turned earth.
It's superb with pot roast and all
kinds of game meat.
$16–18
Alto Adige, Italy
Imported by Polaner

D'Angelo
AGLIANICO DEL VULTURE
**Medium-bodied.
A savory, approachable
Aglianico with good balance.**
Aglianico is a dark-skinned Italian
grape of Greek origin. This 100%
example is grown in volcanic soils
that impart a unique mineral
quality reminiscent of baked
bricks or clay. The wine is a
fitting partner for a mushroom
risotto or anything baked slowly
under layers of cheese. $16–18
Basilicata, Italy
Imported by Opici

Di Meo
IRPINIA AGLIANICO
**Medium-bodied.
Fruitier than most Aglianicos
and well balanced for food.**
This is a soft, voluptuous version
of Aglianico—full of those
brickish, roasty aromas that
characterize the grape but with
a surprising amount of cherry
fruit at its core. Try it with crusty
pork chops, polentas, and pastas
with sausage. $16–18
Campania, Italy
Imported by Supreme

Franck Peillot
MONDEUSE
**Light- to medium-bodied.
Enticingly perfumed,
then pleasantly astringent
in the finish.**
The grape is
Mondeuse,
known as
Refosco in
Italy. Grapey
and raspberryish, the wine has a
piquancy that makes it a great fish
and white meat accompaniment.
Or try it slightly chilled with Thai,
Vietnamese, or other Southeast
Asian dishes. $16–18
Savoie, France
Imported by Louis/Dressner

Luis Pato
BAGA
**Medium-bodied. Nice, rustic,
fruity stuff with firm tannins.**
Baga is "berry" in Portuguese,
so this wine's flavor is self-
explanatory. Unfiltered, un-fined,
and a little gruff in character, it's
just right for fried pork or chicken
and hearty Iberian specialties like
paella, *puerco asada* (roasted
fresh ham), and braised pork
with clams (the traditional dish
of Algarve, Portugal's southern-
most region). $16–18
Beira, Portugal
Imported by Tri-Vin

Le Terrazze
ROSSO CONERO
**Medium-bodied. Fragrant,
dry, and elegant—a feasting red.**
From Montepulciano
grapes grown on the
central eastern shore
of Italy, this finely
balanced wine,
briefly aged in large
casks, sports smoke-
scented red fruit and a juiciness
that begs for food. It's a savory
companion to chicken or pork

dishes and pasta with hearty red sauces. $17–19
Marches, Italy
Imported by Marc de Grazia

Gianni Gagliardo
DOLCETTO D'ALBA
Light- to medium-bodied.
A soft and juicy red with delicious fruit and no hard edges.
This young Italian winemaker crafts a refreshingly unpretentious Dolcetto that's fragrant with cherries and mint. It's not only a terrific wine for sipping but also an easygoing companion for pasta and pizza. Chill it first. $17–19
Piedmont, Italy
Imported by Enotec

Coturri
ALBARELLO
Full-bodied. Red-wine density and ripeness, white-wine acidity.
This blend-of-all-blends from Sonoma is 40% Petite Sirah and 40% Zinfandel, with Carignan, Barbera, and Alicante-Bouschet, Early Burgundy, Sauvignon Vert, Sémillon, and Muscat topping it off. A joyful jumble of crushed berries, passion flowers, and marmalade, it excites your palate with intense, juicy character. Drink it lightly chilled with a steaming bowl of gumbo, grilled chicken with roasted red peppers, or a citrusy ceviche. $17–20
Sonoma

Cascina Tavijn
RUCHÉ
Medium-bodied.
Bright, fruity, and forceful.
Ruché (pronounced roo-KAY) is a marvelously obscure Piedmontese wine that somehow allows bright, grapey fruit to emerge through a haze of alcohol and tannins. By making your mouth water one

moment and then drying it out the next, it has something of a vodka-and-cranberry quality about it. Serve it with sweet/salty things like pork with fruit or sausages packed with sun-dried tomatoes and fennel. $17–20
Piedmont, Italy
Imported by Louis/Dressner

Pecchenino
DOLCETTO DI DOGLIANI
"San Luigi"
Medium-bodied.
Purplish, low-acid, fruity— a mouthfilling pleasure.
Piedmontese locals say that if you analyze a sample of their blood, half of it will turn out to be Dolcetto. They drink this kind of wine young with savory Italian cooking: antipasti, veal and pork dishes, baked pastas, and soft buttered noodles with sage. While Dogliani isn't the preferred zone of production for Dolcetto, this is one wine that far exceeds its appellation. $18–20
Piedmont, Italy
Imported by Vias

Cline Cellars
MOURVÈDRE "Ancient Vines"
Medium- to full-bodied.
Flavorsome and firm, with rich tannins and an exotic perfume.
Fred Cline has rescued Mourvèdre from extinction in California with his carefully crafted, savory interpretation. (Mourvèdre produces very dark wines, hefty to the point of carnality.) It may not be quite as black as you hope, but it's always a mouthful of tarry, dusty, dried blueberries and black currants— not to mention a nice touch of cocoa from the oak; some vintages are more tannic than others. Cellar it a few years and

then unveil it with a five-spice Cantonese roast duck. $18–20
Contra Costa, California

Foradori
TEROLDEGO ROTALIANO
Medium-bodied. Fascinating rarity with savory character and excellent concentration.
This is 100% Teroldego—a grape that covers fewer than three hundred acres of soil in the world. Elisabetta Foradori has made it her life's work to turn this forgotten variety into serious wine worthy of cellaring. Low yields and forty-year-old vines lend ample depth and complexity to its herby, red fruit palate. Serve with meaty lasagnas, osso buco, a rich risotto, or steak. $18–20
Trentino, Italy
Imported by Polaner

Domaine de Lagrezette
CAHORS
Medium-bodied. A strapping red for the cellar.
Scented with black licorice, iron, and dusty black fruits, this blend of 75% Malbec and 25% Merlot is in no sense a cute little sipper. It's a commited carnivore's red, with tannins that need a few years to mellow. Tackle it at the table with the stuff the locals eat in Cahors: duck confit and cassoulet. $18–21
Southwest France
Imported by Martin Scott

Mionetto
RASO SCURO
Medium-bodied. Succulent, balanced, and surprisingly easy to drink for such a complex wine.
Inside the flamboyant flask bottle dwells a unique blend of Cabernet Sauvignon and Teroldego, one of the rarest grape varieties in Italy. Raspberries and roasted beef notes appear subtly in the bouquet and seem to expand through the finish. It's an exciting, unusual choice for rich pastas, pepper steak, and northern Italian cheeses like Fontina and Tallegio.
$18–22
Veneto, Italy
Imported by Mionetto

$20 to $30

Renwood
BARBERA
Medium-bodied. Ripely sweet and succulent, with abundant fruit.
Renwood Winery is more famous for its Zinfandels, but we prefer its Barbera, which shows less oak and plenty of cherry, blueberry, and sweet cola flavor. Don't expect anything remotely Italian-tasting. Just pour it with a bacon burger, other grilled fare, or spicy Thai or Vietnamese and enjoy the ride.
$20–22
Amador, California

COS
CERASUOLO DI VITTORIA CLASSICO
Medium-bodied. Creamy-textured and very plush.
An important wine made in the Vittoria growing zone at the southeast corner of Sicily. (The "COS" is formed from the initials of the three proprietors' first names.) Cerasuolo is a traditional blend of Nero d'Avola and Frappato, which adds a fruity, peppery note. Serve this mouthfilling mix of roasted cherries and berries with roast pork, salty cheeses, and game birds. $20–22
Sicily
Imported by Domaine Select

Marietta Cellars
PETITE SIRAH
Very full-bodied.
**One of the heartiest, most
decadent red wines in
California.**
Marietta's old-vine Petite Sirah
usually goes into other blends.
But when Chris Bilbro bottles it
alone, it's an opaque black elixir
that lusciously coats the glass.
It's hard to specify fruits here;
just imagine a stew of mixed
berries reduced to their essence.
A magnificent barbecue wine
and a perfect duck partner.
$20–22
Sonoma

Taurian Vineyards
PETITE SIRAH
"Proprietors Reserve"
**Full-bodied. Rustic, juicy,
and unpretentious.**
Elso Taurian has been growing
small amounts of ruddy Petite
Sirah for more than thirty years
on his two-acre plot of old vines
in the Russian River valley. The
wine's appealing gaminess and
tart black fruit are just what you
want at a summer cookout
starring home-grown vegetables
and fresh tomatoes. $20–24
Sonoma

Marziano & Enrico Abbona
DOLCETTO DI DOGLIANI
"Papa Celso"
**Full-bodied. An opaque purple
super-Dolcetto with soft tannins
and grapey fruit that lasts.**
This surprising wine swiftly
overtakes your palate and
cleverly distracts you with
gorgeous aromas of violets and
truffles. That's why you'll want
to keep it around for your next
Piedmontese feast of sheep
cheeses and braised lamb or
beef. If you can't find the Papa

Celso, Abbona's regular **Dolcetto
di Dogliani** ($15–17) is an
excellent alternative.
$20–25
Piedmont, Italy
Imported by Polaner

San Giuliano
BARBERA D'ALBA
"Fiore di Marcorino"
**Full-bodied. Mouthfilling ripe
tannins and a huge finish.**
Barrel-aged, high-octane,
and magnificent! All the slurpy,
sexy mouthfeel you could want—
a palate of ripe cherries and
grenadine with a cool
sort of leathery rusticity
underneath—makes for great
drinking and serious food
matching. Explore this Barbera
with meat lasagnas, ducks,
roast pig, or timbale.
$20–25
Piedmont, Italy
Imported by Summa Vitis

Domaine de la Marfée
COTEAUX DE LANGUEDOC
**Full-bodied. A super-
concentrated, complex wine—
as good as Carignan
gets.**
The deep purple,
high-tannin Carignan
originated in Spain
but is now the most

widely grown grape in France.
Very limited production and extra
bottle age make this wine—a
magnificent old-vines Carignan
from a century-old vineyard—an
artisanal effort. It is intense,
rustic, peppery, wild, and purple
bordering on black. At the dinner
table, think sirloin, rack of lamb,
or smoked sausage.
$20–25
Languedoc, France
Imported by European Cellars

TWO KNOCKOUT PRIMITIVOS

Primitivo di Manduria is an Italian DOC in sun-roasted Apulia, and one of its estates—the ultramodern Vinicola Savese—makes some of the best Primitivos around. **Vinicola Savese Primitivo di Manduria "Terrarossa"** ($22–24) is an earthy draught that drinks like a particularly savage red Zinfandel. Notes of dark chocolate, black licorice, raspberry, and damp soil crowd into the glass, jockeying for your attention. Come dinner-time, team this full-bodied red with a no-nonsense red meat extravaganza.

Primitivo (and Zin) lovers should go to extraordinary lengths to locate **Primitivo di Manduria Dolce Naturale** ($30–35), a sweet, late-harvest rarity. Pour it (sparingly, we advise) alongside bittersweet chocolate desserts or a deluxe triple-crème cheese. *Both wines imported by Tricana*

Mastroberardino
TAURASI "Radici"
Full-bodied.
A bold, firm-textured, old-fashioned red that needs aging.
Mastroberardino is the most renowned interpreter of the Aglianico grape, which accounts for 100% of this wine. With its formidable battery of tannins and pungent palate of scorched earth, dried fruits, and cinnamon, this is not for New World wine fans (though your great-grandfather would probably love it!). It's ideal for traditional southern Italian cuisine, has tremendous cellar potential, and is pricier in older vintages.
$20–30
Campania, Italy
Imported by Martin Scott

Summers
CHARBONO "Villa Andriana"
Full-bodied. Miraculously well-balanced and low-alcohol for such a thick, lush wine.
This red is made from Charbono, an obscure Italian grape barely grown in Italy anymore but lovingly nurtured by a few fanatics in California. Vividly purple and exploding with

blueberry fruit, it's very versatile at the table. Grilled salmon or tuna, bean salads, blue cheeses, barbecue, and spicy fare of all kinds would be delicious with this exotic tipple. $22–24
Napa

Arnaldo-Caprai
MONTEFALCO ROSSO
Full-bodied. A powerful red that in the old days would've been described as "manly."
This heady blend has 70% Sangiovese and 15% Merlot—plus 15% Sagrantino, the most tannic red wine grape in the world. And while that makes for pretty muscular stuff, the wine is also deep, earthy, leathery, and wonderful. A match with a beef tenderloin and earthy ingredients like mushrooms, truffles, and roasted root vegetables would be fantastic.
$22–24
Umbria, Italy
Imported by Villa Italia

Zenato
RIPASSA DI VALPOLICELLA
Full-bodied. Thick and velvety, extravagantly ripe, and almost impossible to resist.
In the Ripassa method, fresh Valpolicella wine is pumped over the spent skins of Amarone

(basically, raisined grapes), giving it a richer, sweeter, dried fruit character. In both taste and texture this version drinks like chocolate sauce—yet it reveals an intriguing complexity if you pay attention. Match it with roast beef or venison, a prune-stuffed pork roast, or aged, crumbly blue cheeses. FYI, Zenato's basic **Valpolicella** ($10–12) is a cheap, pleasing spaghetti red. $22–25
Veneto, Italy
*Imported by Winebow/
Leonardo LoCascio*

Girard
PETITE SIRAH
Full-bodied. Jet-black and powerful yet wholly smooth.
Run by various owners since its founding in 1978, Girard is now turning out great powerhouse wines from some of Napa's oldest vineyards. Their Petite Sirah, grown on a rescued plot of hundred-year-old vines, tastes like a bowl of sun-ripened figs with a little Rhônish earth lurking beneath. A great match for barbecue ribs and slow-smoked meats. $22–25
Napa

Cellers Unió
PRIORAT
"Tendral"
Full-bodied. Sun-roasted, luscious, and complex.
This is our favorite release from this quality-driven Spanish co-op. A blend of 60% Carignan and 40% Grenache, it is aged in a combination of used sherry casks and American oak, an interesting recipe for Priorat. The wine is powerful, no question, but its fine balance makes it elegant as well. Let it breathe a bit and pair it with maple-glazed ham, kielbasa, or anything big and gamey. $22–25
Priorat, Spain
Imported by OmniWines

Bodegas Balcona
MONASTRELL
"Partal" 2000
Full-bodied. Very powerful on the palate, sun-ripened but not overripe—in a word, classy.
With its enticing, earthy black currants and the ripe tannic backbone that makes it suitable for long cellaring, this thought-provoking artisanal wine makes one wonder just how high Spain's star will rise in the pecking order of wine nations over the next decade. Try it with chorizo sausage or aromatic Spanish cheeses like Cabrales and Idiazabal.
$23–25
Bullas, Spain
Imported by Tempranillo

Domaine du Gros Noré
BANDOL
Full-bodied. A serious, satisfying, flamboyantly rich dinner wine.
That Provençal treat—the Old World big taste of Mourvèdre—is yours when you pour this red. Alain Pascal's version of Bandol is fruitier and smoother than many, with extraordinary elegance. Still, this is no casual sipper. It shows its best side with steaks, duck, and strongly flavored sausages.
$24–26
Bandol, France
Imported by Kermit Lynch

Giuseppe Mascarello
BARBERA D'ALBA
"Santo Stefano di Perno"
Medium-bodied. Graceful, yet incredibly full-flavored and fragrant.
Here's an ultratraditional Barbera whose expression of its *terroir* is unparalleled. Aromatic

AMARONE: WORTH EVERY PENNY

MARONE is a *recioto* (reh–CHAW–toh), or dried grape, wine. And like all reciotos, it is a labor of love for the winemaker. In hot, dry years in Italy's Veneto region (maybe three or four in a decade), the three grapes of the Valpolicella blend—Corvina, Molinara, and Rondinella—are left on the vines until they are super-ripe, almost raisined. They're then air-dried on straw mats to concentrate their flavors. The few drops of juice pressed from them is fermented to dryness, emerging as a robust, high-alcohol red wine for long-term aging.

Amarone doesn't come cheap, but it's worth every penny on the right occasion. **Allegrini Amarone della Valpolicella** ($60–65), is a big-hearted wine booming with notes of smoke, prune, dried cherry, leather, and sandalwood. We like it in its first ten years, while some connoisseurs will insist on waiting at least that long. But there's no disputing its magnificence with roast duck and game. It's also an after-dinner luxury with a hunk of Parmigiano-Reggiano.

Less pricey but still superb is **Allegrini's "Palazzo della Torre"** ($20–22), a smooth, full-bodied red made from 70% regular grapes and 30% raisined ones. *Both wines imported by Winebow/Leonardo LoCascio*

---

clouds of sage, wild mushroom, rich loam, and damp straw float temptingly above a basketful of super-ripe cherries. Vividly fruity when young and earthier and more complex after six to eight years, it's compelling either way. Serve it with lasagna, salty cheeses, and stuffed roasts of pork or veal.
$25–30
Piedmont, Italy
Imported by Polaner

Prunotto
BARBERA D'ALBA
"Pian Romualdo"
Medium- to full-bodied. Succulent, deep-fruited, matured in oak, and built to last. Sometimes Barbera is a light little drink. At other times it's rich and kirschlike—red meat required. This one falls into the latter category, so uncork it when carnivorous company comes to dine. $28–30
Piedmont, Italy
Imported by Winebow/ Leonardo LoCascio

Over $30

Château Bouscassé
MADIRAN "Vielles Vignes"
Very full-bodied. Big and meaty, with pure Old World character and ferocious tannins.
Alain Brumont crafts his mightiest Madiran from fifty-year-old vines of Tannat grown near the Pyrenees. (Tannat is among the most tannic of grapes, which may explain its name.) Baked earth, tar, leather, and prunes dominate in this red, with high notes of black tea. It easily lasts (and often needs) fifteen to twenty years in the cellar, and wines from the mid-'90s are quite interesting now; as food wines they make exceptional partners for roast duck. For earlier consumption we recommend the vineyard's slightly more approachable regular **Madiran** ($14–16), blended with Cabernet and Merlot. $30–35
Southwest France
Imported by Lauber

Ercole Velenosi
ROSSO PICENO
"Roggio del Filare"
Full-bodied. The ultimate Rosso Piceno and one of the best wines in Italy.
Artisanally crafted from Montepulciano and Sangiovese grown on the Adriatic shore, this wine is redolent of earth, currants, sweet cherries, and roasted coffee, with more flavors surfacing as it breathes. Ripe but not overbearing, big but not muscle-bound, it perfectly balances grace with power. If you can't find it, look for its less expensive sister, **"Il Brecciarolo"** ($13–15), equally compelling at its price. Neither wine garners

the attention it deserves because it's hard to compete with the overhyped wines from Tuscany and Piedmont (more's the pity). Enjoy either wine with a steak or your Sunday roast. $32–35
Marches, Italy
Imported by Domaine Select

Bonny Doon
OLD TELEGRAM
Full-bodied.
Broad, deep, black as pitch.
This red shows the maverick winemaker Randall Grahm at his best. Made from Mataro (a.k.a. Mourvèdre), it is his tip of the hat to Vieux Telegraphe from Châteauneuf-du-Pape—but it trumps that wine with more sweet fruit and texture. It's sourced from old vines and tastes of prunes, smoke, black pepper, and lavender. Be forewarned: Only 1,500 cases are made, and only in good vintages. When it comes to food, it's a rare treat with grilled lamb or game. $33–35
California

Domaine Tempier
BANDOL "Classique"
Full-bodied. Vibrant, powerful, and seemingly very dry.
A wine in need of time.
Tempier's Bandol, arguably the benchmark for this Provençal appellation, defies both easy drinking and easy description. While its fantastic, aromatic mixture of earth, exotic florals, and stewed plums is tempting, its unrelenting power on the palate suggests that you'll have to be patient and cellar this stern red wine. It's a classic choice for southern French fare like Provençal *ragout de boeuf* (beef stew) and leg of lamb seasoned

with rosemary. $34–36
Bandol, France
Imported by Kermit Lynch

Di Majo Norante
MONTEPULCIANO
"**Don Luigi**"
**Full-bodied. A flamboyant,
barrel-aged, deep-fruited
"super-Monte."**
The finest wine of its appellation,
Don Luigi (80% Montepulciano
and 20% Tintilia, another local
grape) is a kingly red wine,
modern-seeming with its vanillin
new oak and languorous black fruit
but still expressive of its Italian
coastal origins. While it can be
cellared, it drinks just fine now
with roasted lamb, venison fillets,
or a broiled strip steak topped
with Gorgonzola. $35–40
Molise, Italy
*Imported by Winebow/
Leonardo LoCascio*

Château Montus
MADIRAN
"**Cuvée Prestige**"
**Very full-bodied.
One of the deepest,
most intensely saturated
red wines in the world.**
Alain Brumont's famed Château
Montus is constantly compared to
the Premier Cru wines of
Bordeaux. Where his Bouscassé
wines are all about soil and
tradition, Montus is more about
pure power. It is matured over
two years in new Tronçais oak
barrels (Tronçais is a forest in
southwestern France), which
influences its intense palate of
prunes, truffles, and jet-black fruit.
No telling how long this wine
might evolve in the bottle, but
let's just say you might have to
leave it to your children. The
richest duck confits, pâtés de fois
gras, and game meats do it justice.
Try the less expensive, basic

Madiran ($23–25) to get the
general idea.
$45–55
Southwest France
Imported by Lauber

Agricole Vallone
SALENTO ROSSO
"**Graticciaia**"
**Full-bodied. Late-harvested
and utterly intense.**
This 100% Negroamaro is vinified
by the *passito* method—that is,
concentrating the sugars and
flavors of grapes by drying the
grapes before they are crushed.
The wine is perhaps the ultimate
expression of Apulian winemaking—
the molten essence of black figs
complicated by roasted beef and
tar. Serve with the haunch of
some great beast. $60–70
Apulia, Italy
Imported by William Grant

Paolo Bea
SAGRANTINO DI MONTEFALCO
Secco "**Pagliaro**"
**Full-bodied. Muted by
tannin when young, this red
becomes hugely flavorful
with long cellaring.**
Here we have a bottle of India ink
spilled from the tough-skinned
Sagrantino grape, exclusive to
Umbria's vinous hot zone. With a
long, exceedingly dry finish of
black fruits, tree sap, and tar, this
red definitely needs time in the
cellar to soften. Once properly
matured (at least 5–10 years),
it's great with beef and venison.
The rare and expensive **Passito**
($250–300) is exceptionally long-
lived and a raisiny, liqueurlike
masterpiece. Dessert would only
diminish it; pair it instead with a
simple dish of dried fruits and
Gorgonzola Dolce.
$65–80
Umbria, Italy
Imported by Rosenthal

CHOICE ROSÉS

A ROSÉ is a rosé is a rosé. Or is it?

Modern rosé wines are usually made by one of two methods. The most common involves a shorter maceration period of the skins with the juice after the grapes have been crushed. (It's the skins that give red wines their color—so when they are separated from the juice, the pigment source goes out the window.) Fermentation then proceeds as in the making of white wine. A second technique is to simply blend a small amount of red wine into a white wine—something you can even try at home if you are so inclined. Rosé styles also differ from country to country, as a comparative tasting of those we've chosen to feature here will clearly show.

Rosés excel in the warmer months—a nice change of pace from heavier reds and the everyday whites. And the fact that these refreshers are light in color doesn't mean they're lacking in character. With rosés, the secret is in knowing which ones to pick. Once you've stocked up, chill a bottle, kick back, and enjoy!

Pinord
REYNAL ROSÉ
"Crackling Wine"
Fun, fun, *fun!* "Crackling wine" is an apt description for this Spanish *frizzante*, lightly fruity rosé. An icy cold refreshment, it's also great for spicy foods, Tex-Mex, and tapas. A good Sangria base, too! $5–6
Imported by Pleasant

Les Lauzeraies
TAVEL ROSÉ
Tavel, from Provence, is arguably the most famous rosé in the world and also happens to be the traditional choice for serving with bouillabaisse. This version of Tavel is very dry and full-bodied. $9–11
Imported by Monsieur Touton

Señorio de Sarria
NAVARRA ROSADO
"Vinedo No. 5"
From the Navarra region of Spain comes this strawberryish, soft, fresh rosé. It's particularly pleasing with hors d'oeuvres, tomato salads, tapas, and omelets. $9–11
Imported by Spain Wine Collection

Château de la Guimonière
ROSÉ D'ANJOU
Here's a cherry-packed Cabernet Franc rosé from the Loire. With a touch of sweetness and a modest 11% alcohol, it's the best spicy food partner among the rosés recommended here. $9–12
Imported by T. Edward

Château de Pourcieux
CÔTES DE PROVENCE ROSÉ
This rosé from Provence is juicy and perfectly balanced, with clean, delicate fruit. It's a rosé that behaves like a white, so pair it with fish and crudités. $10–12
Imported by Baron François

Producteurs Plaimont
CÔTES DE SAINT-MOUNT ROSÉ
"Les Vignes Retrouvées"
This co-op is the star of its region, in the heart of Armagnac country. The blend is 50% Tannat, 30% Pinenc, and 20% Cabernet, which makes for a hearty pink wine indeed. Lots of muscle and fruit for pâté, charcuterie, and similarly meaty eats. $10–12
Imported by V.O.S.

Bodegas Castano
YECLA ROSÉ
Made from Monastrell grape (the Spanish name for Mourvèdre), this dark seductress from Spain's Yecla wine zone wins you over with a hint of spice. It couples well with the rich, crisped fat of roasted lamb. $11–13
Imported by Polaner

Antichi Vigneti di Cantalupo
COLLINE NOVARESE ROSATO "Il Mimo"
A 100% Nebbiolo from Italy's Piedmont and as serious a food wine as you could wish for. Dark in color, full-bodied, and laden with fruit, it's a hit with northern Italian cuisine. $14–16
Imported by Polaner

Kir-Yianni
AKAKIES ROSÉ
Made from the Xinomavro grape, native to Greece, this rosé is a chunk of ripe cherry-berry fruit bolstered by great, spritzy acids and a touch of tannin. You'd do well to pair this Greek beauty with barbecues or an assortment of olives and pâtés.
$14–16
Imported by Polaner

Domaine Bart
MARSANNAY ROSÉ
Class up a picnic with this gorgeously aromatic, dry rosé made with Pinot Noir from Burgundy. It's brilliant with grilled fish, chicken, cold cuts, and honey-baked ham. $14–16
Imported by Polaner

Torre Dei Beati
MONTEPULCIANO D'ABRUZZO "Cerasuolo"
This deeply colored Italian rosé from the Montepulciano grape is really more like a light red. Replete with dark cherries, cocoa, coffee, and leather, it's especially good with pepper steak and the like.
$14–16
Imported by Artisan

Wölffer
ROSÉ
Wölffer Estate, located on the South Fork of Long Island, New York, makes rosé by shamelessly mixing Merlot and Chardonnay. It's lovely (go figure!), and a lively, copper-colored refresher with steamed mussels and other breezy coastal fare. $14–16

Château Mourgues du Gres
COSTIÈRES DE NIMES ROSÉ "Les Galets "
This rosé from the Rhône is boisterous, full-bodied, and ripe with formidable fruit and alcohol; save it for the grill. If you prefer a gentler style, opt for the "Fleur d'Eglantine" ($13–15), very nice with cold sliced meats.
$15–17
Imported by Weygandt/Metzler

Muri-Gries
LAGREIN ROSATO
Fabulously rich and concentrated, this Italian/German rosé from Alto Adige is a little earthy and firm in the finish—like a pale, dry red. Great with sausages, salmon, and savory vegetable classics like ratatouille.
$16–18
Imported by Polaner

Domaine Tempier
BANDOL ROSÉ
This legendary rosé from Provence is made from 100% Mourvèdre in a bone-dry, full-bodied, cellarable style. Drink with a cold sliced filet mignon and a dollop of Dijon mustard. $27–30
Imported by Kermit Lynch

TO BREATHE OR
NOT TO BREATHE?

*T*RY THIS EXPERIMENT: Gently pour half a glass of wine, then sniff it. Now give the glass a few seconds of vigorous swirling, then sniff again. You'll find the aromatics have increased dramatically. Why? Because you've just "opened up," or aerated, the wine by exposing it to oxygen. Besides creating the wine's bouquet, you've also softened the texture, making the wine more palatable.

Breathing Wine

A more gradual period of aeration is called "breathing." But don't repeat the same mistake so often made in restaurants. Uncorking a bottle and leaving it open for half an hour (or half a day, for that matter), is no way to breathe wine. Because the neck of the bottle is too narrow, only a dime-sized surface of the wine is exposed to air. Instead, use a decanter or carafe, which instantly aerates the wine as it's poured and then allows the wine more air contact because of the wide neck and fat bowl of the vessel.

Another surprise for wine lovers who aren't up on their breatheology: Few wines really need it. Breathing helps tannic young reds to soften, aromatically complex whites to blossom, and long-cellared wines of both colors to awaken from their slumber. But the simple Merlot or Pinot Grigio you pour for a pre-dinner cocktail needs no breathing time. Nor does Champagne, whose aromas ride piggyback on the bubbles.

A word of caution about very old bottles. Wine is unpredictable sometimes, and the beauty of an older wine—especially a delicate one like red Burgundy—can occasionally fade within minutes (even seconds!). For that reason, always taste a just-uncorked bottle to see whether it needs to be aerated at all. It's also instructive to witness the blossoming of a mature wine as it transforms itself in the glass.

Decanting Wine

To decant a wine, all you need is a large glass pitcher or jug. True believers have been known to pour a wine from one pitcher to another several times, but chances are that this method is as likely to ruin a good red as bring out its best.

Most wines are simply poured into the decanter. But those that contain sediment—normal occurrence in mature reds, wines with little or no filtration, and Vintage Port—require lighting a candle.

To decant for sediment, stand the bottle up for several hours before opening it so the sediment settles at the bottom. At pouring time, light a candle at the table and hold the decanter in front of it. Then decant the wine in one slow, continuous stream, keeping the neck of the bottle backlit. That way you can watch the flow of wine and stop it when you see the first traces of sediment. If you're careful, virtually all the sediment will be left in the bottom of the bottle and your wine will be ready to enjoy.

CHAPTER THREE

Primary White Grapes

Most wine drinkers believe that whites are outclassed by inherently "more serious" reds—a major misconception. Truth be told, few reds have as many dimensions as the greatest whites. White wines are also better able to translate the complexities of *terroir* because they are almost never overburdened with oak, alcohol, and tannins.

This chapter uncovers the secret side of the most popular white wines—the truth about Chardonnay, the marvelous diversity of Riesling (much of it as dry as you please), and the reason you shouldn't tuck away that bottle of Sauvignon. We also suggest some of the foods people think are for reds only but in reality improve with the right white.

Chardonnay

*Chardonnay is currently the most popular wine in the world,
but does that mean it's the best? No. Like any wine,
it can be made well or it can be made poorly.*

AT ITS BEST, Chardonnay is a complex white that ages well and acts as a dramatic vehicle for its *terroir*. At its worst, it has excessive oak and alcohol and either lacks beneficial natural acidity or is deprived of it through tricks of winemaking.

A decade or so ago it seemed as if American wine drinkers preferred California "Chard" over any other white. Never mind that the vast majority were over-oaked, far too alcoholic, and heavily manipulated. Perhaps many consumers were lured by the magic word "buttery," which consistently crops up in magazines' tasting notes.

The tide is finally turning. Less new oak is being used at some wineries and winemakers are more concerned about balancing acidity. Better growing sites are being identified, and complexity is taking precedence over oak-derived flavors. Mainly, though, it's consumers who are veering away from the oaky wines of yesteryear.

In Oregon's Willamette Valley and Long Island, New York, the movement toward leaner, more elegant styles is strikingly evident in the glass, with both places producing subtly sculpted Chardonnays. Also heartening is the flood of "unwooded" Australian Chards, especially those from Western Australia. Tropical-tasting, juicier, more adept with food, and priced for everyday use, the new-style Chardonnays are made to please wine lovers, not wine writers.

Then there's Burgundy, in eastern France—to most people the region where Chardonnay reaches its apogee. Indeed, white burgundies, with their complexity and opulence, can be very impressive. Are they the finest white wines in the world? No, because some are mediocre or even awful, just as in every wine region. Yet a few (including many of those described here) are great wines both in their own right and to serve with food. Crafted with skill and dedication by growers who work to express the character of their hallowed vineyards in Chablis, Meursault, and the Montrachets, they are perhaps some of the purest examples of Chardonnay in the world. Still, don't forget: The true standard for judging any wine is how well it suits *your* palate.

Under $12

Carta Vieja
CHARDONNAY
Light-bodied. Balanced, smooth, and far better than the price suggests.

Why this delicious, varietally correct Chardonnay from Chile comes at a bargain-basement price is a continuing mystery—but that's just another reason to snap it up. Its apple and cream flavors work well with any light fare, and it's also ideal for spritzers or sangria. $4–6
Maule, Chile
Imported by Frederick Wildman

Hardy's
CHARDONNAY
Light-bodied. A smooth and pleasant Aussie.
This one's dependable, and good value to boot. A little oak, a little orchard fruit, and a clean, healthy finish make this our favorite of the many inexpensive Chardonnays from Down Under. Try it with fried shrimp, chicken fingers, and other breaded snacks. $6–8
South Australia
Imported by International Cellars

Señorio de Sarria
CHARDONNAY
Medium-bodied. Silky, golden in color, and full of fruit.
This wine has a nice balance of acidity and body—what European wine writers refer to as "harmony." Non-oaked (rare in a Spanish wine) and rich with pears and honey, it's a perfect accompaniment for polenta, egg dishes (including Spanish tortillas and Italian frittatas),
and other soft foods. $9–11
Navarra, Spain
Imported by Spain Wine Collection

Domaine Jean Touzot
MÂCON VILLAGES
Light-bodied. Lively, refreshing, and elegant.
Here's the ideal light Chardonnay from southern Burgundy: fragrant with flowers, crisp at the finish, and marvelous at brunch with quiches and sandwiches. $9–11
Burgundy
Imported by V.O.S.

Wyatt
CHARDONNAY
Light- to medium-bodied. A juicy, light-textured, extremely food-friendly Chard.
This California wine is sourced mainly from Carneros and fermented in 40% new oak—just enough to soften the edges without rendering the wine, well . . . wooden. At dinner it's a sassy match for salmon and white meat chicken. It's also quite nice on its own. $10–12
California

Blackstone
CHARDONNAY
Medium-bodied. Suavely oaked and easygoing.
This is a classic mid-coast California Chardonnay that's better balanced than most. Smooth and appealing, it boasts a light shot of butterscotch in the finish. Serve it with fish steaks or corn chowder. $10–12
Monterey, California

Novellum
CHARDONNAY
"Reserve Cuvée"
Medium-bodied. A moderately plump, ripe sipper.
This pleasing Old World 100% Chardonnay hails from the Languedoc village of St. Chinian. It radiates a floral, bready perfume and is the right stuff for your next shore dinner: grilled fish, kebabs, corn-on-the-cob, potato salad.
$10–12
Languedoc, France
Imported by European Cellars

$12 to $20

Jean-Paul Brun
BEAUJOLAIS BLANC
"Terres d'Orées"
Light- to medium-bodied. Succulent mouthfeel, no oak.
White Beaujolais? Yes, a kind very rarely seen in the U.S. This 100% Chardonnay, naturally vinified with wild yeasts and minimal sulfur, is clean, juicy, and has a flowery bouquet. A classy bistro-style sipper on its own or with quiches and omelets.
$12–14
Beaujolais
Imported by Louis/Dressner

Selaks
CHARDONNAY
Medium-bodied. Smooth, savory, and bright in the finish.
This Chardonnay is only lightly oaked and is imbued with that green, savory New Zealand character. We find it a comely accompaniment to vegetables (especially au gratin), the Greek spinach-and-feta pie *spanakopita*, and herbed chicken or pork.
$12–14
Marlborough, New Zealand
Imported by American Estates

Ferngrove
CHARDONNAY
Medium-bodied. Exceptional fruit, vibrancy, and balance.
This comes from the spectacular and unusually cool Frankland region of Western Australia. Fermented in 70% stainless steel and 30% French oak, it boasts a pure tropical fruit palate. A perfect Chardonnay for the grill.
$13–15
Frankland River,
Western Australia
Imported by Bayfield

Domaine Maillet
MÂCON VERZÉ
Medium-bodied. Fresh, plump, and incredibly appealing.
With its vibrant combination of green melons, apples, and cream, all held aloft by great acidity, this drinks better than some $50 Chassagnes. Rich enough for roast hens and fish but simply delicious on its own.
$13–15
Burgundy
Imported by Bayfield

Toad Hollow
CHARDONNAY
"Francine's Selection"
Medium-bodied. Fruity and fun to drink.

Todd Williams's whimsical, quality-driven winery in Sonoma turns out delicious, fruit-forward, food-friendly wines. The Chardonnay is non-oaked and full of ripe melon and poached pear—a fine partner for grilled white meats and seafood bisque.
$13–15
Sonoma

Domaine Billaud-Simon
CHABLIS
Light- to medium-bodied. Very dry, vivacious, and minerally.
At the table this well-priced Chablis performs like a twist of cold, fresh lemon for fish and mixed green salads—not to mention oysters, for which Chablis is the traditional Gallic partner. Fans of richer Chablis should try any of this estate's Premier Cru or Grand Cru selections, all of them superb. $14–16
Burgundy, France
Imported by Langdon Shiverick

Colterenzio
CHARDONNAY
"Altkirch"
Light- to medium-bodied. Delicately perfumed and lively.
This winery has a graceful touch with white wines. The Altkirch is an elegantly made Chardonnay, with subtle apple fruit all over and nice mineral etching in the finish. Enjoy it with Italy's lemony pasta, veal, and chicken dishes. $15–17
Alto Adige, Italy
Imported by Avatar

Fitz-Ritter
CHARDONNAY
Spätlese Trocken
"Durkheimer Spielberg"
Medium-bodied. Rich, tangy, bone-dry, and refreshing.
German Chardonnay? Don't panic. This outstanding wine is picked very ripe but vinified totally dry. Elegantly balanced with a lovely apricot flavor, citrusy acidity, and a rich vein of minerals, it's delicious with vichyssoise or other creamy soups and is especially useful for smoked meats or fish. $16–20
Pfalz, Germany
Imported by Chapin Cellars

Alex Gambal
BOURGOGNE BLANC
Medium-bodied. A juicy, elegant Chardonnay with a fresh perfume.
Alex Gambal is an American working in Burgundy and making

WINES WITHOUT WOOD

A new word has been popping up on Australian wine labels for the past few years: "unwooded." It describes a wine that has had no contact with oak barrels, oak chips, or any wood whatsoever, leaving a clearer, lighter, and fresher-tasting drink in the bottle. The majority of these wines are in the lower to middle range of the price scale (barrels are expensive, you see) and not only offer excellent value but also stand as refreshing alternatives—especially to the usual buttery, oaky Chardonnays. With the trend growing apace Down Under, expect to see several unwooded examples on wine store shelves in the future.

One that already awaits your pleasure comes from McLaren Vale, South Australia: **Rockbare Chardonnay** ($12–14; *imported by Martin Scott*). It drinks like a wondrous cross of a stony French Chablis and a glass of papaya juice and pairs nicely with tuna and yabbies (Australian for crayfish). Another hails from Victoria: **Plunkett Chardonnay "Blackwood Ridge"** ($14–16; *imported by Verdoni*). Oak-free, splendidly balanced, and rather Euro in style, it has a fresh melony flavor and an affinity for shellfish and piquantly spiced dishes.

splendid wines from several appellations (see page 53). His white Burgundy is as intricate as lace—a graceful Chardonnay threaded with green apple and citron. It's nice on its own or teamed with a soup, salad, or fresh trout. $17–19
Burgundy
Imported by House of Burgundy

L'Abbaye de Petit Quincy
BOURGOGNE EPINEUIL
Medium-bodied.
Like a hybrid of Chablis raciness and Côte d'Or richness.
A captivating wine, naturally made in the far north of Burgundy near Chablis. Its mineral spine hides behind almondy, appley flavors and a smooth, enticing mouthfeel. Trout amandine would be perfect with this. $17–19
Burgundy
Imported by World Wide Wine

Roberto Cohen
POUILLY-FUISSÉ
Light- to medium-bodied.
An extremely elegant kosher wine for delicate fare.
The American Roberto Cohen, arguably the best *négociant* of kosher French wine, selects a very traditional Pouilly-Fuissé from his sources in Maconnais, in southern Burgundy. Minerally, citrusy, scintillating, and devoid of oak, it's ideal for halibut or other firm white fish. $18–20
Burgundy
Imported by Roberto Cohen

Patricia Green
CHARDONNAY
Medium-bodied. A slender wine that shows how elegant Pacific Northwest Chardonnay can be.
Patty Green and Jim Anderson (formerly of Oregon's Torii Mor Winery) produce small

quantities of delicious, refined Chardonnay. With its wisps of fragrance from ocean and orchard, this clean, jazzy wine is for those tired of the oaky butter bombs from California. Try it with a steaming bowl of clam chowder or pan-Asian fish and veggies. $18–20
Oregon

Mount Eden
CHARDONNAY
"MacGregor Vineyard"
Medium- to full-bodied.
Succulent, boldly flavored, and mouthfilling.
This melony, savory Chardonnay hails from the Central Coast's Edna Valley, an oval-shaped shelf of vines watered each morning by the cool fogs off the Pacific. Smoky oak and sweet herb flavors complement chicken and seafood salads. $18–20
Edna Valley, California

Cockfighter's Ghost
CHARDONNAY
Medium-bodied.
Creamy and complex.
There's a refreshing modesty of oak and alcohol here, which allows the wine's deep veins of tropical fruit and glazed citrus to burst forth. Think swordfish and mahi-mahi steaks for partners. This producer also offers a fruiter second label from Adelaide (in the state of South Australia) called **"Firestick"** ($15–18), which we love with greasy stuff like fish fritters and fried plantains. $18–20
Hunter Valley, New South Wales
Imported by Ravensvale

MONSIEUR GUFFENS, *PETIT NÉGOCIANT*

Négociants are wine merchants who buy grapes, wines, or must (the juice and pulp of crushed grapes that have yet to be fermented), then create wine sold under their own labels. They thrive in Burgundy because so many individual growers produce minuscule quantities from so many different appellations. Numerous *négociants* now have vineyard holdings of their own. A cadre of smaller winemakers of this sort, colloquially known as *petits négociants*, aspire to high art in their boutique–style wines. One such wine is Jean–Marie Guffens at Domaine Verget.

This busy producer makes dozens of wines, ranging from very expensive Grand Cru Puligny and Chassagnes–Montrachet to bargains from Mâcon, St. Veran, and Pouilly Fuissé. His pure, unalloyed Chardonnays from Chablis, however, show his signature style. The medium–bodied **Verget Chablis "Terroir de Chablis"** ($21–23) is cool and concentrated, with laserlike acidity in most years. An exercise in minimalism, it has clean character, vibrant mouthfeel, enticing leafy aromas, and a rich complement of melony and green appley fruit. Look too for Guffens's more opulent **Verget Chablis "Terroir de Fleys"** ($21–23) and any Premier Cru offerings you can find. Pair them with oysters and fine-flaked fish such as sole; they also make complex partners for the cold noodle dishes of Chinese, Thai, and Vietnamese cuisine. *Imported by Stacole*

Domaine Servin
CHABLIS
"Cuvée Massale"
Medium- to full-bodied. Astonishingly ripe and exciting Chablis.
All of Servin's Chablis are superb, including a very complex and full-bodied **1er Cru "Vaillons"** ($28–32). The hidden jewel, however, is the Massale, an exotic Chardonnay filled with such atypical flavors as pineapple, tangerine, and jasmine. It's also blessed with scintillating acidity and a long finish. Asian or Pacific Rim seafood dishes excel alongside. $19–21
Burgundy
Imported by Weygandt/Metzler

$20 to $35

Au Bon Climat
CHARDONNAY
Medium-bodied. Fruit-driven and satisfyingly rich.
At this idyllic Central Coast estate, Jim Clendenen crafts a graceful Chardonnay with tropical-tasting fruit, ample oak, and vibrant texture. Match it with glazed fish or pork tenderloin. $20–22
Santa Barbara, California

MacRostie
CHARDONNAY
Medium- to full-bodied. One of the best-balanced Chardonnays in California.

This is one of the few American wineries that achieve perfect synergy between fruit, oak, and acidity on a year-to-year basis. Drunk on its own, it's a rich, refreshing glass of wine. Served

WHITE BURGUNDY

AY "BURGUNDY" to wine drinkers, and ninety-nine out of one hundred will think "red." But the whites of this famous winegrowing region include some of the most important names in winedom. Although they are all made from Chardonnay, they divide basically into two camps: the crisp, austere wines of Chablis, grown in cool, northerly, limestone vineyards, and the opulent, barrel-aged wines of the Côtes de Beaune.

A textbook Chablis vintner is Jean-Marc Brocard. His **Jean-Marc Brocard Chablis Vielles Vignes "Domaine Sainte Claire"** ($20–22) is organically farmed and, like almost all Chablis, devoid of oak. Stony, lemony, and floral in the nose with a crisp, refreshing finish, it's a classic match with flaky fish and oysters. The Premier Cru **"Fourchaume"** ($26–29) is creamier, richer, and elegant with lobster. Tasters with a scientific bent should also explore Brocard's special bottlings named for geologic eras—**Jurassique** ($18–20), for one. *Imported by Lauber*

In the Côtes de Beaune, opulence is the goal, oak is the rule, and the debate rages between tradition and modernism. Vincent Girardin is the quintessential modernist, making forward wines (wines that taste good young) with lots of new oak and very ripe fruit. His **Vincent Girardin Puligny-Montrachet "Les Enseignères"** ($45–50) is plump and pleasing with zooming aromas of pear, honey, and papaya and an expansive vanilla-oak finish. Other stars in his repertoire are an almost lurid **Meursault 1er Cru "Les Charmes"** ($34–36) and a silky, sensuous **Chassagne-Montrachet "Clos de la Boudriotte"** ($35–40). All are great for grilled seafood or poultry with fruity sauces. *Imported by Vineyard Brands*

Traditionalists prefer the long-heralded wines of Domaine Leflaive, now run as a biodynamic estate by Anne-Claude Leflaive and the formidable winemaking talent Pierre Morey. Whether it's **Domaine Leflaive Puligny-Montrachet** ($70–80) or rarer bottlings of Batard-Montrachet, Chevalier-Montrachet, and Le Montrachet, these are some of the most long-lived, subtly crafted, *terroir*-driven white Burgundies of all. They work best with rich haute cuisine—lots of cream, butter, and white meats on the bone. *Imported by Wilson Daniels*

with baked ham and buttered noodles, its peach-pineapple fruitiness emerges all the more. At Thanksgiving, this white could elevate your turkey and dressing, cranberry sauce, and candied yams to food-and-wine heaven. $20–23
Carneros, California

François d'Allaines
MONTAGNY
Medium-bodied. Traditional, forceful, earthy, Burgundian style.
François d'Allaines is one of a cadre of Burgundian *petits négociants* who produce top-quality wines from purchased grapes. We recommend his minerally, exquisitely balanced Montagny—a fabulous complement for chicken, pork, and earthy dishes based on potatoes, mushrooms, or root vegetables. Monsieur d'Allaine's plumper, smokier **Montagny 1er Cru "Les Derrieres Vignes"** ($20–24) and lighter **Rully 1er Cru "La Fosse"** ($24–26), both made from sixty-year-old vines, are also superb. $20–25
Burgundy, France
Imported by Polaner

Clos du Bois
CHARDONNAY Reserve "Calcaire"
Medium- to full-bodied. The opulent, richly oaked Cal style.
The top Chardonnay of the California giant—rich pear fruit, plenty of French oak, buttered toast flavors, and a heady finish; in some vintages it's nicely thick. Among the foods it goes well with are grilled or broiled salmon and double-crème cheeses such as Brie and Petite Gervais. $20–23
Alexander Valley, California

Clos Pegase
CHARDONNAY "Mitsuko's Vineyard"
Medium- to full-bodied. A creamy white wine smartly balanced by acidity.

Better balanced than many of its peers, this Chardonnay is an attractive mouthful (and noseful) of pears, honey, and floral perfume. A third of the production is aged in new French oak before being blended with the remainder. Serve with richly sauced white meats (it's excellent with pork in an apricot-mustard glaze) and sea bass, red snapper, and other saltwater faves. $22–24
Carneros, California

Foxen
CHARDONNAY
Medium-bodied. A gentle, elegant style with a rich finish.
This is one of the best small-production Chardonnays in California. Cool breezes off the ocean, a late-season harvest, and reasonable use of oak result in a flavorsome wine with a light, buttery quality that goes particularly well with fish steaks and Dungeness crab. $22–24
Santa Maria, California

The Ojai Vineyard
CHARDONNAY "Bien Nacido"
Full-bodied. Abundant fruit and earthiness, plus a juicy finish.
We like winemaker Adam Tolmach's small-production, noninterventionist winemaking philosophy: His Chardonnay comes from vines more than thirty years old, and no new oak is used. The toasty aromas, pear fruit, and clayish minerality are just the ticket for herby

roast chicken and a buttery sauté of sliced Vidalia onions. $28–30
Santa Barbara, California

Gary Farrell
CHARDONNAY
Medium-bodied.
Firm and opulent, with a very complex finish.
Gary Farrell's Chardonnays and Pinots really thrive in the vernal, misty landscape of Sonoma's Russian River valley. Honey, peach, pear, and fresh-sawn wood permeate his Chardonnay in its youth, with a little more alcohol and sweetness evident in the '02 and '03 vintages. For cellaring, some prefer Farrell's flashier, oakier effort from the Bien Nacido vineyard in Santa Maria: **Bien Nacido Chardonnay** ($35–38), which gets nuttier as it ages. Sautéed skate or monkfish would go great with either wine. $30–32
California

Over $35

Domaine Colin–Delèger
ST. AUBIN 1er Cru "Les Combes"
Medium-bodied. Nervy, mineral-rich, fish-friendly perfection.
One could opt for Michel Colin's great, cellar-worthy Chassanges—but dollar for dollar, the brisk, flinty, reliably elegant wine he makes next door in St. Aubin is the savvy choice. Sport fishermen should keep a few bottles on hand in the wine rack. $35–42
Burgundy
Imported by Kermit Lynch

Fernand & Laurent Pillot
CHASSAGNE MONTRACHET
Medium-bodied. Redolent of the vineyard and terrifically succulent and vigorous.
This is real Chassagne, with steely, minerally, complex aromatics that initiate conversation at the table. Serve it now or in the next two or three years with classic whitefish dishes—say, broiled flounder topped with dill butter or herby mustard. $38–40
Burgundy
Imported by New Castle

Domaine Vincent Prunier
PULIGNY-MONTRACHET
"Les Garennes"
Medium- to full-bodied.
Fragrant, elegantly balanced, and minimally oaked.
As revered as they are, wines of the Puligny-Montrachet appellation in Burgundy are either magnificent or terribly disappointing. So let's opt for the former to describe this wine from an estate worth watching— a Puligny that's exceptionally ripe, practically dripping with minerals, and persistent on the palate with lively apple/pear fruit and lilies. Any firm-but-flaky fish like cod will team well with it. $42–50
Burgundy
Imported by Martin Scott

Domaine Maroslavac
PULIGNY-MONTRACHET
"Clos du Vieux Chateau"
Medium-bodied. Excellent balance, unusually good acidity, and much minerality.
Masters of restraint, this domaine makes Chardonnay wines closer in style to Chablis than to modern-day Pulignys. The oak is barely perceptible in this lean, tightly knit white, and the flavor of crisp green apples lingers nicely. Enjoy it with crab, squid, mussels, or any other denizens of the briny deep. $46–50
Burgundy
Imported by Lauber

Domaine Bonneau du Martray
CORTON CHARLEMAGNE
Grand Cru
Medium- to full-bodied. Velvety, and a blue-chip choice for the cellar.
A flagrant display of nuts, cream, toffee, and butterscotch that lasts from the startling initial aroma to the rich, pulsating finish, this white Burgundy is always worth trying, even in poor vintages. You should also know that few whites go better with the creamy, butter-rich dishes of French haute cuisine.
$55–65
Burgundy
Imported by Diageo

Domaine Jean-Noel Gagnard
CHASSAGNE-MONTRACHET
1er Cru **"Morgeot"**
Full-bodied. Lusciousness, succulence, and great staying power.
For some, this top-tier Burgundy producer makes the definitive rendition of Chassagne. There's real harmony and balance here, plus clear expression of the clay and chalk of the Morgeot vineyard. Loaded with pear and complex mineral flavors, the wine drinks beautifully young, but also ages well (we're cellaring the '98). A serious meal match for cod, monkfish, or lobster tails. $65–75
Burgundy
Imported by Martin Scott

Domaine Remi Jobard
MEURSAULT 1er Cru **"Le Poruzot-Dessus"**
Full-bodied. One of the ripest, most honeyed, and opulent French whites we know.
At one of the very best sites in Meursault, the Poruzot vineyard (which some think should have been classed a Grand Cru long ago), young Remi Jobard makes a creamy, superlative white Burgundy. He ages it in 15–25% new oak and gives it a good long soak on the lees to add richness and complexity. Unfiltered and unfined, it is redolent of smoke, baked bread, and apple/pear fruit. Cellar for two to five years and serve with salmon, swordfish, or traditional French cuisine, whether "country" or "haute."
$70–80
Burgundy
Imported by Weygandt/Metzler

Talbott Vineyards
CHARDONNAY **"Sleepy Hollow"**
Full-bodied. Plush and exuberant, flooding the mouth with flavor.
This media darling from the Santa Lucia highlands leads the Chardonnay pack in Monterey, with no serious contenders in sight. Boasting a huge concentration of tropical fruit and pungent butter and oak tones throughout, it's practically more food than wine. Show it off with foods that won't compete: simply prepared poultry, pork roasts, and ham are good choices. Robb Talbott makes many other Chardonnays as well, like the zesty, non-oaked **Kali Hart Vineyard Chardonnay** ($18–20), named for his daughter. $70–80
Monterey, California

Chenin Blanc

Though plantings exist in cool climate areas throughout the world, Chenin Blanc is a superstar in only one place: the Loire Valley of France, its bucolic ancestral home.

UCH LIKE A TALENTED SINGER, Loire Valley Chenin Blanc has range. Lots of range, with its wines running the scale from bone–dry (*sec*) to off–dry (*demi-sec*) to syrupy sweet (*moelleux*)—a side of the grape revealed in Sweet Wines, pages 208–215. It is also found in sparkling versions, though very few of them make their way across the Atlantic.

At all sweetness levels, good Loire Chenins exhibit a pungency and penetrating earthy quality stronger than that of any other white wine in the world. They also possess tremendous natural acidity, which in drier versions can be something of a shock to new tasters. For these reasons, and because we admire Loire Chenin's stubborn refusal to be hip or trendy, we refer to it jokingly as "the world's most adult white wine."

Anyone interested in this grape will do well to learn the characteristics common to its wines' various Loire appellations. Vouvray, in the area of Touraine in the middle Loire, produces wines with aromas of ripe orchard fruits and intense minerality. Across the river, Montlouis produces lighter, less dramatic wines in its sandy soils. Farther west in Anjou, Saumur offers light, juicy bargains (usually in a dry style)—but just a few miles down river, tiny Savennières produces some of the most powerful (and driest) wines known to man. Sweet wines are the forte of the Coteaux du Layon, Quarts de Chaume, and Bonnezeaux districts, which lie farther south.

Besides joining Sauvignon Blanc and Riesling as one of the top three most acidic wines (white or red), Chenin is also one of the best whites to cellar. The most age–worthy Chenins are Vouvray and Savennières, which sometimes need ten years to come around!

As for food pairing, dry Chenin has a special affinity for seafood—especially crab, shrimp, lobster, and other crustaceans. *Demi-sec* versions go best with sweet or spicy cuisine. *Moelleux* wines are intended for dessert—although a mature, fully sweet Coteaux du Layon can be one of the world's greatest matches for foie gras.

Under $12

Caves des Vignerons
SAUMUR BLANC
Light-bodied. An extremely crisp, vivid Chenin Blanc.
Lemony and somewhat grassy around the edges, this terrific little white adds zest to fried fish, calamari, shrimp cocktail, omelets, and steamed veggies. A steal at this price! $6–8
Loire, France
Imported by House of Fine Wines

Domaine de Vaufuget
VOUVRAY
Light- to medium-bodied. A simple, soft Chenin with lip-smacking fruit.
Reminiscent of fresh apple cider, this white teams handily with foods that need a little fruit: spicy Southeast Asian dishes, Cajun–seasoned seafood, and Indian or Thai curries. It's also pleasant with autumnal soups made from pumpkin or butternut squash.
$6–8
Loire, France
Imported by Monsieur Touton

Baron Herzog
CHENIN BLANC
Light- to medium-bodied. A fruity and refreshing kosher wine with many uses at the table.
This may be the best value in kosher wine on the market. It's Chenin of the fruity sort—apple-accented and succulent, with a lingering touch of sweetness. Great for spicy foods and gefilte fish.
$6–8
California

Chateau de Montfort
VOUVRAY
Light- to medium-bodied. A fun, off-dry intro to Loire Chenin Blanc.
This Chenin, with fresh apples and green leaves mingling on the palate and a touch of sweet lemon crème in the finish, is practically the ultimate wine for spicy foods. Lovers of fruity wine will find it delightful on its own.
$8–10
Loire, France
Imported by Diageo

A DISTINCTIVE CHENIN

It's not easy to find on a map, let alone at your local wineshop. But if you're lucky enough to come across a bottle from the Coteaux du Loir (that's right—*Loir*, sans "e") or its principal town of Jasnières, grab it. This  wild-and-woolly appellation on the Loir, a northern tributary to the greater Loire, is home to a species of Chenin Blanc that's fascinating, utterly distinctive, and yes, a bit challenging. Flavors of nuts, straw, and apple cider are recognizable as Chenin, but the steely backbone of acids that propels them is a characteristic only a Chenin freak could love. Look for **Domaine de Bellivière Coteaux–du–Loir "l'Effraia"** ($18–20) and explore it with a nutty aged Loire goat cheese like Saint Maure. *Imported by Louis/Dressner*

Domaine Saint Vincent
SAUMUR BLANC
"La Papareille"
Medium-bodied.
Bone dry, rich, and creamy.
This amazing wine drinks like a baby Savennières or Vouvray Sec, both of which sell for at least twice the price. Flavors of apples and earth gradually emerge in the glass as the wine is exposed to air. Try it with poached salmon or linguini in white clam sauce. $9–12
Loire, France
Imported by Winebow/Origine

Vinum Cellars
CHENIN BLANC
"Wilson Vineyards Cuvée CNW (Chard–No–Way)"
Medium-bodied.
Plump, creamy,
and amiable.
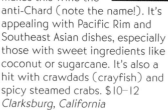
Rich tropical fruit and a pleasing underlying layer of stoniness makes this wine the anti-Chard (note the name!). It's appealing with Pacific Rim and Southeast Asian dishes, especially those with sweet ingredients like coconut or sugarcane. It's also a hit with crawdads (crayfish) and spicy steamed crabs. $10–12
Clarksburg, California

$12 to $20

François Pinon
VOUVRAY
Medium-bodied. Fruity, friendly, and gently balanced.
Here's a spring blossom of a wine, made in the *tendre* ("tender") style—that is, halfway between dry and sweet. Aromas and flavors of apples, melons, and lilies combine

with creamy texture and gorgeous length of flavor to make this wine perfect for salmon in a miso glaze and vegetables of all kinds. $14–16
Loire, France
Imported by Louis/Dressner

Olga Raffault
CHINON BLANC
"Champ–Chenin"
Medium- to full-bodied.
A big, dry, earthy white for hard-core Chenin fans.
This austere Chenin, with its firm mouthfeel, is fermented in steel and then aged in

barrels. Green leaves and steely notes swirl through the aromas. We think it's a delicious lobster wine, but some tasters find it too dry for that particular crustacean; scallops in cream would please most anyone. $14–16
Loire, France
Imported by Louis/Dressner

Domaine Deletang
MONTLOUIS SEC
"Les Batisses"
Medium-bodied. A very dry, richly textured Chenin.
The classic textural descriptor for wines such as this is "waxy," referring to the mouthcoating quality of the beeswax combs found in all-natural honey jars. (Taste it and see what we mean.) This estate's Sec, with its bright lemon-zest finish, goes splendidly with crab cakes and firm-fleshed fish like halibut; the sweeter **Demi–Sec** ($20–22) is more appropriate for sweet 'n' sour shrimp, roast pork with apples, or other rich, sweetish foods. $16–18
Loire, France
Imported by Daniel Johnnes

Paumanok
CHENIN BLANC
Medium-bodied.
Wickedly dry, fresh-flavored,
and bracingly acidic.

Here is one New
York State
producer who
understands Long
Island's potential
to create crisp,
food-friendly

wines along European lines.
Charles Massoud's fiercely juicy
Chenin has no oak in sight—just
the way we like 'em. Cool and
limelike, it's a natural shellfish
and ceviche partner. Drink it
young. $16–18
North Fork of Long Island,
New York

Domaine des Aubuisières
VOUVRAY DEMI-SEC
"Les Girardières"
Medium-bodied. Sweet, creamy-
smooth, and best drunk young.
In this decadent Chenin from
one of Vouvray's best interpret-
ers, caramelized lemon peel,
honey, and custard flavors fill
the mouth with tongue-
titillating richness. It's a delicious
complement to spicy dishes like
blackened red snapper, shrimp
gumbo, and Maryland crabs with
plenty of Old Bay. $16–18
Loire, France
Imported by Weygandt/Metzler

Domaine Bourillon–Dorléans
VOUVRAY SEC Vielles Vignes
"La Coulée d'Argent"
Medium-balanced. One of the
most pleasingly balanced dry
Chenin Blancs available.
Subtly scented with Granny
Smith apples and fresh cream,
Vouvray Sec is sometimes
austere, but this wine is so
pleasantly smooth that anyone
would enjoy it. It's a triumph

with fresh greens and cracked
crab. Try the estate's alluring
Demi-Sec ($18–20) with
creamier, sweeter seafood.
$17–19
Loire, France
Imported by Europvin

Domaine des Baumard
SAVENNIÈRES
"Clos du Papillon"
Medium- to full-bodied.
Firm, very dry, intensely
minerally, and long.
Papillon ("butterfly") is the
entry-level wine from this
estate, but it may be their best
food partner. Penetrating on the
palate with aromas of green
leaves and fresh citrus, it cuts
like a knife through oily mackerel
and sardines and complements
the brininess of oysters. For
sheer drama, the **"Trie Spéciale"**
($30–35) is a full-bodied barrage
of minerals, baked apple, and
ginger, though it needs about
five years of bottle aging (and
can cellar for twenty or thirty
more). Chill slightly, decant, and
serve with shrimp or crab risotto,
lobster with drawn butter, or
roast Christmas goose.
$18–20
Loire, France
Imported by Monsieur Touton

François Chidaine
MONTLOUIS "Clos Habert"
Light- to medium-bodied.
Gently sweet, fresh-tasting,
and elegant.
Here's a Chenin Blanc in the half-
sweet, half-dry *tendre* ("tender")
style, with a finishing touch of
extra sweetness. Creamy and
succulent, with ripe apple/pear
fruit and a hint of white honey,
it is lighter than a typical Vouvray
(its more famous neighbor) and
a delicate food partner. Try it
with mild squash or pumpkin

dishes, stuffed whole fish, or shrimp scampi. $18–20
Loire, France
Imported by Louis/Dressner

Domaine du Closel
SAVENNIÈRES
"La Jalousie"
Full-bodied. Offers freshness and steely firmness.
This crisp Chenin Blanc is vibrant with apple and grapefruit flavors, plus minerally qualities reminiscent of quinine—at least when the wine is young. With age come more baked biscuit-and-honey flavors and a softer, more complete mouthfeel. It's the quintessential Savennières, and elegant with poached fish of all kinds. $19–22
Loire, France
Imported by Louis/Dressner

$20 to $40

Thierry Puzelat
VOUVRAY
Medium-bodied. Off-dry and intense, with superlative acidity keeping it fresh.
Organic vinification, tiny production, and manic attention to quality make this producer a cult favorite. Puzelat makes several cuvées, and all are worth trying. Serve them with exotica like stuffed zucchini blossoms, roast turkey with oyster dressing, or barbecued oysters. $20–25
Loire, France
Imported by World Wide Wine

Clos Baudoin
VOUVRAY
Medium- to full-bodied. Richly textured, ripe, and hefty on the palate.
This historic estate dates from the Napoleonic era, when it was established by the first Prince Poniatowski (1763–1813). The grapes come from a small plot of old vines located in the Vallée de Nouys, directly above the estate. The wine sees a long, cool fermentation with natural yeasts, leaving it marvelously rich and honeyed. What's more, the sheer mass of fruit creates an impression of sweetness—yet this white is essentially dry. Cellar it to golden maturity and enjoy with buttery seafood and very fatty sausages.
$20–60
Loire, France
Imported by Sussex

Château Soucherie
SAVENNIÈRES
"Clos des Perrières"
Medium- to full-bodied. Powerful and firm in the mouth, yet graceful.
You may have to cellar this for a few years before it is ready—but what a wine! A 100% Chenin from vines over thirty years old enclosed in a centuries-old walled vineyard, it's leafy green in the nose and redolent of apples, spring flowers, and a twist of lemon peel. Its citric backbone can handle any fish you choose, not to mention wine-challenging foods such as asparagus. $23–25
Loire, France
Imported by Rosenthal

Foreau
VOUVRAY SEC
Full-bodied. Powerful and expansive in the mouth, with a deep, dry finish.
An exciting, full-throttle Chenin Blanc from a master, with fresh and baked apples dominating an

A CHAMPION OF BIODYNAMISM

Winemaker Nicolas Joly is the preeminent defender of biodynamics, the holistic, decidedly mystical approach to farming created a century ago by Rudolph Steiner—but also the "newest new thing" in winedom. Some think Joly's approach too doctrinaire, but who's to argue when his are some of the most impressive white wines made in the world?

The ultimate Chenin Blanc may be **Nicolas Joly Savennières "Clos de la Coulée de Serrant"** ($70–100, more for older vintages)—a full-bodied, bone-dry, wildly fragrant wine with a deep golden color and a creamy, complex palate. We've also often enjoyed Joly's **Savennières–Roche Aux Moines "Clos de la Bergerie"** ($60–80), a shimmering, minerally, crystal chandelier of a wine and a Dover sole's best friend.

The wine from the historic Coulée de Serrant, a twelfth-century vineyard of chalk and gravel, earns Monsieur Joly most of his admirers. Vintages from the '60s and '70s are gentle and silky now, offering tealike flavors that range from mint to gunpowder to chamomile. "Younger" vintages, such as the '89, are dry as a gin martini yet discreetly honeyed—and about as minerally as Chenin can get. (Drinking anything younger may make you miss the magic of these wines.)

Seafood is the main course of choice, with the focus on oysters, shrimp, and scallops served unadorned or in the most delicate of creamy sauces. Blini with sour cream and Iranian black caviar grow even more tempting when served with these meticulously made wines. *Imported by Paterno*

amazingly complex palate that lasts and lasts. This is a very "adult" wine for a whole roasted fish wrapped in fresh herbs. The glossy, deep golden **Demi-Sec** ($24–26), with its glazed-fruit sweetness and deep earth-and-honey layers, can evolve in the bottle for decades; it's also particularly suited to duck confit and foie gras.
$24–35
Loire, France
Imported by Rosenthal

Domaine de la Sansonnière
ANJOU "La Lune"
Full-bodied. Richly layered, with penetrating ripeness and great length of flavor.
To call vintner Mark Angéli quality-driven and meticulous is an understatement. His methods are biodynamic, a mode of organic winemaking based on the holistic theories of Rudolph Steiner. Angéli's production is minuscule, his vine plantings incredibly dense so that the vines will compete to survive, and his late-harvest wines (like this one) are actually picked one grape at a time. In the La Lune, it isn't sweetness that makes an impression but rather depth, both of *terroir* and structure. Dried apricots, vanilla, and a bready aroma lurk intriguingly in the finish. Among the foods that do the wine justice are broiled lobster and salty blue cheeses.
$35–40
Loire, France
Imported by Louis/Dressner

Gewürztraminer

Most think it German, and indeed it once was. But most modern "Gewürz" comes from France's Alsace region, where it makes profound, perfumed dry whites.

*A*LSACE'S VERSIONS of the exotically scented wine Gewürztraminer are huge in every respect—taste, alcohol, perfume. And with the exception of the late-harvest wines, most are very dry. German Gewürzes, on the other hand, are lighter, juicier, more minerally, and not so wildly fragrant.

Does that make one superior to the other? Well, as with any wine, it all depends on what you like. What we *can* say is that as food wines, the German Gewürztraminers win hands down.

That needn't be seen as heresy in a day when Alsace is ground zero for great Gewürz. On its own, the Alsatian version is a big-boned, flamboyant beauty whose alluring flavors, finesse, and complexity are rarely matched. Yet it is simply indisputable that the wines that best complement food are those that approach it gently, which largely has to do with what they are *not*: too heavy, too alcoholic, too sweet, too acidic. The bolder the wine, the more likely it is to hang around on the palate and overpower, rather than enhance, the taste of food.

Gewürztraminer (geh-VURTZ-tra-mee-nuhr) is a particular clone of Traminer, a lighter-skinned grape named for Tramin, a town in the Alto Adige—the DOC zone that covers the northern portions of Italy's Trentino and is home to a German-speaking majority. The word *gewürz*, German for "spicy," was added to the name, though in this case "spicy" refers to the multiplicity of flavors packed into the grape—among them lychee, gingerbread, and roses.

Because it's such a characterful wine, Gewürztraminer can challenge wine lovers, most of whom seem to either love it or hate it. Not surprisingly, our picks on the next few pages are based on which currently-sold versions go best with food, though several are also great sippers on their own. The ideal dinner (or lunch) pairings are the Germanic classics, including leek-and-onion tart, ham and German sausages (wursts), potatoes and other root vegetables, and rich fish dishes such as whitefish with apples and onions.

Under $12

Alexander Valley Vineyards
GEWÜRZTRAMINER
"New Gewürz"
Light- to medium-bodied.
At a modest 12% alcohol,
a fruity, easygoing sipper.
It's easy to like this clean, balanced
glass of sunny fruits and perfume—
the opposite of the "more-is-
better" style. It's also terrific for
curries and pad Thai. $9–11
North Coast, California

Hugelheim
GEWÜRZTRAMINER
Spätlese Dry
"Hugelheimer Hollberg"
Medium-bodied. Surprisingly
dry and subtle for Gewürz
and more elegant than many.
This wine is an exercise in
minerality. While its bouquet
is blessed with a kitchen rack
full of spice, it's not a spicy-food
wine. Try it instead with firm-
fleshed fish like skate and
halibut, creamed potatoes
with parsley, or lemony veal
or chicken cutlets. $11–13
Baden, Germany
Imported by Wines for Food

$12 to $20

Martin Zahn
GEWÜRZTRAMINER
Medium-bodied. Soft, smooth,
and prettily perfumed.
As Gewürz goes, this is styled fairly
modestly—yet it's still a gorgeous-
smelling drink with peppery, floral,
honeyed qualities to spare. The
traditional partner for Alsatian
leek-and-onion tart, it also works
wonderfully with pâté, fried
potatoes, and fish steaks. $13–15
Alsace, France
Imported by Michael Lerner

Von Franckenstein
GEWÜRZTRAMINER Kabinett
Medium-bodied. Delicately sweet,
exotic, and scintillating.
Don't let the name
scare you:
The only thing
brought to life
in this German
winery is great
Gewürz. This one's

particularly delicious, teeming
with tropical fruits dusted with
jasmine and rose petals. Its exotic
palate and low-to-modest alcohol
make it a willing partner for
cuisines that span the globe,
from India to West Africa to the
Caribbean. $14–16
Baden, Germany
Imported by Wines for Food

Domaine Trimbach
GEWÜRZTRAMINER
Medium-bodied. Firm, fleshy,
and dry at the finish.
This giant of Alsace makes a
full range of high-quality white
wines. Their surprisingly dry
Gewürz is perfumed with flowers
and talcum and shows just a
touch of fruit—a fine wine for
baked ham and potato salad.
Collectors prize the sweet
Gewürztraminer Vendanges
Tardives ("late harvest," priced
at $60–80); we've enjoyed
examples that dated back to the
1950s and were still fresh-tasting
and deliriously rich. $14–16
Alsace, France
Imported by Diageo

Lucien Albrecht
GEWÜRZTRAMINER
Medium-bodied. Weighty
style with earthy complexity
in a wine to cellar.
Jean Albrecht, representing the
nineteenth generation at this
estate, works in a grand,
traditional style. His Gewürz is

enormously concentrated and dry, more akin to Grand Cru Burgundy than anything recognizably Germanic. Cream, dried apricots, and minerals pulse through the finish. Serve with the traditional sausages, tarts, and creamy dishes of Alsace. Albrecht's sweeter *vendange tardive* Gewürzes are expensive but sensational. $15–20
Alsace, France
Imported by Pasternak

Fitz-Ritter
GEWÜRTZTRAMINER Spätlese "Durkheimer Nonnengarten"
Medium-bodied. Pleasing and plump, with good ripeness.
Here's a great introduction to Gewürz from the large, historic estate of Konrad Fitz and his American wife, Alice. An amiable jumble of apple/pear fruits, flowers, and minerals, it's wonderfully refreshing with hot 'n' spicy Hunan pork, garlicky sausages, and chicken satay. $17–19
Pfalz, Germany
Imported by Chapin Cellars

Willm
GEWÜRTZTRAMINER Reserve "Cuvée Emile Willm"
Medium-bodied. Fragrant, deeply flavorful, and lasting.
What an aroma! Roses and more roses, with a little lychee,

honeydew, and gardenia floating around. Also, the wine's acids and

alcohol are in good balance— rare to find in a Gewürz. It's an exotic (yea, erotic?) wine for savory tarts and authentically pungent Alsatian Münster cheese. $18–20
Alsace, France
Imported by Monsieur Touton

$20 to $30

Jean-Baptiste Adam
GEWÜRTZTRAMINER "Kaefferkopf-Cuvée Jean-Baptiste"
Medium-bodied. A sleeper in most years, this graceful, dry wine is nicely lifted by acidity.
Though he works from a Grand Cru site, Monsieur Adam pursues a subtle, mineral-driven style that seems under-appreciated by the wine press. That's a pity, since the wines perform heroically at the table. Relish this flinty, floral Gewürz with rich fish dishes, white meats, and vegetables in fragrant sauces. $20–22
Alsace, France
Imported by Chapin Cellars

GRAPEFRUIT AND ROSES
Young Bernard Schoffit, a pioneer at Domaine Schoffit in Alsace, is making his mark in the world of wine. The Rieslings, Tokays, and Gewürztraminers from the domaine's Harth vineyard are late-ripened and possessed of incredible density, opulence, and an appealing natural sweetness. **Domaine Schoffit Gewürztraminer "Harth"** ($20–25) is dizzyingly aromatic and rich—all grapefruit and roses on a steely spine of minerals. At the table, it's best paired with sturdy foods like *choucroute garni* (Alsatian sausages and sauerkraut) and roasts of veal or pork. *Imported by Weygandt/Metzler*

GEWÜRZ THAT WOWS

Maurice and Jacky Barthelme, who succeeded Albert Mann (Maurice's father-in-law) in the 1980s, have catapulted their predecessor's estate onto every top ten list in Alsace. Their **Domaine Albert Mann Gewürztraminer Grand Cru "Furstentum"** ($33–36), grown organically and late-harvested from old vines, smells like some improbable distillate of liquid wildflowers. In the mouth, its concentration of flamboyantly ripe peach, papaya, and passion fruit lends an impression of sweetness but stops short of becoming a dessert wine (a formula that's just right for foie gras). You'll also find this Gewürz so full-bodied that it practically coats the wineglass. *Imported by Weygandt/Metzler*

Pierre Frick
GEWÜRZTRAMINER
Medium-bodied. Fantastically flavorful and succulent, with a bright finish.
Biodynamically farmed, this superb, small-production Gewürz bursts forth with floral aromas mixed with red berries and lychee. Thanks to its unusually fine acids, it's balanced beautifully for seafood. Try it with a baked bluefish wrapped in bacon or pancetta. $20–22
Alsace, France
Imported by Louis/Dressner

Over $30

Domaine Weinbach
GEWÜRZTRAMINER
"Clos des Capucins–Cuvée Theo"
Medium- to full-bodied. Some of the classiest, driest, most elegant wine in Alsace.
Colette Faller and her two daughters, Laurence and Catherine, produce great whites that eschew the heaviness and perfumy excess of some of their Alsatian peers. This Gewürz, often needing four to five years to blossom, is prettily scented with lychee and pear and shows a bit of tannin in the tail. Decant to

breathe and then serve with veal, chicken, or duck dishes.
$35–40
Alsace, France
Imported by Vineyard Brands

Domaine Zind-Humbrecht
GEWÜRZTRAMINER
"Herrenweg de Turckheim"
Full-bodied. Densely concentrated and glycerous in texture, with a whopping finish.
The king of Alsace wine, Olivier Humbrecht is a perfectionist, obsessed with eliciting the essence of each vineyard in which his wines are grown. Even the Herrenweg, his basic Gewürz, is a powerhouse— heady and thick-textured with caramelized-tasting fruit and a bouquet straight from the rose garden. It's an excellent choice for lobster, braised pork loin, or your favorite smelly cheeses. Olivier's multiple single-vineyard selections from **Hengst, Heimbourg,** and **Clos Windsbuhl** ($50–150) are all extremely rich and generally have over 15% alcohol. Such wines don't need food; they *are* food.
$35–45
Alsace, France
Imported by Kermit Lynch

Pinot Grigio/ Pinot Gris

*On the white wine stage the spotlight has been turning
to the light, fresh wines of this European grape,
but the reviews of its performance are mixed.*

A **MASTER OF DISGUISE**, the grape most folks know as Pinot Grigio has at least four different identities. It is Pinot Grigio in northern Italy, Grauburgunder in Germany, and Pinot Gris in Alsace and Oregon (and most other places). Not surprisingly, the wines from each region are distinctly different, mainly because of the vast differences in *terroir*.

The Pinot Gris of Alsace, formerly known as Tokay Pinot Gris until the laws changed in 2004, is the most flamboyant. Very rich, very floral, high in alcohol, and often vinified in a sweet, perfumy style, it demands the attention of the taster from first sip to last. The Alsatians themselves use it only for very rich fare or, in sweeter versions, for pastries and cheeses. (Mysteriously, although the grape was known as Tokay, it has no relation to the Hungarian wine Tokaji, pronounced the same but spelled differently.) Oregon Pinot Gris seems to take its inspiration from Alsace, but offers less in the way of honeyed richness and more in the way of fresh fruit—mostly stone fruits like peach and apricot. The German version is mostly of local interest to the Germans, the best examples emanating from Baden. Grauburgunder is invariably bone-dry and often rather earthy and austere on the palate.

By far the most popular is Italian Pinot Grigio, grown abundantly in the northern provinces of Alto Adige, Friuli, and the Veneto. Some versions (including several noted here) offer interesting character and pair well with fish, pastas, and any dishes that take a light, dry white. But as a rule, Pinot Grigio is a cocktail wine, inexpensive and conveniently made for chilling and swigging. Just like vodka, it offers itself as a neutral, inoffensive beverage you can pitch a couple of ice cubes into without a hassle. It is no surprise that it is catching up to Chardonnay as the bar pour of choice, both in America and internationally.

Under $12

Graffigna
PINOT GRIGIO
Medium-bodied.
Lavish, round,
and ripe-fruited.

This big wine is
made at the
hundred-thirty-
year-old Graffigna
estate in the San Juan region of
Argentina. Despite the "Grigio" in
its name, the peach, pear, and
perfume character makes it more
similar to an Alsatian Pinot Gris
than to its Italian counterparts. It's
a likely pick for ham salad, deviled
eggs, and other picnic classics.
$8–10
Tulum, Argentina
Imported by TGIC

Villa del Borgo
PINOT GRIGIO "Forchir"
Medium-bodied. Fine silkiness
and succulent character.

What is it that makes
this bargain Italian
Pinot Grigio taste so
expensive? Answer:
It's more earth-
driven than fruity
(characteristic of

Pinot Grigios from Friuli) and
has a pleasing hint of fresh
cream capping the finish. Drink it
as an apéritif or as a table wine
with *pasta con vongole* (pasta
with clam sauce). It also nicely
complements any food dressed
with aioli, the Provençal garlic
mayonnaise.
$10–12
Friuli, Italy
Imported by Vin Divino

Di Lenardo
PINOT GRIGIO
Light- to medium-bodied.
Crisp, vivid, and refreshing.

A real bargain from a hip young
winemaker who comes up
with delightful whites in every
vintage. Aging on the lees lends
hints of nuttiness and hay, but
mostly this is just a nice, clean
sipper—the right wine with
some chips 'n' dips at the end
of a long, hard day.
$10–12
Friuli, Italy
Imported by Martin Scott

Joachim Flick
PINOT GRIS
Medium-bodied. Perfectly
balanced and juicy.

This German Pinot
Gris falls some-
where between
the super-wrought
Alsatian style and
simpler Italian Pinot
Grigio. It is vividly

minerally throughout, with a
little grapefruit sneaking in now
and then. Delicious with tuna
salad and an interesting choice
for risotto. $11–13
Rheingau, Germany
Imported by Wines for Food

$12 to $20

Villa Girardi
PINOT GRIGIO
"I Mulini"
Medium-bodied. A
plump, enticingly
aromatic pleasure.

Here we have a Venetian-style
Pinot Grigio—i. e., fruitier and less
minerally than the norm. It's a
friendly, appley wine suited to
gnocchi or cheese ravioli. $12–14
Veneto, Italy
Imported by Verdoni

Jean-Baptiste Adam
PINOT GRIS
Medium-bodied.
Dexterously balanced,
bright, and mouthfilling.
This fine, reasonably priced
Pinot Gris has a pretty floral
fragrance and a tendency to
stimulate the appetite. Bring a
bottle to your next potluck
supper, where it will probably
go with everything and delight
the crowd. $13–15
Alsace, France
Imported by Chapin Cellars

Terlano
PINOT GRIGIO
Medium-bodied.
Very bright, very pure-tasting,
and a firm finish to boot.
This excellent producer of long-
standing is, for some, the best
interpreter of Pinot Grigio in
Italy. The wine has an aroma like
an Alpine breeze and fills the
mouth with minerals and citron.
It's a fairly elaborate white for
just sipping, but it makes a
perfect partner for seafood
pasta and steamed mussels.
$13–15
Alto Adige, Italy
Imported by OmniWines

Domaine Trimbach
PINOT GRIS "Reserve"
Medium-bodied. Sleek, superbly
balanced, and easy to enjoy.
Market-savvy Jean Trimbach
figured out how to make an
irresistible, soft Pinot Gris in a
snazzy package at a great price.
Packed with pear and passion
fruit and just minerally enough,
it's not too heavy for new-
comers but will still satisfy die-
hard Alsace aficionados. Whip up
a ham-and-cheese sandwich and
enjoy. $14–16
Alsace, France
Imported by Diageo

Lucien Albrecht
PINOT GRIS
Medium- to full-bodied.
A satiny, golden-hued white
with a subtly sweet touch.
This Alsatian
classic comes
from one of the
oldest, noblest
estates in the region. Richly made,
with deep drafts of lilies and
gardenia in the nose, it's a glorious
salmon partner and rich enough
for lobster and Dungeness crab.
Anything Chardonnay can do,
this white can do better. $14–16
Alsace, France
Imported by Robert Kacher

Elena Walch
PINOT GRIGIO
Medium-bodied. Impressively
layered and lasting.
Elena Walch, a former architect,
became a wine producer in 1985
after marrying Werner Walch,
heir to one of the oldest wine
families in the Italian Alps. Hers is
a particularly ripe Pinot Grigio,
with pleasing pear aromas and
lush texture. It's a knockout with
buttery herbed fish. $15–17
Alto Adige, Italy
Imported by Artisan

Marco Felluga
PINOT GRIGIO
Medium-bodied. Rich and
satisfying—a serious dinner wine.
Working from vineyards in Collio,
hard against the Adriatic shore,
Roberto Felluga (proprietor
Marco's son) crafts an excellent,
flavorsome wine with a ripe,
sea-briny palate. It's a fine
companion for sardines or the
tomatoless *pizza bianco*. For a
profound upgrade, try **Russiz
Superiore** ($20–22), a full-blown
dry white for stuffed fish. $16–18
Friuli, Italy
Imported by Dalla Terra

$20 to $40

Colterenzio
PINOT GRIGIO "Praedium"
Medium-bodied. Fresh aromas, nice concentration, great length.
Here's a Pinot Grigio for grown-ups. Even though it's crisply made and has the variety's typical citrus-and-mineral scents, it winds up richer and earthier than most of its peers. Poached chicken, fatty fish, and mushroom cream sauces are good partners. $20–22
Alto Adige, Italy
Imported by Avatar

Domaine Albert Mann
PINOT GRIS Grand Cru "Hengst"
Full-bodied. Powerful and thick, with an impression of sweetness.
The wines from this estate, which are less alcoholic and heavy-handed than many Alsatian Grand Crus, still maintain intense flavor propelled by juicy acidity. The Hengst is a flamboyant, almost syrupy elixir whose voluptuous perfume of daylilies, mango, and orange sherbet can overwhelm. It's a magnificent statement at dinner, but only with the richest of fare. $22–26
Alsace, France
Imported by Weygandt/Metzler

Joachim Heger
PINOT GRIS Trocken
Medium- to full-bodied. Aggressive and rich, this is dinner wine, not a simple sipper.
Propelled by vivid acidity, this virile Hessian attacks the palate with complex slate and ripe citrus. Succulent and totally dry, it's a particularly fine match for bouillabaisse. $25–28
Baden, Germany
Imported by Cellars International

Domaine Schoffit
PINOT GRIS Grand Cru "Rangen de Thann–Clos Saint Theobald"
Full-bodied. The distilled essence of Pinot Gris— and almost over-the-top.
Fruit-saturated, intensely perfumed, and multidimensional, Bernard Schoffit's rococo variation on Pinot Gris is sourced from the steep volcanic slopes of the Rangen, a legendary Alsatian site. Briny, minerally, and meticulously balanced, it leaves a strong impression of sweetness (more precisely, intense ripeness) and a little skin tannin in the finish. It's more of a wine to contemplate after dinner than during, so try serving it with triple-crème cheeses or pâté de fois gras. $38–40
Alsace, France
Imported by Weygandt/Metzler

PRIME PINOT GRIS FROM OREGON

At ElvenGlade Winery in Oregon's North Willamette Valley, owner Bill Kelley and winemaker Chris Worth turn out a Pinot Gris that's impressive all around: the medium- to full-bodied **ElvenGlade Pinot Gris** ($18–20), a white with a huge, opulent palate. Soulfully rich and varietally true, it hits you with up-front flavors of pears, whetstone, and spice. Try it with its regional food match of cedar-planked salmon or, barring that, broiled fish of any kind. We love it in the autumn with roast turkey and acorn squash.

Riesling

*Learning to relish wine made from this German grape
requires a little work—but only in finding the style that
best suits your taste. That done, prepare to fall in love.*

HERE'S A REASON for our unbounded enthusiasm for
Riesling, and we're more than happy to share it: It's simply the
best food partner in the world.

There are several reasons why. First, there is no wine grape translated with such variety. Riesling can be rich or light; simple or profound;
intensely dry or voluptuously sweet. You can match it to every course of
a meal, appetizer through dessert. Its aromatic range is, for all intents
and purposes, infinite. That means it is as complex as any wine you care
to mention. Technically speaking, it has better acidity than any other
wine grape, which makes it mouthwatering, which in turn makes it an
aid to digestion and palate sensitivity. High acidity also means Riesling
cellars better than any white wine on earth—and many reds. It is usually lighter than other wines, thus serving as a graceful partner for food
rather than an adversary. Its lower alcohol, averaging 7% to 11%, makes
it a balm for the spicy dishes that few other wines can handle.

Above all, Riesling is a completely transparent vehicle for its
terroir. Granted, it is picky, and won't thrive everywhere. But on its home
turf, in the vineyards of Middle Europe, it triumphs. In Alsace it makes
rich, sensuous wines with a certain "Frenchness" about them, exotic yet
still earthbound, sunny wines from sunny climes. In Austria, the wines
reflect the austere, rocky slopes of the Danube—dry, zestful Rieslings
with restrained character and significant alcoholic strength. Then there's
Germany, where arguably the finest wines are made. In brown bottles
from the Rhine come the historic, firm, nervy wines of the Rheingau; the
friendlier, sometimes berryish offerings of the Rheinhessen; and the fat,
slurpy fruit bombs of the Pfalz, where the slopes are gentler and the
weather warmer. To the west flows the River Nahe, home of graceful, citrusy wines that never shout but whisper persuasively. Finally comes the
wild squiggle of the Mosel, where sunlight is scarce and the pebble-
strewn vineyards slope down at seemingly impossible angles to the river
below. Wonderfully delicate wines flow from green–glass bottles here,
balletic balancing acts of fruit and slate. The Saar and the Ruwer, the
Mosel's tributaries, are sources of the most ethereal wines of all.

Under $12

Willm
RIESLING
Light- to medium-bodied. Hints of fruit and mineral, and a dry, zippy finish.
This is easily the best deal in Alsace Riesling. Lively, fresh-tasting, and light-handed in style, it pairs well with any food that likes a dry white with a bit of fruit to it, from chips 'n' dips, shrimp cocktail, and pâtés to entrée salads and poultry. $9–11
Alsace, France
Imported by Monsieur Touton

Jul. Ferd. Kimich
RIESLING Kabinett Trocken "Paradiesgarten"
Light- to medium-bodied. Brisk, steely, and dry.
This tiny, 250-year-old estate makes wines (all of them dry) by very traditional methods. The wines are a bit austere, but just the ticket for fresh shellfish and sushi. The pricing is attractive, too. $9–11
Pfalz, Germany
Imported by Chapin Cellars

Esk Valley
RIESLING
Light-bodied. From New Zealand, an example that's crisp, simple, and slightly fruity.
Gordon Russell crafts fine, modern Riesling with a refreshing citrus and floral quality—rather Mosel-like, in fact. A great pick for shrimp cocktail. $9–11
Hawkes Bay, New Zealand
Imported by Vineyard Brands

Max Ferdinand Richter
RIESLING "Estate"
Light-bodied. Pure, fresh, and delicate, with a faint hint of sweetness.

Made in an old-fashioned style at a three-hundred-year-old estate on the River Mosel, this ethereally delicate wine is kissed with green apples and honeysuckle. It sips easily with seafood salads, boiled shrimp with remoulade sauce, and cold cuts. The aromatic **Kabinett "Wehlener Sonnenuhr"** ($14–16) is a textbook rendition at a great price—and fantastic with rare tuna. **Spätlese "Brauneberger Juffer–Sonnenuhr"** ($18–20) is

---

TRANSLATING A GERMAN WINE LABEL

When buying a German wine, the most important thing to understand is the difference between ripeness (the amount of sugar at harvest) and sweetness (the amount of sugar in the finished wine). German wine labels tell you both! The first level of ripeness is **Qualitatswein** or "quality wine," light and fruity. **Kabinett** is riper at harvest than Qualitatswein, usually off-dry and light to medium–bodied. **Spätlese** (literally "late picked") is riper, richer, and usually sweeter. **Auslese** is handpicked when very ripe, definitely sweet, and may have botrytis (noble rot). Here's the catch: Any of the above may be fermented to total dryness (labeled **Trocken**), or near total dryness (**Halbtrocken**). In practice, a Kabinett Halbtrocken tastes about as "sweet" as Brut Champagne. See Sweet Wines (pages 208–215) for **Beerenauslese** (BA), **Trockenbeerenauslese** (TBA), and **Eiswein** (ice wine).

earthier and more honeylike—an unlikely but perfect companion to southern soul food.
$10–12
Mosel, Germany
Imported by Langdon Shiverick

Johannes Ohlig
RIESLING Dry "Nikki"
Light- to medium-bodied. Zing! A bone-dry, generously fragrant pleasure.

This excellent, affordable Rheingau Riesling comes from a four-hundred-year-old family estate. It's a bright little wine— pear-scented and a great match with sushi. The Spätlese Halbtrocken "Johannisberger Erntebringer" ($14–16) is a riper, fuller-bodied jumble of oranges, minerals, and cloves; good partners for this one are paella, shrimp gumbo, and stir-fries.
$10–12
Rheingau, Germany
Imported by Wines for Food

Joachim Flick
RIESLING
Medium-bodied. Fruity, firm, and lasting.
Flick wines (bottled in liters!) owe their filigreed character to a rare vein of pure limestone found in the estate's corner of the Rheingau. The Riesling is graceful, plump with apricot/peach notes, and balanced on a dime. It's an astonishing value and seems almost made to order for Chinese food.
$10–12
Rheingau, Germany
Imported by Wines for Food

Dr. Loosen
RIESLING "Dr. L"
Light- to medium-bodied. Sleek, balanced, and easy to like.
Because of its consistent quality and availability, this wine has been many wine lovers' introduction to fine German Riesling. Ernie Loosen's entry-level version offers a glimpse of his craftsmanlike style. Its precise flavors, juicy acids, and off-dry fruity character are just what the doctor ordered for pâtés, fried fish, and summer seafood.
$10–13
Mosel, Germany
Imported by Valckenberg

Stephan Reuter
RIESLING Dry "Krettnacher Altenberg"
Light- to medium-bodied. Very dry, with razorlike acidity.
Here's a wine that hits you with an icy laser beam of apple-pear fruit and citrus—a waker-upper, for sure. It is also one of the juiciest, driest, most penetrating Rieslings around. Use it as a racy match for oysters, salads, and salmon roe. $11–13
Saar, Germany
Imported by Wines for Food

Freiherr Von Schleinitz
RIESLING Dry "Slatestone"
Light- to medium-bodied. A sturdy dry white for sipping.
This estate at the far north end of the Mosel has found success with this minty, fresh-tasting, lovely Riesling (as it has with a mildly sweeter version for the same good price). Pop one open for Middle Eastern takeout like tabbouleh, stuffed grape leaves, and falafel. $11–13
Mosel, Germany
Imported by Cellars International

$12 to $20

Dr. F. Weins-Prüm
RIESLING Halbtrocken
Medium-bodied. Dry, stony,
refreshing, and firm.
Crafted by Bert Selbach at his
tiny, ten-acre Mittelmosel estate,
this Mosel Riesling is dry as you
please, with suggestions of
mineral water and citron. It's a
zestful apéritif or a cool mate to
crab or shrimp salads and smoked
trout. This estate also makes a
delightfully refined **Kabinett**
($20+) and a vibrant, sherbety
Spätlese "Wehlener Sonnenuhr"
($25+). $12–14
Mosel, Germany
Imported by Cellars International

Gysler
RIESLING Kabinett
"Weinheimer Hölle"
Medium-bodied.
A blast of fruit
that awakens
the palate.
Never have we
tasted a Kabinett
Riesling with such high sugar
and acidity levels: It may remind
you of the most intense,
delicious lemonade you've ever
had. Food isn't needed—
just chill and enjoy.
$12–14
Rheinhessen, Germany
Imported by Michael Skurnik/
Terry Thiese

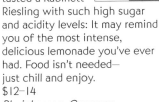

Joh. Haart
RIESLING Kabinett
"Piesporter Goldtröpfchen"
Light- to medium-bodied.
Enticingly fresh, pale, and lovely.
This gossamer wisp of a wine
comes from a legendary Mosel
vineyard. Crystalline flavors of
flowers and green apples abound,
supported by a touch of enticing

sweetness. Hard not to like! Drink
it for refreshment or serve with
light fish, vegetables, and main-
course salads. $13–15
Mosel, Germany
Imported by Chapin Cellars

Dr. Konstantin Frank
JOHANNISBERG RIESLING Dry
Light- to medium-bodied.
Fresh and zesty.
You wouldn't guess it from the
German-sounding name, but this
is a delicious American Riesling
from a New York wine pioneer.
Green apple and melon fruit
tickle your taste buds all the more
as you savor pâtés or smoked
fish. Fans of sweeter whites
could try the **Riesling Semi-Dry**
($12–14), perhaps with a New
York State blue cheese. $13–15
Finger Lakes, New York

Josef Leitz
RIESLING
"Rudesheimer Drachenstein"
Medium-bodied. Sexy, luscious,
and a.k.a. "Dragonstone."
If fresh ripe pears were picked
and reduced to their purest
essence, you'd come close to the
jolting flavor of this wine. Few
wines are this complex while
staying so downright *fun*. Any
spicy food will excel. Those
curious about Leitz's "serious" side
can search out the liqueurlike
Spätlese Rudesheimer Berg
Schlossberg ($32–40), a sweet
wine for the cellar. $13–15
Rheingau, Germany
Imported by Michael Skurnik/
Terry Thiese

Schloss Gobelsburg
RIESLING
Medium-bodied. A firm, fleshy
white with a dry finish.
Any of Michael Moosbrugger's
white wines are worth drinking,
but his value wines are a boon to

THE TOP GERMAN VINEYARDS

We talk a lot in this book about *terroir* and its significance for the quality of all wine. In Germany, wine producers are wrestling with this very concept as the industry there attempts to classify its vineyards using a Grand Cru system to identify its best sites.

Following is an alphabetical list, broken down by regions, of what we believe are the historically important German *terroirs* (vineyards with ideal natural conditions) for Riesling. As in Burgundy, multiple estates often share these vineyards; the names shown in parentheses are the finest or largest producers who derive great wines from them today.

MOSEL
Bernkasteler Doktor (Thanisch, Wegeler)
Brauneberger Juffer (Fritz Haag, Richter)
Enkircher Batterieberg (Immich–Batterieberg)
Erdener Pralat (Loosen, Mönchhof)
Graacher Himmelreich & Domprobst (Joh. Jos. Prum, Willi Schaefer)
Piesporter Goldtröpfchen (Reinhold Haart, Joh. Haart)
Ürziger Würzgarten (Joh. Jos. Christoffel, Loosen, Mönchhof, Weins– Prüm)
Wehlener Sonnenuhr (Joh. Jos. Prüm, Loosen, Studert– Prüm, Weins– Prüm)
Zeltinger Sonnenuhr (Joh. Jos. Prüm, Selbach-Oster)

SAAR
Saarburger Rausch (Wagner, Zilliken)
Scharzhofberg (Egon Müller, Von Hovel, Kesselstatt, Von Volxem)

RUWER
Maximin Grünhaus (Von Schubert)
Karthäuserhofberg (Karthäuserhof)
Kaseler Nies'chen (Karlsmühle, Kesselstatt)

NAHE
Niederhäuser Hermannshöhle (Dönnhoff)

MITTELRHEIN
Bacharacher Hahn (Jost)

RHEINGAU
Erbacher Marcobrunn (Schloss Schönborn)
Johannisberg (Schloss Johannisberg)
Kiedricher Grafenberg (Weil)
Oestricher Lenchen & Dooser (Spreitzer)
Rauenthaler Baiken (Kloster Eberbach)
Rudesheimer Berg Schlossberg (Breuer, Kesseler, Leitz, Wegeler)

RHEINHESSEN
Nackenheimer Rothenberg (Gunderloch)
Niersteiner Pettenthal (Strub, Heyl Zu Herrnsheim)

PFALZ
Forster Kirchenstuck, Pechstein & Ungeheuer
    (Bassermann–Jordan, Bürklin–Wolf, Von Buhl, Müller)
Ruppertsberger Gaisböhl (Bürklin–Wolf)

anyone who loves Austrian wines. This affordable Riesling is very Burgundian—that is, graced with good, earthy minerality and a rich finish. It would soar with a crab casserole. Still more impressive is the **Riesling "Vom Urgestein"** ($18–22), a mix of fruit from the Grand Cru vineyards of Gaisberg and Heiligenstein. Mouthwatering, dry, and herbal, it's a fine partner for lobster ravioli in pesto. $14–16
Langenlois, Austria
Imported by Michael Skurnik/
Terry Thiese

Mönchhof
RIESLING "Estate"
Medium-bodied. A succulent wine jammed with fruit.
From a classic, four-hundred-year-old estate under the visionary custodianship of Robert Eymael, this Riesling dances seductively on the palate and explodes with peaches at the finish; enjoy it with curries and salty snacks. For more drama, try the ripe, rich, cellar-worthy **Spätlese "Urziger Wurzgarten"** ($25–28), an incredible wine for glazed game birds. $14–16
Mosel, Germany
Imported by Cellars International

Bert Simon
RIESLING "Estate"
Light-bodied. Slender, lightly sweet, and fine.
This pastoral estate on the Saar River makes easy-to-like, peachy, minerally wines from two monopole (estate-owned) vineyards, an unusual opportunity for Simon to keep costs down and quality high. Try the basic wine with fried foods or sandwiches. Enjoy the **Spätlese "Serriger Herrenberg"** ($18–20), a graceful, silky offering with some sweetness, when you need a wine for vegetarian Indian food. $14–16
Saar, Germany
Imported by Cellars International

Kurt Darting
RIESLING Kabinett
"Dürkheimer Michelsberg"
Medium-bodied. Thick, honeyed musings on Riesling's outer limits of ripeness.
Kurt Darting always serves up super-ripe Rieslings at great prices from several Rheinpfalz vineyards in Bad Dürkheim, with Michelsberg the class of the field. Dripping with broiled peach, cherry, and honey, this Kab is a good choice for hot Szechuan specialties and spicy Buffalo chicken wings. Also try Darting's Spätleses, which are lush across the board. $14–16
Pfalz, Germany
Imported by Michael Skurnik/
Terry Thiese

Meulenhof
RIESLING Kabinett
"Wehlener Sonnenuhr"
Medium-bodied. Greenish in hue, zesty on the palate, and delicate in the finish.
The best vineyard in the small Mosel-Saar-Ruwer town of Wehlen is Sonnenuhr, named for the huge sundial that stands on the property. Both this delicate and tingly Kabinett and the sweeter **Erdener Treppchen Spätlese** ($18–20) are textbook examples of their type. Green fruits and lime-blossom freshness are pleasing in both wines. The Kab goes with light pan-Asian and Nuevo Latino cuisine. The Spätlese refreshes with sweeter fare like plantains and well-sauced barbecue. $15–18
Mosel, Germany
Imported by Michael Skurnik/
Terry Thiese

145

THREE FROM MAXIMIN GRÜNHAUS

Rising abruptly from Germany's Mosel plain, the thousand-year-old Maximin Grünhaus vineyards in Ruwer are a formidable sight: eighty acres of steep, terraced vineyards divide the Brudersberg (Brothers' Hill), the Herrenberg (Gentlemen's Hill), and the Abtsberg (Abbot's Hill)—each a legendary slice of German *terroir*.

At the center of the estate owned by Baron Carl von Schubert is the imposing Maximin Grünhaus itself, a monastery until 1802. Even von Schubert's everyday wines are an exercise in grace and precision. The **C. von Schubert Riesling "Maximin Grünhauser"** ($16–18) is supremely delicate and scintillating, with a lithe, fruity finish. Its winsome lime-and-apple flavors pair well with all kinds of tasty fare, from Thai noodles to lobster

rolls to cold cuts with mustard. The estate's **Kabinett "Maximin Grünhauser Herrenberg"** ($14–16) is more age-worthy—a tender, minerally nugget of perfection. In very ripe years the **Spätlese "Maximin Grünhauser Abtsberg"** ($18–20) is at once powerful and elegant, a slurpy combo of guavas, candied apples, wildflowers, and pebbly minerality. (For the record, the 2003 vintage was fantastically ripe.) Those wines will probably need five to ten years of bottle aging and will last for several decades. *Imported by Valckenberg*

Bonny Doon
RIESLING
"The Heart Has Its Rieslings"
Medium-bodied.
Lavishly ripe and slurpy.
Here's one-of-a-kind California winemaker Randall Grahm's ode to German Spätlese. A mouth-watering flood of sweet peach, nectarine, and baked apple, it's a great match for traditional Thanksgiving fare and Cantonese roast duck.
$16–18
California

Eugen Wehrheim
RIESLING Spätlese
"Niersteiner Orbel"
Medium-bodied. Fun, frolicsome, and loaded with fruit.
Ribbons of ripe peach and apricot swirl through the core of this Spätlese, giving it an almost sherbety character. It's a balm for

spicy ethnic dishes and highly seasoned sausages—German currywurst and Spanish chorizo, for two.
$16–18
Rheinhessen, Germany
Imported by Chapin Cellars

Willi Schaefer
RIESLING
"Graacher Himmelreich"
Light- to medium-bodied. Very concentrated, with profoundly ripe fruit, silky texture, and a long, tapering finish.
An off-dry and exquisitely textured delight, this Riesling suggests a very flavorful

apple confection topped by a scoop of lime sorbet. It's near-perfect, whether by itself or

with light fish of any kind. Schaefer's wines are scarce and worth searching out, with the **Spatlëse "Graacher Domprobst"** ($25–35) often considered the most important by collectors. $16–20
Mosel, Germany
Imported by Michael Skurnik/ Terry Theise

J. & H. A. Strub
RIESLING Kabinett **"Niersteiner Pettenthal"**
Medium-bodied. A scrumptious, juicy Riesling that demands food.
"All grapefruit all the time," backed by peach and cranberry and the unmistakable earthy timbre of Rheinhessen's red sandstone soils. Walter Strub clearly loves acidity, and his wines ricochet wildly off your palate (with some bottle aging, they smooth out). For now, try one young with sweet-and-sour fish, fried calamari, or crab. The wildly ripe **Spätlese "Niersteiner Paterberg"** ($18–22), albeit from a lesser site, is a tempting glassful of pure apricots. $18–20
Rheinhessen, Germany
Imported by Michael Skurnik/ Terry Theise

Gunderloch
RIESLING Kabinett **"Jean-Baptiste"**
Medium-bodied. Gorgeous balance and elegance.
Fritz Hasselbach creates monumental wines, often ranked best in the Rheinhessen. In the Jean-Baptiste, piercing aromas of ripe peach and evergreen lead the way in an exquisitely balanced, off-dry wine destined for the dinner table. Try it with white meats or Asian or Latino fusion cuisine. The rarer

Spätlese "Nackenheim Rothenberg" ($32–35) is sweet, plush, and practically phosphorescent in its key lime finish. It's a special wine for the cellar, worthy of a full-scale Chinese banquet. $18–20
Rheinhessen, Germany
Imported by Cellars International

Keller
RIESLING Kabinett **"Florsheim-Dalsheim"**
Medium-bodied. Beautifully balanced and consistent from nose to finish.
Like Gunderloch, Keller ranks as a top Rheinhessen winemaker. Though he's better known for his excellent dry wines, we love this fruity Kab. Jasmine aromas and a palate of peach, orange, and slate are enticing, while the acid and fruit are integrated in perfect harmony. A succulent salmon and tuna partner, it's also a classic with sausages, sauerkraut, and potatoes. $18–20
Rheinhessen, Germany
Imported by Sussex

Franz Künstler
RIESLING Kabinett **"Hochheimer Reichestal"**
Medium- to full-bodied. Some of the ripest, most sensuous wine in the Rheingau.
Gunter Künstler picks ultra-ripe fruit every vintage, barrel-ages his wines on the lees, and proves better than anyone that acidity is what drives flavor in wine. Sweet grapefruit, mango, peaches, honey—the flavors seem not only hedonistic but endless. Look for the astonishing **Riesling "Estate"** ($14–16), which drinks like a Spätlese for a fraction of the price. Pair both with such salty or spicy fare as

curries, glazed ham, Cantonese roast meats, kimchi, and barbecue. $18–20
Rheingau, Germany
Imported by Cellars International

Ratzenberger
RIESLING Spätlese Trocken **"Steeger St. Jost"**
Light- to medium-bodied. Very dry, very penetrating.
Jochen Ratzenberger is one of the most talented winemakers in his region. His orangey Spätlese Trocken, rich and devoid of sweetness, is a precise wine with an earthbound, clayish minerality. The balance is gorgeous. Try it with a serious piece of baked fish, a gratin of potatoes, or good old-fashioned corned beef and cabbage. $18–20
Mittelrhein, Germany
Imported by Moore Brothers

Karlsmühle
RIESLING Kabinett **"Kaseler Nies'chen"**
Medium-bodied. Driven and intense.
Made complex by the intense minerality of the Grand Cru Nies'chen vineyard, this wine crafted by Peter Geiben is magnificent, though invariably muted for the first year or two. It then erupts with cascades of sherbety citrus and apple. The wine will also cellar well for several years—but if you can't wait, go for Geiben's **Kabinett "Lorenzhöfer Mäuerchen"** ($18–22), whose leafy, lovely, lime-blossom nose and rippling acidity elevate even the simplest fish dishes. $18–22
Ruwer, Germany
Imported by Michael Skurnik/ Terry Thiese

$20 to $40

Von Hövel
RIESLING Kabinett **"Oberemoneler Hütte"**
Light-bodied. A likely bid for the prettiest Riesling in Germany.
So delicate, so fine-boned, and so crystalline in color and mineral clarity is this wine that it seems to have captured the essence of a May afternoon in a bottle. Its wildflower, river water, and lemon crème scents also bewitch us into writing silly and romantic tasting notes! No matter. Drink this with sashimi or poached trout and thank us later. $20–23
Saar, Germany
Imported by Cellars International

Georg Breuer
RIESLING **"Montosa"**
Full-bodied. Bone-dry, mineral-rich, and powerful.
This is a blend made from fruit grown biodynamically at two of Breuer's mountain vineyards— the gravelly Rüdesheim Bert Schlossberg, which provides intense slaty character, and the Rauenthal Nonnenberg, which adds citrusy brightness. Dry and strong, it's a serious partner for richly sauced ocean fish and scallops. $20–24
Rheingau, Germany
Imported by Classical Wines

Joh. Jos. Prüm
RIESLING Kabinett **"Wehlener Sonnenuhr"**
Medium-bodied. Perfectly balanced and lasting.
The wines of J. J. Prüm are the benchmark for Sonnenuhr, Mosel, and possibly German wine itself. This Kab is delicate at first but expands into a shimmering, lemony, pear-drop diamond of a

wine; it's particularly nice with fresh trout. The **Spätlese "Wehlener Sonnenuhr"** ($25–35) offers more sweetness and powerful slate that completely takes over the finish; it holds its

own with fish like salmon and marlin. Those fond of more pungent, earthy Riesling should opt for the **Spätlese "Zeltinger Sonnenuhr"** ($25–35), which somehow has a darker, less tamed character—great with pork, veal, and light game. Best for drinking young is plump, sultry **Kabinett "Graacher Himmelreich"** ($20–25), which shows lots of red berry fruit and pineapple—a nice flavor profile for curries and spicy seafood. (Note: Prüm's wines are invariably fizzy and unsettled when they first arrive in the United States but soon calm down and cellar for decades.) $20–25

Mosel, Germany
Imported by Cellars International

Kruger-Rumpf
RIESLING Spätlese
"Münsterer Dautenpflanzer"
Medium- to full-bodied. Outrageously ripe, vividly flavored, and succulent.
Green apples are the hallmark of Stefan Rumpf's graceful Granny Smith-scented wines, which practically balloon with flavor on the palate. All the wines are good, but the Spät— with its endless ribbons of green apple, slate, vanilla, and pears—is incomparable. It achieves wine-food nirvana with roast pork and apples but also pairs well with fish, lobster,

and mixed grill. $20–25
Nahe, Germany
Imported by Michael Skurnik/ Terry Thiese

J. J. Christoffel Erben
RIESLING Kabinett
"Ürziger Würzgarten"
Medium-bodied. Complex, fine, and silken.
His estate is now leased to Robert Eymael, but Hans Leo Christoffel still makes the family wines. The Rieslings are among the best—delicate, subtly deep, cut with rivulets of minerals, and haunting. Here, the *terroir* of the Würzgarten ("spice garden") adds its exotic, floral flair. Try it with an *herbes de Provence*–dusted roast hen or Thai shrimp with basil. The riper **Spätlese** ($30+) is a good candidate for dishes served with chutney or mango salsa. Note: Erben's **Ausleses** ($30–65), of which there are several versions each year, are wines to meditate upon.
$20–25
Mosel, Germany
Imported by Michael Skurnik/ Terry Thiese

Reinhold Haart
RIESLING Kabinett
"Piesporter Goldtröpfchen"
Medium-bodied. Lively, juicy, ripe, and sophisticated.
Winemaker Theo Haart is a benchmark producer in the Mosel. His Piesporter is like an Easter basket of flowers, oranges, and candied ginger, with crisp acids and perfectly expressed *terroir.* It excels with fried, salty foods but also makes a great choice for a full-scale lobster dinner. Buy a case for drinking and a case for cellaring.
$20–25
Mosel, Germany
Imported by Cellars International

Fritz Haag
RIESLING Kabinett
"Brauneberger Juffer–Sonnenuhr"
**Medium- to full-bodied.
A magnificent, dense Riesling that's slow to evolve.**
Famed for his unerringly superb wines and bone-crushing handshake, Wilhelm Haag is the master and commander of the Brauneberger Juffer vineyard— and some might say the Mosel itself. His wines need time to soften their crunchy, powerful structure and unfold their layers of white peach, citron, slate, and cream . . . but we're willing to wait. Serve the Kabinett with sliced veal or pork in mustard. Serve Haag's formidable **Spätlese Brauneberger Juffer Sonnenuhr** ($35–40) with a whole roast goose or duck. $22–25
Mosel, Germany
Imported by Cellars International

Franz Prager
RIESLING Federspiel
"Weissenkirchner Steinriegl"
**Medium- to full-bodied.
Concentrated, bone-dry, and cellar-worthy.**
About as traditional as Austrian Riesling gets, the Riesling from the Steinriegl vineyard seems cool (almost minty) in character, with deep mineral layers. Its acidity is so finely integrated into the wine that it's hard to detect right away. Superb with lemony fish, breaded veal cutlets, and rich crab or lobster dishes. $23–25
Wachau, Austria
Imported by Vin Divino

Karthäuserhof
RIESLING Spätlese
"Eitelsbacher Karthäuserhofberg"
Medium-bodied. A vibrant, authoritative Riesling with rich sweetness and depth.
Centuries old, highly regarded, and one of the "big three" in the Ruwer River valley, this estate makes wines deeply anchored in red slate—and while they're often ungiving in their youth, they're built to age. Appropriate food choices include white-meat chicken teriyaki and a rolled pork roast with apricots. $25–30
Ruwer, Germany
Imported by Cellars International

H. Dönnhoff
RIESLING Kabinett
"Norheimer Dellchen"
**Light- to medium-bodied.
Some of the most graceful Rieslings in Germany.**
Helmut Dönnhoff, the undisputed king of the Nahe, has a motto: *"Das ganze Ding muss klingen!"*

THE SPÄT TO BEAT
Robert Weil is on everyone's short list of the best winemakers in the Rheingau (or possibly all of Germany), and his **Robert Weil Riesling Spätlese "Kiedricher Grafenberg"** ($50–60) is the top of his line as far as dinner wines are concerned. With sheer power wedded to flamboyant fruit, this full-bodied Spät is endlessly long on flavor—the *ne plus ultra* of modern Riesling. Sweet pears and white peaches, clover honey, ginger, and passion flower are only the start of its aromatics—but it's that great minerality that's the big reward. Ham, game birds, and whole fish are good food mates. Incidentally, Weil's simply labeled but powerfully built **"Estate" Trocken** ($20+) is one of the best dry wines in Germany. *Imported by Cellars International*

("The whole thing must harmonize"). This particular wine has been taut and firm in some years, delicate in others, yet it always sustains that precious harmony of acidity, sweetness, and mineral backbone. Perfumed with tangerines and potpourri, it goes well with light food—even the raw kind (ceviche, sushi, sashimi). The collector's wine from the estate is the **Spätlese "Niederhäuser Hermannshöhle"** ($55–65), so cellarable it might outlive you. $25–35
Nahe, Germany
Imported by Michael Skurnik/ Terry Thiese

Schafer-Frohlich
RIESLING Spätlese "Bockenauer Felseneck"
Medium-bodied.
A Spät to reckon with.

This startlingly ripe peach-and-tangerine bomb comes from Tim Frohlich, a wunderkind on the ascent. The acid structure and sheer clarity of this and all of Frohlich's wines are nothing short of remarkable. Those who prefer their wines less sweet can try his perfectly balanced **"Estate" Halbtroken** ($16–18), a nice choice for steak tartare or even simple sandwiches. Save the full-blown Spät for white meat stews and sauerbraten. $28–32
Nahe, Germany
Imported by Cellars International

Bründlmayer
RIESLING "Zobinger Heiligenstein"
Medium- to full-bodied.
Powerful, with perfectly integrated acidity.
Willi Bründlmayer, considered a top-tier winemaker in Austria

by many wine writers, makes huge, dry Rieslings that have a tendency to age well for many years. This one is dense with earth and apples, but hints of tropical fruits emerge in warm vintages like '03; it's also great with mustardy swordfish or salmon. Also look for the cellarable, extravagant **"Alte Reben"** ($50–65), made from old vines, or **Langenloiser Steinmassel** ($25–30), a friendlier, fruitier cuvée with just 12% alcohol and an incredibly pure streak of pear in the finish. $29–34
Kamptal, Austria
Imported by Michael Skurnik/ Terry Thiese

Egon Müller
RIESLING Kabinett "Scharzhofberger"
Medium-bodied. Firm, subtle Riesling in need of cellaring.
This legendary winery (est. 1797) owns seven hectares of the Scharzhofberg, one of Germany's top vineyards. The wines need years in the cellar but reveal a crisp, citron-and-stone palate and supreme class. Best served with simply-prepared trout, sole, or cod. $35–40
Saar, Germany
Imported by Frederick Wildman

Domaine Zind-Humbrecht
RIESLING "Herrenweg de Turckheim"
Full-bodied. Dry and headily perfumed, with more soil on display than fruitiness.
Olivier Humbrecht is the king of Alsace wines, thanks to his obsession for detail and quality. His Riesling is redolent of stones and fresh earth, underwritten by ripe citrus and fruits, and surprisingly high in alcohol. Save

this for richly sauced fish, white meats, and sweetbreads. His **Riesling Grand Cru "Rangen de Thann"** ($80–100), from old vines in volcanic soils, is the one you see most often at auctions. $36–40
Alsace, France
Imported by Kermit Lynch

Josef Hirsch
RIESLING
"Gaisberg Old Vines"
Medium- to full-bodied. Tremendous "cut" and mouth-filling intensity in a dry style. Johannes Hirsch is bottling everything in screw caps, inventing crazy new cuvées, and winning legions of fans with his amazing wines. We love his Gaisberg, a savory, salty, concentrated dry white gently simmering with straw, pepper, and peaches; enjoy it with your best salmon or chicken dish. $38–45
Kamptal, Austria
Imported by Michael Skurnik/ Terry Thiese

Over $40

Dr. Bürklin–Wolf
RIESLING **"Gaisböhl"**
Full-bodied. Formidable richness and strength; finishes dry. This four-hundred-year-old estate makes world-class dry Riesling in a voluptuous style. The Gaisböhl (formerly "Ruppertsberger Gaisböhl") is the equivalent of a Spätlese Trocken, late-picked but vinified dry. It's a bold, tropical fruit-scented white with earthy complexity. Serve with smoked fish, sweetbreads, or pork. $45–50
Pfalz, Germany
Imported by Classical Wines

Domaine Schoffit
RIESLING Grand Cru
"Rangen de Thann"
Full-bodied. Riesling writ large! Creamy and pulsing with flavor. This should convince red-only wine lovers that white wine can be complex and sensational. The litany of fruits and flowers is secondary here. This wine is about *texture*—so satiny on the palate it seems all-enveloping. Enjoy with foie gras or especially pungent cheeses such as Port Salut and Limburger. $50–60
Alsace, France
Imported by Weygandt/Metzler

Sauvignon Blanc

*The grape of Sancerre and Pouilly-Fumé makes wines
that shift shape in different parts of the world but
rarely lose their signature hint of grassiness.*

*T*HINK *young*, THINK *green.* That's it in a nutshell for
wines made from Sauvignon Blanc, best drunk as young and
as fresh as possible. The flavor profile is "green" in that the
usual comparisons in tasting notes are to herbs, grass, green olives, and
green peppers—all in all, "vegetal." Another famous comparison is to the
gooseberry, which tastes a bit like tart green grapes.

For the wine lover the drink-it-young rule means that Sauvignon
Blanc takes the worry out of whether to cellar or not to cellar, while
"green" is a mnemonic for the wine's natural food partners—green salads and leafy veggies, herbed dishes, and the like, though decidedly
nongreen foods like fish are deliciously eligible as well.

Euro-style Sauvignons often lend a citrusy note (usually grapefruit)
and minerality to the hallmark grassiness. More fruit-saturated, warm-
climate Sauvignons tend toward a melon flavor or peachiness.

The Loire is the most important center for Sauvignon, with those
from the vineyards of Sancerre and Pouilly-Fumé leading the pack. Next
most important is the South Island of New Zealand, specifically the
Marlborough district. How do the wines differ? Loire examples are more
elegant, understated, and mineral-driven, while the New Zealanders are
more aggressive, fruitier, and greener—and less pricey, by and large. A
less important growing area is Bordeaux, specifically the pebbly soils of
Graves (also known as Pessac-Leognan) and Entre-Deux-Mers (from
which come cheaper, everyday wines). Here the grape is usually blended with Sémillon and frequently oaked.

California makes decent Sauvignon Blancs when vintners go easy
on the oak, but the climate is a bit too warm for the grape to succeed
regularly. South Africa also makes Sauvignon Blanc, but with widely
varying quality and puzzlingly high prices.

As with Merlot, most Sauvignon growers usually offer only one
version—the reason for the absence of second labels and other "extras"
in the following recommendations. If you especially like a Sauvignon
from a certain winery, contact the importer (pages 227–230) or winery
(pages 223–226) to see what else they might offer.

Under $10

Carta Vieja
SAUVIGNON BLANC
Light-bodied. A Chilean wine perfect for everyday sipping.
Only the worst wine snobs would scorn this varietally true Sauvignon. For its price, it is fresh, juicy, non-oaked, and it has an herby, citrusy snap. Brilliant for a party, it's also good at the table with salads and appetizers. $4–6
Maule, Chile
Imported by Frederick Wildman

Barefoot Cellars
SAUVIGNON BLANC
Light-bodied. Crisp and cheerful.
For a California Sauvignon, this party/picnic wine is atypically light, bright, and devoid of oak. Now owned by Gallo, the estate will hopefully continue to produce wines that are good value. $6–8
California

Domaine La Prevote
TOURAINE
Light-bodied. A brisk, easygoing cocktail sipper.
This 100% Sauvignon Blanc offers a lemon-fresh apéritif style from the Loire at an amazing price. Whether it's drunk on its own or with salads or crudités, it's a nice choice for whenever you feel like relaxing. It's also a good base for a Kir cocktail (white wine with a little cassis, the black currant liqueur). $7–9
Loire, France
Imported by Monsieur Touton

Château Tour de Goupin
BORDEAUX BLANC
Light-bodied. Dry, delicate, and pretty on the palate.
Half Sauvignon Blanc, half Sémillon—and all refreshment.

A lovely sense of citrus brightens the finish of this wine. Pair it with light fish and appetizers. $8–10
Bordeaux
Imported by Baron François

William Cole
SAUVIGNON BLANC
Light-bodied. A Chilean bargain that's pungent and lively.
This Sauvignon is fresh-tasting, peppery, grassy—green joy with perfect acidity and no oak. The greenness makes it a super leafy vegetable or tabbouleh match. $8–10
Casablanca, Chile
Imported by Metropolis

Château de la Presle
TOURAINE BLANC
Medium-bodied. Fiercely aromatic, boldly flavored, and zingy.
Now this is the kind of Sauvignon we like: *sauvage*, as the French say, totally dry, and loaded with minerals, acidity, grassiness, and a little grapefruit. It's an exciting wine for greens, grains, pesto, tomatoes, goat cheeses, and *pizza bianco* (cheese, but no tomato sauce)—and a hit with oily fish like mackerel or sardines. $9–11
Loire, France
Imported by Bayfield

$10 to $20

Château Lamothe de Haux
BORDEAUX BLANC
Light- to medium-bodied. Crisp and elegant.
A citron-scented Sauvignon/ Sémillon blend with a fresh finish. It's a marvelous dry white with first courses, vegetable

dishes, or a creamy pasta tossed with smoked salmon. $10–12
Bordeaux
Imported by Bayfield

Henri Bourgeois
SAUVIGNON BLANC
"Petit Bourgeois"
Medium-bodied.
Crisp and revivifying.
A "baby Sancerre" from Chavignol, an important village in France's Sancerre district. Racy, citrusy, and tinged with an herbal note, this one is fresh and easy with flaky fish, vegetables, hors d'oeuvres, or chèvre. The winery's various Sancerre cuvées are renowned as well. $10–12
Loire, France
Imported by Monsieur Touton

Sacchetto
SAUVIGNON BLANC
Light-bodied. Ethereally delicate—a Mediterranean take on Sauvignon.
This gentle dry white entices you with an elusive floral-herbal theme and fresh flavors throughout. Serve with sautéed greens, gnocchi with pesto, or flaky fish with a splash of lemon. $10–12
Veneto, Italy
Imported by John Given

Blanco Nieva
SAUVIGNON BLANC
Medium-bodied.
Penetrating on the palate.
This Spanish Sauvignon is bold, grapefruity, and unbelievably aromatic, with rapierlike acidity. It's a great solution for such "problem" wine foods as asparagus, artichokes, or sardines and other oily fish. $10–12
Rueda, Spain
Imported by Frontier

François Cazin
CHEVERNY
"Le Petit Chambord"
Light- to medium-bodied.
Crisp, plump, and piquant.
An indigenous blend of 90% Sauvignon Blanc and 10% Chardonnay. Very dry and kissed with herbs and earth, it often shows a light nuttiness in the finish. Try it with endive spears stuffed with goat cheese. $10–12
Loire, France
Imported by Louis/Dressner

Shenandoah
SAUVIGNON BLANC
Light- to medium-bodied.
Seductively fragrant and smooth.
What really makes this fun is a shot of 20% Viognier in the blend, which adds richness and a sexy pear perfume. It's an exotic American white wine with great potential for crab dishes and spicy seafood. $10–12
California

Domaine du Tariquet
SAUVIGNON BLANC
Medium-bodied.
Bright, juicy, and flavorsome.
This bone-dry Sauvignon, from Cognac country in southern France, is an electric jolt to the senses. A winning apéritif at a great price, it's also a hit at the table with foods as varied as shrimp Creole, stuffed grape leaves, and pasta with pesto. $10–12
Côtes de Gascony, France
Imported by Baron François

A GO-WITH-EVERYTHING SAUVIGNON

It wasn't until the 1980s that Marlborough, the winegrowing region on the northern tip of New Zealand's South Island, came to the wine world's attention—and then because of one grape: Sauvignon Blanc, which thrives on the area's combination of warm days, cool nights, light rainfall, and lots of sunshine. A wine that lives up to the region's growing reputation is **Vavasour Sauvignon Blanc "Dashwood"** ($12–14), an addictive combo of freshness, grace, and lively fruit. Zesty and fragrant, it offers grass and minerals in the nose and threads of grapefruit and kiwi on the palate.

Practically the paradigm of a great food wine, it goes with everything: fish, fowl, vegetables, and even red meat dishes—particularly roast leg of lamb with garlic and rosemary. *Imported by Lauber*

Red Hill
SAUVIGNON BLANC
Medium-bodied. Enticingly fragrant and versatile.
The moment you open the bottle, this Sauvignon fills the room with its melon and fresh citrus perfume. A vibrant and succulent wine, it exhibits a balance and integrity of flavor that benefits "green" food of any kind, from herbal cheeses to bitter greens to pesto.
$10–12
Marlborough, New Zealand
Imported by Bayfield

Jean-Marc Brocard
SAUVIGNON DE ST. BRIS
Light- to medium-bodied. Savory and crisp.
A bit of a rare bird, this Sauvignon is sourced near Chablis, which is usually Chardonnay's turf. The producer does with Sauvignon what he perfects in Chablis, making a crisp, slightly earthy, and very interesting wine with no oak and plenty of pleasure to offer. A great choice for an omelet or Cobb salad. $11–13
Burgundy
Imported by Lauber

Château La Blancherie
GRAVES BLANC
Light- to medium-bodied. Juicy, dry, and elegant.
This blend of Sauvignon Blanc and Sémillon is made in a crisp, non-oaked style, with a dash more complexity than simple Bordeaux Blanc. It is versatile for foods that like a rich, dry white—among them, white meat chicken, seafood terrines, and pâté.
$12–14
Bordeaux
Imported by Bayfield

Babich
SAUVIGNON BLANC
Medium-bodied. Fresh and juicy mean "no worries, mate."
This kinder, gentler New Zealand Sauvignon is very melony in flavor and quite refreshing overall. It's a natural with vegetables, chowders, and seafood salads. $12–14
Marlborough, New Zealand
Imported by Martin Scott

Stoneleigh
SAUVIGNON BLANC
Medium-bodied. Tingly and refreshing, with lots of flavor.
A widely available old favorite. This wine remains as tasty and grassy as it should be, with that

grapefruity Sauvignon character coming through in spades on the finish. A super white for vegetable lasagna, Greek salad, or *moules meunière* (mussels cooked with lemon, herbs, and white wine). $13–15
Marlborough, New Zealand
Imported by Allied Domecq

Henry Marionnet
TOURAINE BLANC
Light- to medium-bodied.
Bright, pure, and radiant with Sauvignon character.
This ultra-organic producer makes a fresh, vibrant, exciting Sauvignon Blanc that rivals anything coming from the more rarefied precincts of Sancerre or the middle Loire. Alive with grapefruit and exotic floral aromas, it's a zestful match for goat cheese pizzettes and chilled shellfish. $13–15
Loire, France
Imported by Weygandt/Metzler

Selaks
SAUVIGNON BLANC
Medium-bodied. Pungent, richly textured, and mouthwatering.
One of the pioneers of New Zealand Sauvignon, the Selaks winery (est. 1934), consistently crafts assertive, take-no-prisoners wines. If you love "dirty martinis" (with olive brine), you'll love this white. It's unique and delicious with fish steaks, tarragon chicken, or any herby, savory fare. $13–15
Marlborough, New Zealand
Imported by American Estates

Villa Maria
SAUVIGNON BLANC
Medium-bodied.
Vibrant and savory, with a lip-smacking finish.
This is penetrating stuff, bursting with grapefruit, juniper, and gooseberry. It's particularly good with "green" foods like veggies and pesto and mesclun. And, like many noteworthy New Zealand wines, it's a screwcap! $14–16
Marlborough, New Zealand
Imported by Vineyard Brands

Framingham
SAUVIGNON BLANC
Medium-bodied.
Boisterously ripe, fruity, and well-rounded at the finish.
Sourced from the Wairau Valley in New Zealand's Marlborough region, Framingham Sauvignon is more plump and fruit-driven than its peers, with limeade and melon aromas aplenty. A superb salmon partner (especially for gamier wild salmon), it also pairs well with garlicky foods. $14–16
Marlborough, New Zealand
Imported by Bayfield

Goisot
SAUVIGNON DE ST. BRIS
Light- to medium-bodied.
A bright, rich rarity that excels at the table.
This Sauvignon Blanc from Burgundy, the ancestral home of Chardonnay, has a Chablis-like minerality tacked onto Sauvignon's minty, grapefruity varietal character. The wine is not only organic but extremely well made. Try it with lemon sole or a leek-and-goat-cheese tart. $15–17
Burgundy
Imported by Polaner

Thelema
SAUVIGNON BLANC
Medium-bodied. Silkiness balanced with some earthy complexity.
From one of the highest and probably coolest vineyards in South Africa comes a

Sauvignon with no oak but plenty of grapefruit, citrus zest, and steely character—all capped with a juicy finish. Serve with flaky fish, veggies, or chicken pot pie. $15–17
Stellenbosch, South Africa
Imported by Cape Classics

Nautilus
SAUVIGNON BLANC
Medium- to full-bodied.
Ripe and rather intense.
Nautilus works in a rich style, crafting wines for the table. Their Sauvignon boggles the palate with waves of lime, kiwi, green olive, and cut grass. (Sip it as an apéritif only if you're in the mood for something really gutsy.) Exciting with lobster, monkfish, or grilled seafood sausages. $15–17
Marlborough, New Zealand
Imported by Négociants USA

Domaine Mardon
QUINCY
Medium-bodied.
Elegant,
generous, and
lingering.

Quincy, situated on the river Cher in the southern part of the Loire Valley, is the savvy wine lover's alternative to Sancerre and Pouilly-Fumé. Mardon's version is a fat, flinty delight. The perfect goat cheese partner, it's also a nice complement for salmon and shellfish in cream. $15–17
Loire, France
Imported by Daniel Johnnes

Allan Scott
SAUVIGNON BLANC
Medium- to full-bodied.
An electrifying, wildly
fragrant Sauvignon.
The intensity of this wine is almost unimaginable given its acidity, martini olive aromas, and salty minerality. It's the answer for foods that need aggressive wine pairings: smoked or oily fish, spicy ceviche, and entrée salads full of greens and zesty dressings. $15–17
Marlborough, New Zealand
Imported by Uniqco

Domaine Sautereau
SANCERRE
Medium-bodied.
Utterly elegant and
well made, yet barely known
in the United States.
This wine always evolves the same way. Its first few weeks on the U.S. market see it through a lemony, "jumpy" phase; the edge then relaxes and it becomes one of the great Sancerres. Its bracing mineral bouquet is like a blast of fresh air. Crisp, racy, and dry, it's a fish wine par excellence. $15–17
Loire, France
Imported by Grand Cru

Girard
SAUVIGNON BLANC
Medium-bodied. Very finely
balanced and succulent.
A clean, bright, minimalist white. In high contrast to the oaky style popular in Napa, this Sauvignon is built more like a Loire wine but shows the melon, orange, and saturated fruit quality of its warmer origins. Serve with tuna steaks, baked Brie, or cracked crab. $16–18
Napa, California

Brancott Vineyards
SAUVIGNON BLANC
"Reserve"
Medium- to full-bodied.
Rather hearty for white wine.
This frequently intense dry white is packed with herb,

olive, grapefruit, and fresh cut grass flavors. It's heart-racing with salmon or spinach pie. When your guests drink *only* white wine but you're serving red meat, this white is up to the job. $16–18
Marlborough, New Zealand
Imported by Allied Domecq

Frank et Jean-François Bailly
SANCERRE
"Cuvée Chavignol"
Medium-bodied.
As elegant and impressive a Sancerre as any we've tasted.
In this artful Sancerre, fabulous aromatics of herbs and flowers are accompanied by gorgeous, mouthwatering texture and a long, full finish. A classic fish wine, it's also able to handle asparagus. $16–19
Loire, France
Imported by Daniel Johnnes

Dalton
SAUVIGNON BLANC
Medium-bodied.
Fruity and seductively aromatic, it's dry—but just barely.
This is our favorite kosher wine for food: marvelously juicy, with exquisite green melon and lime flavors, an aroma that billows out of the glass, and a crisp, lip-smacking finish. Drink it with anything from the sea or the vegetable garden. $17–20
Galilee, Israel
Imported by Allied Importers

Koura Bay
SAUVIGNON BLANC
"Whalesback"
Full-bodied. An impressively bold, perfumy wine that commands attention.
This outlandishly ripe, succulent wine has a huge bouquet of the "greenness" (grass, green

peppers, etc.) that makes New Zealand wines such wonderful partners for vegetables and herbed fish and fowl. It can even work with lamb! $18–20
Marlborough, New Zealand
Imported by Weygandt/Metzler

Domaine de Chatenoy
MENETOU-SALON
Medium-bodied. Sometimes drier, sometimes fruitier, but always vivacious.
This intriguing Sauvignon hails from centuries-old vineyards abutting Sancerre. More pungent than typical Loire Sauvignon, it is almost aggressively herbal. Pair it with fresh vegetables, stuffed peppers, smoked salmon, and tomato dishes. $18–20
Loire, France
Imported by V.O.S.

Philippe Raimbault
SANCERRE "Apud Sariacum"
Medium- to full-bodied.
Dense, vigorous, full-flavored.
Here's Sauvignon at its purest, made complex by the gravelly, chalky soils of the Loire Valley. The nautilus shell on the label suggests what to serve: anything fresh and briny from the sea. It's also splendid with poultry—say, chicken breasts in a tarragon cream sauce. $18–20
Loire, France
Imported by T. Edward

Domaine Girard
SANCERRE "La Garenne"
Medium- to full-bodied. Rich, round, and highly elegant.
A "complete" wine from start to finish, this Sauvignon is for people who appreciate balance and evidence of *terroir* in their wines. Mineral layers and deep, creamy fruit invite thoughtful sipping. A grown-up choice for crab cakes, halibut and other

firm fish, or Montrachet and other creamy goat cheeses. $18–20
Loire, France
Imported by Louis/Dressner

Domaine Hervé Seguin
POUILLY-FUMÉ
Medium-bodied.
A Pouilly notable for
its delicacy and
underlying strength.
Hand-harvested from vines over thirty years old, then minimally handled, this wine is delightfully crisp and lemony, with a distinct vein of minerality. Think seafood salads (especially spooned into avocado halves) and fillets of sole or other flaky fish. $18–20
Loire, France
Imported by Robert Kacher

Over $20

Domaine Cailbourdin
POUILLY-FUMÉ "Les Cris"
Medium- to full-bodied.
Astonishingly fragrant and
rife with refreshing acidity.
This drinks like a dry gin and tonic—easy on the lime. Wonderfully refreshing and true to its *terroir*, it's an aristocratic choice for lobster or soft cheeses. $20–22
Loire, France
Imported by Lauber

Pascal et Nicolas Reverdy
SANCERRE "Les Coutes"
Medium- to full-bodied.
That elusive creature:
a Sancerre with assertive
Sauvignon Blanc character.
Exquisitely balanced, rich, and pulsing with fruit and minerality, this Sancerre is almost startling to drink. It is hand-harvested from fifty-year-old vines, bottled without filtration, and has a

tremendously long finish. Enjoy with rich seafood (lobster!) or aged goat cheeses. $20–22
Loire, France
Imported by Weygandt/Metzler

Henry Pellé
MENETOU-SALON
"Moroques"
Medium-bodied. Full-flavored
and savory, with palpable fruit
in the finish.
A vivid Sauvignon Blanc awash with lime, crushed mint, and mineral notes. While certainly dry, it is fruitier than Sancerre or Pouilly-Fumé. Mediterranean and Middle Eastern foods are among its best partners. $20–23
Loire, France
Imported by Peter Vezan

Russiz Superiore
SAUVIGNON BLANC
Full-bodied. One of the
most complex and
full-flavored Sauvignons.
Aromas of grapefruit, green pepper, and sage waft strongly from this special wine, made by the Marco Felluga estate in Collio. Incredibly firm and densely layered, it has an earthy *terroir* expression some call aggressive; we just call it great winemaking. Drink with broiled fish, asparagus au gratin, or pasta tossed with sausage and fresh sage. $20–23
Friuli, Italy
Imported by Polaner

Grgich Hills
FUMÉ BLANC
Medium- to full-bodied.
Savory, soft, and judiciously
enhanced by oak.
This is Californian Mike Grgich's perennial classic Sauvignon, marketed as "Fumé"—a term coined by Robert Mondavi. Mild vanilla and marjoram notes from the barrel are layered within

melony fruit in this luxurious white. Try it with chicken-and-almond stir-fry, mustardy veal cutlets, or swordfish. $20–23
Napa

Domaine Thomas–Labaille
SANCERRE "Les Monts Damnés"
Medium-bodied. Subtly intricate and slow to evolve.
Real wine geek stuff, this. Loire fans swear by the tiny *lieu-dit* (a vineyard with no Premier or Grand Cru designation) near Chavignol, from which the wine derives its pungent chalk-and-earth character and surprising longevity—both on the palate and in the cellar. Black bass, skate, monkfish, and other substantial seafood suggested. $22–25
Loire, France
Imported by Louis/Dressner

Château de France
GRAVES Blanc
**Medium- to full-bodied.
Assertive, abundant, and elegant.**

Half of this Sauvignon/Sémillon blend from Pessac-Leognan, in northern Graves, is aged in new oak and half in one-year-old barrels. Its fruity freshness is accented by lime and honeysuckle, making it a lively partner for creamy-rich fish dishes, white meat chicken, or a gratin of vegetables. It benefits from a bit of aging. $28–30
Bordeaux
Imported by Bayfield

Roberto Cohen
POUILLY-FUMÉ
Medium-bodied. Subtle, elegant, and very dry.
Anyone who enjoys a dry white with no oak would most likely relish this graceful Sauvignon with citrus and cool steel in its veins. Serve it with baked, steamed, or sautéed fish, greens of all sorts, or goat cheese. While it is kosher, the wine's greatness as a Sauvignon is what makes it stand apart. $30–32
Loire, France
Imported by Roberto Cohen

DID YOU SAY *SCREWCAP*?

Yes, we did, and wine lovers will do well to listen. Folks in New Zealand and its Sauvignon Blanc–friendly winegrowing region of Marlborough have been particularly enthusiastic about high–quality screwcap wines—and with good reason. A properly made cap is a far better seal than a cork, thereby cutting down on spoilage. (The estimates of how much wine is sold spoiled, or corked, vary from three to ten percent.) Other advantages are the ease with which screwcap wines are opened and resealed and their ability to be stored standing up. Screwcaps are also preferred over plastic corks, which can't always guarantee an airtight seal.

The leading maker of the caps is French: Pechiney, whose Stelvin aluminum "capsules" come with liners of glass or varying combinations of polyethylene, PVDC, and tin. Their product has made short work of the perception that screwcaps are déclassé or worse. Plenty of top European and California producers have brought out screwcap lines, with some of the wines costing more because their winemakers think the cap a superior closure.

"BARNYARD" AND OTHER
CURIOUS TERMS

*N*EWCOMERS and seasoned wine lovers alike are often scornful of the terms they find in the tasting notes of certain writers. "Why would I want to taste rocks?" they cry when a wine is described as "minerally." "And what on earth does a barnyard taste like?!"

To paraphrase Thelonius Monk, writing about wine is like "dancing about architecture." Indeed, the limitations of mere words are soon revealed any time you try to describe a physical sensation like taste.

Two facts can help clear things up: 1) Taste isn't everything; smell is equally important. So when we say a wine evokes roses, it's not because we've ever chomped on a rose; it's the aroma that triggers the connection. 2) Words can suggest a wine's character through connotation rather than literally describing its flavor; "earthy," "woodsy," and "perfumy" are good examples. Remain skeptical or even laugh if you wish; but an open imagination and a quick lesson in traditional wine shorthand will soon have you reading wine notes like a pro. And where better to start than the barnyard?

Bequeathed to us by the French, **barnyard** describes a rustic or fecund character, either a literal smell of horses and hay (which can be pleasant) or just a "country" feel; it's often applied to red Burgundy and southern French reds. The less threatening **earthy** is a useful word that can either liken a wine's aroma to fresh, moist soil or describe the wine's overall character—rustic, funky, unpolished. **Minerally** conveys the aroma of wet stones, a rocky stream, or a clean sidewalk after a rain. (Minerality is a defining component of the world's best white wines and a few of its reds.) **Dusty** is used for dry wines (usually Bordeaux reds and Cabernet Franc) that bring to mind sawdust or a dusty country road.

Chewy is a textural descriptor of tannic or very concentrated wines (typically full-bodied reds), tongue-in-cheekily suggesting that one has to chew the wine before swallowing. As for **fat**—and the maddeningly opaque term **structure**—we'll have to ask you to turn to the Glossary (pages 217–222), where you'll also find everything you always wanted to know about **oak.**

CHAPTER FOUR

Other Choice Whites

The overflowing bounty of white grapes can easily confuse the casual wine drinker because very few have entered the pantheon occupied by Chardonnay and Sauvignon Blanc. Should that matter? No. Keeping white wines straight takes a back seat to enjoying their many charms.

Poetic license is at play in calling these wine grapes "white," as their color ranges from pale green to gold to pink. The light color of the wines they yield comes from the separation of the pigment-producing skins during fermentation, so that even a black-skinned grape can bring forth a pale but no less interesting white wine. That understood, read on!

Other Choice Whites

Get ready for a dizzying but very pleasant ride on the white-wine roller coaster. Even hard-core red lovers will likely be excited by the variety in tastes and styles.

AT THAT FUN PARTY you went to last week, was the Viognier the white wine that swept you off your feet or the one from Austria—um, Grüner something, with the second word starting with "V." And then there are all those other "V" whites to get straight: Verdicchio, Vernaccia, Vermentino, Vinho Verde . . .

A confusing jumble indeed. Yet it's worth sorting out, because the wines of many lesser-known white grapes are no less noteworthy in taste and aroma than the famous varieties; it's just that many are made from blending grapes that rarely or never get top billing—either that, or the grapes have only recently been grown on U.S. soils.

Alabariño, Arneis, Aligoté. Muscadet, Müller-Thurgau, Malvasia Bianca. Mostly from Europe, the endless parade of white wine grapes has marched our way since before medieval times. Most modern varieties no doubt have roots in ancient Greece, Rome, Persia, or other wine-growing civilizations, but tracing them back is a fruitless endeavor. Natural mutation occurs even in a couple of generations, and migration and crossbreeding make it even harder to pierce the mists of history.

More to the point is getting acquainted with the less familiar white grapes, including the delicate, nutty Chasselas, native to Switzerland; grapefruity Scheurebe (SHOY-ray-buh), the German cross between Riesling and Silvaner (the parent of many German hybrids); Tocai, the interesting bruiser from Friuli; and fresh-tasting Pinot Blanc, which excels in Alsace and Alto Adige. And almost any wine lover who has yet to explore the pear perfume of Viognier and the peppery vibrance of Grüner Veltliner has a real treat in store.

When it comes to dining, white wines aren't just for serving with foods that are "light and white." Some of the bolder whites feel more at home with a richly sauced cut of meat than with a filet of sole. The ability of a wine to match well with food depends less on its color than on its weight, balance, and acidity—and in that respect, whites are actually more versatile than reds.

Under $10

Sogrape
VINHO VERDE "Gazela"
Light-bodied. Ultra-crisp, ultra-light, and absolutely refreshing.
This is a sit-by-the-pool or picnic-in-the-park wine. Especially refreshing on a hot day, it treats you to floating clouds of lemon and apricot. A touch of carbonation makes it a particularly nice foil for spicy foods. $5–6
Vinho Verde, Portugal
Imported by Evaton

Caves Aliança
VINHO VERDE
Light-bodied. Mild, with creamy texture and a bit of sparkle.
This simple white, best drunk within a year after release, is faintly scented with apples and wafts into your mouth while sending your soul to the beach. In fact, pack a few in your seashore basket; it's only 9% alcohol, so you and your beach-going buddies may want to take more than one bottle. $5–7
Vinho Verde, Portugal
Imported by Tri-Vin

Domaine de la Chanade
LOIN DE L'OEIL "Les Rials"
Light-bodied.
Brisk and full of character.
This venerable wine is made from Loin de l'Oeil (Len de l'El in the old spelling), a grape found near Gaillac in south-central France. Popular in the sixteenth century but little known in the twenty-first, it's a drink worth rejuvenating. Try this graceful, dry bistro sipper (vaguely reminiscent of Sauvignon Blanc) with omelets, quiches, and frites. $6–8
Southwest France
Imported by Monsieur Touton

Producteurs Plaimont
CÔTES DE GASCOGNE
Light-bodied. Lively, modest in alcohol, and very refreshing.
This fruity little number from a Gascony growers' cooperative is made from the local white varieties Colombard and Ugni Blanc—the grapes that give us Cognac. Sip it in warm weather with a salad of tomatoes and mozzarella. $6–8
Gascony, France
Imported by V.O.S.

Domaine Duffour
VIN DE PAYS DES CÔTES DE GASCOGNE
Light- to medium-bodied. A ripe, juicy white with a mineral finish.

This typical regional blend of Colombard and Ugni Blanc (Trebbiano) benefits from the touch of richness imparted by a dose of Gros Manseng. Pears and earth stay the course on the palate. Perfect for mushrooms, hearty salads, and picnic fare. $7–9
Gascony, France
Imported by Charles Neal

Domaine de Cassagnoles
CÔTES DE GASCOGNE
Light-bodied. A touch of fruit and a bright, vigorous finish.
This wine hits the palate running with juicy, jumpy, pearlike fruit. Made in the Armagnac region of France from traditional grapes Ugni Blanc (a.k.a. Trebbiano) and Colombard, it's refreshing both on its own and with Greek *mezedes* (assorted appetizers), picnic fare, sandwiches, and chips 'n' dips. If you want something sweet and exotic, try their "**Cuvee Gros Maneng**" ($10–12), a tangy-rich treat

165

named for its grape; it's perfection with figs, dates, and blue cheeses. $7–9
Gascony, France
Imported by Weygandt/Metzler

Quinta da Romeira
BUCELAS
Light-bodied.
Iridescent with acidity.
This eye-watering, lemony, lively specialty of the Bucelas region, near Lisbon, is made from Arinto, a high-acid local grape. If Portugal's Vinho Verde is too wimpy for you, wrap your lips around this and enjoy the ride. Oysters, anyone? $8–10
Bucelas, Portugal
Imported by Polaner

Auggen
GUTEDEL Trocken
"Gertie and Max"
Light-bodied.
A crisp, delicate aperitif.
Gutedel (rhymes with "fruit ladle," translates as "good and noble") is a German name for the Chasselas grape from Switzerland. The wine's palate of fresh hay and apples is capped by a subtle

nuttiness. Sip it with hors d'oeuvres and broth-based soups. $8–10
Pfalz, Germany
Imported by Wines for Food

Domaine Gaujal de Saint-Bon
PICPOUL DE PINET
Light- to medium-bodied.
Zippy and fresh.
Picpoul (in its original French form, *piquepoul*, or "lip-stinger") is an ancient grape from Languedoc. But don't be put off. The wine from this estate is just marvelously refreshing, jumping with flavors of fresh grapes and lemon crème. And take note: It may be the world's best white for chicken salad. $8–10
Languedoc, France
Imported by Polaner

Cuevas de Castilla
PALACIO DE MENADE RUEDA
"Cuvée RS"
Light- to medium-bodied.
Piquant and refreshing.
Exotically scented with bay leaf and apples, this is a sublime thirst-quencher in the hot summer months. Pair it with chilled soups like gazpacho or the zesty seafood of the Mediterranean. $8–10
Rueda, Spain
Imported by Polaner

GALICIA'S ALBARIÑOS

The noble grape of northeastern Spain's Galicia region, a land of rocky sea-coasts and wet valleys, yields wines that are peachily aromatic, high in acid-ity, and, unlike most Spanish whites, untouched by oak. They can also be expensive. A bargain from Spanish vintner Martin Codax is from the Salnes Valley, a subzone of the DO (appellation) that made Albariño famous: Rias Baixas. **Burgans Albariño** ($11–13) is brisk, juicy, and perfumed with peach, orange, and wildflowers. People often do a happy double take when they try this for the first time—especially considering the price! It's a tradi-tional paella partner. *Imported by Polaner*

The Rias Baixas–grown **Martin Codax Albariño** ($15–17) is a renowned interpretation of the grape. With its floral bouquet, exquisite balance, and lingering finish of apple–pear fruit, it's a glorious lobster wine and a pleasing companion to seafood salads. *Imported by Tempranillo*

Moncaro
ESINO BIANCO "Terrazzo"
Light- to medium-bodied.
Lively, boldly scented, and dry.
Here's a briny little white from
the Verdicchio
grape, with its
inescapable
licorice and
lemon drop
character. Drink it in carafes by
the seashore, with mussels,
or with cioppino, the Italian fish
stew adopted by Californians.
$8–10
Marches, Italy
Imported by Matt Brothers

Château de Chesnaie
MUSCADET
Sèvre et Maine sur Lie
Light-bodied. Snappy, feather-
light, and vividly refreshing.
The original oyster wine,
Muscadet has a citrusy, talclike
freshness that makes it a fine
predinner drink. At the table it's a
bracing counterpoint for salads
and one of the very best wines
to serve with mussels, clams, and
oysters. Must be drunk fresh!
$8–10
Loire, France
Imported by Monsieur Touton

Domaine du Tariquet
CÔTES DE GASCOGNES
"Cuvée Tardive"
Light- to medium-bodied.
Delicately sweet and succulent.
Made from the Basque grape Gros
Manseng, this "late-picked cuvée"
from an erstwhile Armagnac maker
in southern France is a honeyish,
flowery, mouthwatering white.
Vinified off-dry, it's a gentle
accompaniment to assorted pâtés
and fruits.
$8–10
Gascony, France
Imported by Baron François

Colonnara
VERDICCHIO DEI CASTELLI
DI JESI "Lyricus"
Light- to medium-bodied.
A bright sipper with a
pleasing twist.
The Verdicchio grape has been
grown in the Marches region of
Italy since the fourteenth
century. This Verdicchio, from
vineyards near the coast, is as
precise and full of character as
Italian white wine gets, with
lemons and licorice streaking
across the palate. Try this one
alongside greens, fresh fennel
bulb, or linguine with shellfish
and parsley. $9–11
Marches, Italy
Imported by Winebow/
Leonardo LoCascio

Hatzimichalis
DOMAINE WHITE
Light-bodied. Crisp and
cleansing on the palate,
with faint minerality.
Here you have America's most
popular imported Greek wine.
Pleasantly lemony and good in
every vintage, it's a nice surprise
for many wine lovers, especially
when served with a platterful
of *mezedes* (assorted Greek
appetizers)—stuffed grape
leaves, sardines, green olives,
and taramasalata. $9–11
Opountia Locris, Greece
Imported by Athenée

Casale Marchese
FRASCATI Superiore
Medium-bodied.
Rich for Frascati—almost fat in
the mouth, with staying power.
Tropical, flashy, and evocative of
fresh fruit and almonds, Frascati
could be called the official white
wine of Rome, even though it
originated in the nearby eponymous town. If you can't enjoy a
tumblerful while munching on

crunchy calamari in a sunny Roman piazza, a few sips just might transport you there. $9–11
Lazio, Italy
Imported by Bayfield

Koster-Wolf
MÜLLER-THURGAU Halbtrocken
Light- to medium-bodied.
Soothes and refreshes.
It's hard to imagine anyone not liking this wine made from the Müller-Thurgau grape from Germany. It's dry and palate-pleasing from beginning to end, with just a hint of white peach and a lovely, balanced finish. An unbeatable sipper, it's also nice with tartly flavored dishes of any sort. $9–11
Rheinhessen, Germany
Imported by Chapin Cellars

Blanco Nieva
RUEDA
Light-bodied. Zesty, faintly candied, and almost sparkly.
Vintners in Rueda, on Spain's Duero River, have been uprooting cheaper grapevines and planting the Verdejo grape to make fresh, juicy, exotically perfumed white wines. You might sense a little watermelon-flavored candy in the aromas of this example—a scrumptious addition to a beach party or cookout. $9–11
Rueda, Spain
Imported by Frontier

Sharpe Hill
Vineyard
BALLET OF
ANGELS
Medium-bodied. An
off-dry white with
perfumed character.
A Connecticut wine? You betcha! Apart from the trippy label, this soft, fruity blend of Chardonnay, Muscadet, and Vignoles has a strangely enticing quality, which probably explains why it is one of the few New England wines to become popular. We like its refreshing style with spicy foods. $9–11
Connecticut

VERDICCHIO: THE TART ITALIAN

The eastern Italian region of Marches (Marche in Italian) is home ground for Verdicchio, the ancient yellow–green grape produced in two DOCs, or appellations. Near the Adriatic Sea and the region's only city of size, Ancona, lies Verdicchio dei Castelli di Jesi, whose lemony wines became famous for their green, urn–shaped, two–handled bottles. A good introduction to its wines is also the best bargain Verdicchio on the market: **Marchetti Verdicchio dei Castelli di Jesi** ($7–9). Rather light, zingy, and mouthwatering, it has the typical lemon–zest character that cuts easily through the oily fish dishes of coastal Italy, while its licoricey, herby element makes it a hit with pesto. *Imported by Monsieur Touton*

The Verdicchio di Matelica DOC, farther inland at a higher altitude, produces fuller–bodied wines that are also supremely rich and capable of aging. A prime example is **Bisci Verdicchio Matelica** ($13–15), a wine of crystal clarity, length, and underlying strength. It boasts the telltale Verdicchio "snap" in the finish and a strong anise aroma. It's a great partner for sardines with raisins and pine nuts or pasta with broccoli rabe and sausage. The massive single–vineyard **Bisci Vigneto Fogliano** ($18–29) is for wine lovers seeking powerhouse whites. *Imported by Marc de Grazia*

Argiolas
VERMENTINO DI SARDEGNA
"Costemolinas"
Light-bodied. A popular Sardinian specialty, highly crisp and savory.
Vermentino is an aromatic white grape grown in Sardinia, Corsica, and Liguria in Italy, and the Languedoc-Roussillon region of France (where it is called Rolle). Herbal and snappy, this Italian classic is great with pesto and a fitting partner for grilled veggies and light seafood. $9–11
Sardinia
Imported by Winebow/ Leonardo LoCascio

$10 to $15

Red Newt Cellars
RED NEWT WHITE
Light- to medium-bodied. Bright, fun white with a touch of sweetness and modest alcohol.
The grapes responsible for this white are the East Coast American hybrids Vidal Blanc and Cayuga, so we're way out in left field with this one. But you've got to love its wildly fruity nature. It's also a refreshing foil for grilled fish and spicy dishes like Indian curries. $10–12
Finger Lakes, New York

Rocca di Fabbri
GRECHETTO
Light- to medium-bodied. Gentle, juicy, and faintly floral.
Made from the age-old grape of the same name, Grechetto is less famous than Orvieto (Umbria's other white specialty) but noticeably more aromatic. Its softness and honeysuckle nose make it a pleasure with a light but garlicky clam sauce. $10–12
Umbria, Italy
Imported by Vias

Am Stein
MÜLLER-THURGAU
"Belle Amie"
Light- to medium-bodied. Succulent, clean as a whistle, and totally refreshing.
Müller-Thurgau, the humble work-horse grape of Germany, occasionally gets respectful treatment. This serious version is on the dry side, with an herby, grapefruit palate vaguely reminiscent of Sauvignon Blanc. It comes in a Bocksbeutel, the traditional vessel of the Franken region but whose flagon shape many Americans associate with Mateus. It's a quirky, delicious choice for parties and a good picnic partner. $10–12
Franken, Germany
Imported by Wines for Food

Domaine de Mauvan
CÔTES DE PROVENCE
Light- to medium-bodied. Softly textured and fragrant, with a delicate finish.
This white is made from Marsanne and Roussanne, grapes redolent of the lavender- and rosemary-flecked hills of Provence. Just lovely all around, it can be sipped on its own or paired with creamy dishes, savory tarts, or poultry roasted with herbs. $10–12
Provence, France
Imported by Bayfield

Geografico
VERNACCIA DI SAN GIMIGNANO
Light-bodied. Refreshing with a light, bitter snap in the tail.

This wine was a favorite of Michelangelo, who wrote

in 1643 how it "kisses, licks, bites, tickles, and stings." (Presumably, he'd had a few glasses.) This large producer makes a wine in a simple, brisk style. Faintly nutty, it's a quaffer with pasta *aglio e olio* (garlic & oil), fresh vegetables, or linguini with clams. $10–12
Tuscany
Imported by Matt Brothers

Scarbolo
TOCAI FRIULANO
Medium-bodied. Savory, earthy, and long on flavor.
Some call Scarbolo the definitive Tocai, pointing to its characteristic lime-and-apple flavor and telltale nuttiness. We call it good, savory stuff for mushroomy pasta and stuffed fish. $10–12
Friuli, Italy
Imported by Domaine Select

Ca' del Solo
BIG HOUSE WHITE
Light- to medium-bodied.
A juicy blend of aromatic grapes.
Maverick California vintner Randall Grahm blends Riesling, Muscat, Malvasia Bianca, and red Grenache (hence the faint blush) in this intensely fragrant, pretty wine. It's a surefire hit with spicy Indian dishes and picnic fare. $10–12
California

Botromagno
GRAVINA
Light- to medium-bodied.
Flowery, with a bittersweet snap.
This is a capricious blend of 60% Greco (dry, floral, juicy) and 40% Malvasia Bianca (powerfully aromatic, fruity, and rich). You do the math. Gravina is also one of the only white wines from southern Italy that doesn't weigh your tongue down. As such, it's the perfect

refreshment with spicy seafood and very garlicky fare. $10–12
Apulia, Italy
Imported by Winebow/ Leonardo LoCascio

Bayer
WEISSBURGUNDER
Medium-bodied. Icy-crisp, fragrant, and firm.
This Pinot Blanc from the Neusiedlersee, a vast inland sea in Austria, is a little nutty, a little lemony, and a lot of fun. The opera singer on the label may seem stern and serious, yet the wine within is anything but. This brisk refresher is especially good with such healthful vegetarian fare as brown rice, tempeh, hummus, and falafel. $10–12
Burgenland, Austria
Imported by Wines for Food

Pierre Boniface
VIN DE SAVOIE "Apremont"
Light- to medium-bodied.
A very dry white with an almost-sparkling personality.
Made practically on the Franco-Swiss border from the indigenous grape Jacquere, this white tastes like Champagne without the bubbles. Great with light fish, clams and other mollusks, and greens. Try the richer, more mouthfilling **Roussette** ($14–16) with fondue. $10–12
Savoie, France
Imported by House of Burgundy

Aragosta
VERMENTINO DI ALGHERO
Light-bodied. Pale in color but vigorous and piquant in the mouth.
The rather clinical diagram of a langoustine on the label of this

white suggests serving it with seafood, and we concur. But the piney, savory character shines through even more when the wine complements pasta with pesto. $10–12

Sardinia
Imported by Frederick Wildman

Franzen
ELBLING Dry
Light-bodied. Crystal-clear, bone-dry, and brisk.

Elbling is a German specialty that thrives in ancient soils composed of fossilized seashells. With its delicate neutral palate and zesty finish, it's a good choice for serving with sushi and shellfish. $10–12

Mosel, Germany
Imported by Wines for Food

Domaine Le Mas de Collines
CÔTES DU RHÔNE BLANC
Medium-bodied. Rich, buttery, and balanced, with suave mouthfeel.

Here's a 100% Roussanne, the perfumed, richly textured white grape of the Rhône. Great price, great balance, and no detectable oak make it an interesting alternative to Chardonnay (it shares many of that grape's nutty, buttery aromas). The best food matches? Soups, creamy dishes, and poultry. $10–12

Rhône, France
Imported by Bayfield

P. A. Ohler'sches
SCHEUREBE Kabinett
"Munsterer Dautenpflanzer"
Light- to medium-bodied. The lighter side of "Scheu"— fruity, simple, and appealing.

Funky and *good,* if you like a Scheurebe that has a very strong pink grapefruit flavor

with some Sauvignon Blanc greenness and savor thrown in. Whatever you call it, down it with something spicy or sweet— well-sauced barbecue or Tex-Mex, Hunan, or Szechuan eats. $10–12

Rheinhessen, Germany
Imported by Michael Skurnik/ Terry Theise

Domaine de la Pepière
MUSCADET
Sèvre et Maine sur Lie
Light-bodied. Perhaps the most complex and scintillating Muscadet of all.

Old vines and intense expression of its chalky *terroir* make Marc Ollivier's Muscadet taste like a $30 Savennières. An oyster and shellfish wine of the first order, it's also tasty with a leafy salad, a plateful of fresh mozzarella and tomatoes, and a variety of sushis, ceviches, and crudités. The exceedingly rare **Clos des Briords** ($13–15), which can evolve for a decade or more, virtually breathes minerality. Pair it with oysters or tuna tartare. $10–12

Loire, France
Imported by Louis/Dressner

Liegenfeld
OTTONELLA
Medium-bodied. Ripe, and extravagant in its fruit.

Roughly two-thirds Muscat Ottonel (a cross between an obscure strain of Muscat and Chasselas) and one-third Müller-Thurgau, this wildly aromatic and delicious jumble of peaches, mandarin oranges, and Chinese five-spice is the ultimate answer to curries and

all things Asian. It's also a cool choice for no-holds-barred classics like Chicken with Forty Cloves of Garlic. $10–12
Burgenland, Austria
Imported by Wines for Food

Alois Lageder
PINOT BIANCO
Medium-bodied. Glides over the palate smoothly, then lingers.
Like a glass of little green apples and lemon flowers, this non-oaked wine's scintillating balance and fleshy texture make it a hit with seared scallops, sole Véronique, and other rich, fragrant seafood dishes. The winery's **Hablerhof** ($18+), a powerful wine from a shelf of vines growing at 1,500 feet, improves with brief cellaring and excels with poultry and pork. FYI, Pinot Bianco is Italian for Pinot Blanc. $10–12
Alto Adige, Italy
Imported by Dalla Terra

Sommer
GRÜNER VELTLINER
Kabinett Dry
Light- to medium-bodied.
Crisp and savory,
with surprising length.
This scintillating, herb-kissed Veltliner is refreshingly citrusy. Even better, it's casual enough to start with tuna salad sandwiches at lunch and serious enough to finish with roast chicken and greens at dinner. $10–12
Burgenland, Austria
Imported by Wines for Food

Martine's
VIOGNIER
Full-bodied. A California Viognier of impressive richness and aroma.
The Viognier grape yields legendary wines in the northern Rhône, and this California version has all the pedigreed aromas of ripe pears and gardenias—but without oak. Its relatively high alcohol and sheer concentration of fruit leave an impression of sweetness, so plan your meal accordingly—rich dishes of fish, chicken, or pork with aromatic herbs. $10–15
California

Villa Girardi
LUGANA
Medium-bodied.
Lush, sensuous, and pure.
The Trebbiano clone they grow in Lugana seems to be jet-propelled with flavor and richness. In this wine, notes of stone fruits and mineral recur through a long, smooth finish. It's perfect for pasta in a cream sauce and richer seafood dishes. $11–13
Veneto, Italy
Imported by Verdoni

Aveleda
VINHO VERDE "Alvarinho"
Light-bodied. Crisp with the scents of the garden.
Here's the perfect summer wine. Alvarinho is the Portuguese name for the Spanish Albariño grape, a floral, mouthwatering, Iberian specialty. Enjoy this delicate and gorgeous white with seafood paella, cold crab, or raw shellfish. $11–13
Vinho Verde, Portugal
Imported by Tri-Vin

Stefano Massone
GAVI "Masera"
Medium-bodied. Light in alcohol and dryly refreshing at the finish.
Acidic in a pleasant citrusy way and clean as a whistle, this traditional shellfish wine is equally attractive with flaky

fish, pasta primavera, and feta or goat cheese. $11–13
Piedmont, Italy
Imported by Marc de Grazia

Marotti Campi
VERDICCHIO DEI CASTELLI DI JESI "Luzano"
Medium- to full-bodied. Dry, tangy, and forceful with food.
Citrons, bitter herbs, celery, anisette, stones, sea-brine. . . . Is this a wine profile or a Wiccan's grocery list? This singularly intense white wine zooms over the palate, refreshing as it goes, and elevates the taste of vegetables like broccoli rabe, fennel, cabbages, chard, and the herb cilantro.
$11–13
Marches, Italy
Imported by Villa Italia

Sella & Mosca
VERMENTINO DI SARDEGNA "La Cala"
Light-bodied. A vibrant, simple white with a savory finish.
This limey and juicy white, made from the aromatic Vermentino grape grown in Sardinia, is becoming a staple on Italian restaurants' wine lists. That's hardly surprising, since it works well as both an apéritif and a spirited food partner. Serve it with lemony fish, calamari, or pasta with tomatoes and herbs.
$11–13
Sardinia
Imported by Palm Bay

Zenato
LUGANA "San Benedetto"
Medium-bodied. Characterful dry white with a satiny finish.
Zenato is our favorite producer of Lugana, the formidable white wine made on the south shore of Lake Garda in nothern Italy.

Rich as any Chardonnay, crisp as a Gavi, and delicately fragrant as Pinot Blanc, it's marvelously multifaceted. Serve it as a complement to crab, chicken, or soft cheeses. $11–13
Veneto, Italy
Imported by Winebow/ Leonardo LoCascio

Sessa
LACRYMA CHRISTI BIANCO DEL VESUVIO
Medium-bodied. Dry, lightly acidic, and minerally.
The words *lacryma Christi* in this ancient white wine's name mean "tears of Christ." Made from Coda di Volpe and Verdeca, local varieties of grapes grown in the volcanic Neapolitan soils of Mount Vesuvius, it's a minerally, mildly earthy choice for ocean fish (from the Amalfi coast, if you're lucky!) or a cheese-laden *pizza bianco*. $11–13
Campania, Italy
Imported by Verdoni

Di Lenardo
TOCAI FRIULANO "Toh!"
Light- to medium-bodied. Intriguingly fruity, crisp, and dry.
Friulian Tocai is often a big, hearty wine, but this version is crafted for easy drinking and versatile food matching. A hit with prosciutto and melon, it's also just fine on its own. $11–13
Friuli, Italy
Imported by Martin Scott

Gysler
SCHEUREBE Halbtrocken "Weinheimer Hölle"
Medium-bodied. Dry and zesty, brightly aromatic, and just a little fruity.
Very, very cool. There's something leafy here, and some pink grapefruit, too. Even better, this Scheurebe has terrific balance for

food matching. Enjoy it with your next entrée salad (seafood, Niçoise, Cobb), sausages 'n' sauerkraut, or anything fried and salty. The liter bottle is a bargain. $12–14
Rheinhessen, Germany
Imported by Michael Skurnik/ Terry Theise

Prà
SOAVE Classico Superiore
Medium-bodied. Gently refreshing with a *frizzante,* or faintly sparkling, mouthfeel.
The ancient recipe for refreshment from the Veneto—crisp, clean, apple-scented Soave. Soaves from the Classico Superiore zone must be aged eight months before release, and this super example—packed with plenty of Trebbiano—is delicious with a plate of frito misto or calamari. $12–14
Veneto, Italy
Imported by Vinifera

Kurt Darting
MUSKATELLER Kabinett
"Durkheimer Steinberg"
Medium-bodied. Forceful in perfume and flavor, slightly oily, and brilliant with the right food.
Darting is a master magician of strange grapes. His Muskateller

(Muscat) seems to start out sweet, offering honey, apricot, figs, and flowers in delirious excess—yet it finishes relatively dry. What a curry wine! It may also be the long-awaited answer to such starchy, hard-to-match Eastern European dishes as potato latkes, stuffed cabbage, and *kasha varnishkes* (buckwheat with noodles and egg). $12–14
Pfalz, Germany
Imported by Michael Skurnik/ Terry Theise

Jacky Renard
ALIGOTÉ
Light-bodied. About as light and dry as white wine gets.
The "other white grape of Burgundy," Aligoté is grown in the north of the region in cool climes and chalky soils. It is lighter, more minerally, and more acidic than Chardonnay, making it a perfect oyster white and apéritif. It is also the traditional base wine for a Kir cocktail. $12–14
Burgundy
Imported by Bayfield

Tamellini
SOAVE Superiore
Light- to medium-bodied.
A gentle, creamy white.
The Tamellini brothers produce some of the best Soave around.

A TASTE OF GREECE
The ancient Greek grape Moscholfilero is grown on the high plateau of Mantinia in the Peloponnese and is used to make a perfumy white wine with exotic aromatics reminiscent of Gerwürztraminer. Conditions on the plateau are so cool that the grape harvest is sometimes delayed until late October.

The peachy, plump-cheeked, cherubic personality of **Domaine Tselepos Moschofilero "Mantinia"** ($13–15) makes us smile. Crisp, pleasingly scented, and easy to enjoy, it's great with grilled fish (especially in a salt crust) or any kind of jazzy Greco/Turkish fare—falafel, hummus, tabbouleh, *spanakopita.*
Imported by Wines We Are

Elegant and breezily scented with lemon blossoms and blanched almonds, it's a natural with gnocchi, versatile with mild cheeses, and perfect for oven-baked cauliflower Parmigiana. $12–14
Veneto, Italy
Imported by Vin Divino

Fritz Salomon
GRÜNER VELTLINER "Hochterrassen"
Medium-bodied.
Piquant and savory—and a perfect introduction to Veltliner.
In the world of trend-watchers, just holding a glass of this wine makes you seem chic. Think Sauvignon Blanc with a little hint of white pepper, and you've basically got it down. Citrusy, a little grassy, and incredibly refreshing, it's the choice for salads, sushi, and mixed greens. $12–14
Kremstal, Austria
Imported by Michael Skurnik/ Terry Theise

Cavalchina
BIANCO DI CUSTOZA
Light-bodied. A cheerful white with refreshing character.
A Trebbiano-based blend of varieties from the shore of Lake Garda, this white is similar to Soave (the popular café drink of northern Italy), but grapier and more floral. It's perfect for antipasti. $12–14
Veneto, Italy
Imported by Vin Divino

Ca' del Solo
MALVASIA BIANCO
Light- to medium-bodied.
Smells like a dessert wine but winds up dry and elegant.
With Madeleine on the label and succulent, floral-scented joy in the bottle, how can you resist

this? Pair it with sweet/savory items like prosciutto and melon or Asian dishes seasoned with coriander or lemon grass. $12–14
Monterey, California

Gysler
SILVANER Halbtrocken "Weinheimer Hölle"
Medium-bodied.
Vivid acidity and great, high-toned refreshment.
Rheinhessen winemaker Alex Gysler's Silvaner zigzags across your palate like a pinball. Racy and grapefruity, it's a wonderful meal starter and a vegetarian's friend. The liter bottle is a bargain. $12–14
Rheinhessen, Germany
Imported by Michael Skurnik/ Terry Theise

Giovanni Struzziero
GRECO DI TUFO "Villagiulia"
Medium- to full-bodied. A big wine with an earthy personality.
The grape Greco Bianco, vinified in Campania since the age of the Caesars, is named for the Greeks who brought it there. Smoky and rich, this Struzziero rendition is classic. Pair it with soft, earthy, or oily foods like polenta, fatty fish, and crumbly cheeses. $13–15
Campania, Italy
Imported by Opici

Predio de Vascarlon
RUEDA "Atelier"
Medium-bodied. An atypically rich, pungent Rueda.
Unlike most Ruedas, which are light and spritzy, this terrific non-oaked version from 100% Verdejo grapes has significant body, a luscious tropical

175

perfume, and sackfuls of juicy fruit. It goes well with exotic seafood dishes served with fruit salsa or aioli. $13–15
Rueda, Spain
Imported by Stonepress

Ch. W. Bernhard
SCHEUREBE Kabinett
"Hackenheimer Kirchberg"
Medium-bodied. Ripe, highly aromatic, and mouthfilling.
Hartmut Bernhard specializes in soft yet fruit-saturated whites with gorgeous flavors. Scheurebe, a genetic cross of Riesling and Silvaner grapes, is clearly the thing he does best. The satiny mouthfeel, unique muskiness, and intriguing flavors of mint and red berry are emphasized here by a little sweetness. Serve the Kabinett with sausages or a beet and goat cheese salad. Use Bernhard's fabulously ripe, honeyed **Spätlese** ($15–17) for meats in a cherry glaze or Kung Pao chicken. $13–15
Rheinhessen, Germany
Imported by Michael Skurnik/ Terry Theise

Capay Valley
VIOGNIER
Medium- to full-bodied. Golden-hued, rich, sleek, and flavorful.
The winery's name is pronounced CAY-pay, and its wine is intense. Redolent of pears in syrup, slightly nutty, oaty, and languorous on the palate, it calls for some serious food. Think dishes like roast pork or chicken, salmon stuffed with breadcrumbs and toasted sesame seeds, and turkey cutlets slathered with mustard. $13–15
Capay, California

Colle dei Bardellini
PIGATO
Light- to medium-bodied.
A perfumed, soft, distinctive white with modest alcohol.
A rarity, the Pigato grape is grown in the rocky coastal vineyards just southwest of Genoa. It's a little steely in the nose but surprisingly gentle and subtle in the mouth. If you want to be regionally authentic, enjoy it with fresh ocean fish and dabs of creamy pesto. $14–16
Liguria, Italy
Imported by Vias

Tement
TEMENTO
Light-bodied.
A bright, bracing joy.
Manfred Tement, the finest vintner in Styria (a small wine region in southeastern Austria) mixes this citrusy cocktail of Welschriesling, Grüner Veltliner, and Sauvignon Blanc for his everyday wine. A glass before dinner, another with the crab salad, and the rest capped up in the fridge for lunch tomorrow— that's living! $14–16
Sudsteiermark, Austria
Imported by Weygandt/Metzler

Domaine Thierry Puzelat
MENU PINEAU **"La Pieuse"**
Light- to medium-bodied.
Brisk and pungent.
This ultra-organic *négociant* offers tasty and distinctive wines from ancient local Loire grapes— one being Menu Pineau, most likely a Touraine variant of Chenin Blanc. Whatever the grape's origin, the wine has Chenin's wet stone-and-straw character and fierce acidity. Brilliant for lox and cream cheese or a seafood salad. $14–16
Loire, France
Imported by World Wide Wine

THE TWO SOAVES

Spreading out from the Veneto town of Soave is the vast DOC, or appellation, of the same name. From here hail Italy's most popular dry white wines, most of which come from cooperatives—winemakers who pool their production and marketing costs. This helps explain why Soaves are usually of middling quality.

The dominant grape in Soave is the indigenous Garganega, blended with varying amounts of Pinot Bianco, Chardonnay, and Trebbiano. As a rule, your best bet is to choose a Soave Classico, made in the original (and smaller) Soave zone. Classico wines are drier, more complex, and richer than the often bland, run-of-the-mill issue. One of the best is **Gini Soave Classico** ($14–16), a medium-bodied, golden-hued, heady elixir simmering with the flavors and aromas of poached pears and nuts. What to serve with it? Creamy pastas and fin fish sautéed in butter are a good start. *Imported by Marc de Grazia*

Paul Vendran
VIOGNIER
"La Ferme Saint Pierre"
Full-bodied. A velvety white nectar for hedonists.
Here's Viognier with plenty of alcohol, thick texture, and a bouquet of fresh pears drizzled with caramel—a mixture of sweet and fresh aromas that excites deep-down senses. Serve with triple-crème cheeses, broiled lobster, or roasted chicken or pork with something fruity—say, applesauce. $14–16
Rhône, France
Imported by T. Edward

Sergio Mottura
ORVIETO Secco
Medium-bodied. At once rich, bright, and admirably pure.
At this winery in Umbria, three local grapes—Procanico (believed to be a superior subvariety of Trebbiano), Verdello, and Grechetto—are grown free of chemical additives or fertilizers and then harvested by hand. Though rich, this dry (*secco*) wine from the Orvieto DOC shows exceptional clarity and brightness, making it a real refresher with sole amandine or a plate of garlicky spaghetti. The sweet **Amabile** ($14–16) version is appropriate for fresh fruit and honeyed desserts like baklava. $14–16
Umbria, Italy
Imported by Cadet

Didier Fornerol
ALIGOTÉ
Medium-bodied. Splendidly silken and rich, with vivid acidity in the finish.
Fornerol makes a fetish of delicacy in his Burgundies, yet his Aligoté is lifted by a brilliant lemony freshness. It's "just a dry white wine" in the same sense that Gershwin was "just a piano player." Pair it with oysters simmered in cream, a salad of fresh tomatoes, or crisply fried fish with a squirt of lemon. $14–16
Burgundy
Imported by Daniel Johnnes

$15 to $30

Brüder Dr. Becker
SCHEUREBE Kabinett "Dienheimer"
Medium-bodied. Ripe, honeyed, and pungently aromatic.
The grape Scheurebe, a genetic crossing of Riesling and Silvaner, holds romance and mystery for many German wine fans. And why not? Ripe to a point of oiliness, with additional dimensions of smoke and surprisingly *red* berry fruit, the wines are downright weird. Dr. Becker's version is organic, shamelessly red-fruity, and terrific for ham, glazed meats, squash dishes, and pulled-pork barbecue. Fascinating! $15-17
Rheinhessen, Germany
Imported by Metropolis

Poggio Pollino
ALBANA DI ROMAGNA "Monte di Cambro"
Medium-bodied. A fragrant, strong, dry white with a firm finish.
This is a serious rendition of the wines of Albana di Romagna, the first white wine-growing area to be granted a DOCG— *Denominazione di Origine Controllata e Garantita*, the premium category in Italy's appellation system. Fairly neutral in flavor but equipped with lively acidity and a waxy, balanced mouthfeel, it's a particularly good choice for serving with sardines, mackerel, and other oily and salty fish dishes. $15-18
Emilia-Romagna, Italy
Imported by OmniWines

Broglia
GAVI DI GAVI "La Meirana"
Medium-bodied. An especially pungent Gavi with concentrated fruit and smooth character.

Light, dry whites made from the Cortese grape are the specialty of Gavi di Gavi, a small town in the Piedmont. In this one, a combo of minerals, beeswax, and lemon zest hits the bull's-eye. And what a fabulous food wine! We've found it wonderfully refreshing with edibles as varied as calamari, risotto, mushroom pizza, and artichoke with oil and lemon. $16-18
Piedmont, Italy
Imported by Vias

François Cazin
COUR-CHEVERNY "Cuvée Renaissance"
Medium-bodied. Honeyed, musky, and lightly sweet.
As delicious as it is obscure. Made from Romarantin, a grape that grows essentially in Cheverny and nowhere else, this white has succulent apple fruit, clear minerality, pleasant sweetness, and a luxurious finish. Foie gras works beautifully with it, as do blue-veined and triple-crème cheeses. $16-18
Loire, France
Imported by Louis/Dressner

Txomin Etxariz
TXAKOLINA DE GETARIA
Light-bodied. Fabulously refreshing, with a bright sparkle.
Txakolina ("chock-oh-LEE-nah") is the name of this wine's home turf in the Basque country.
The grapes are equally obscure: Hondarribi Zuri (85%)

and Hondarribi Beltza (15%)— but that just makes us love this exotic tipple even more. Incredibly crisp, lemon-scented,

and a little spritzy, it's the world's most exciting oyster partner. It's also quite good with shrimp, clams, mussels, and salads.
$16–18
Getaria, Spain
Imported by Tempranillo

Marco Felluga
TOCAI FRIULANO
Medium-bodied. Lively, assertive, and lasting on the palate.
Here's a classically made Tocai, with distinctive earthiness, a citrusy middle, and almonds in the finish. It's a natural match for the region's signature antipasto—thinly sliced prosciutto with fresh melon. $16–18
Friuli, Italy
Imported by Dalla Terra

La Giustiniana
GAVI "Lugarara"
Medium- to full-bodied. Ripe-fruited and vigorous.
A full-blown version of the classic Piedmontese white, with strong aromas of minerals and lemon verbena immediately asserting themselves. It's a dramatic white for spicy, garlicky seafood and veal piccata. $16–18
Piedmont, Italy
Imported by Bacchanal

As Laxas
ALBARIÑO
Light- to medium-bodied. Lots of fruit and tangy acidity.
With its signature fragrance of peaches and wildflowers joined with fresh acidity, modest alcohol, and light texture, this happy-go-lucky wine is equally companionable with sushi, a fish on the grill, or a plateful of linguini with red or white clam sauce. $16–18
Rias Baixas, Spain
Imported by Frontier

Di Meo
GRECO DI TUFO
Medium-bodied. Weighty and firm, it's balanced for the table.
The winemakers at the little Di Meo winery in Italy suit our philosophy, making wines from indigenous grape varieties that emphasize grace, balance, and versatility in food pairing. Their Greco is gently floral, expressive of its volcanic soils, and a tasty accompaniment to the local cuisine of ocean fish, earthy pastas, and potatoes.
$16–20
Campania, Italy
Imported by Supreme

Nigl
GRÜNER VELTLINER "Gartling"
Medium- to full-bodied. Rich, dry, and shimmeringly acidic.
Green herb, white pepper, and citrus notes are chiseled into this wine's palate like stone carvings. Though Martin Nigl's entry-level wine, it's still more profound than half the Veltliners out there. For a mind-blowing experience, try his **Senftenberger Piri** ($30–40)—in practically every vintage a mélange of forest aromas and multitiered complexity. Crab, lobster, oily fish like bluefish or tuna, and a vegetable "mixed grill" with high-quality olive oil are excellent partners at the table.
$17–19
Kremstal, Austria
Imported by Michael Skurnik/ Terry Theise

Cantina Il Nurage
SEMIDANO DE MOGORO "Anastasia"
**Medium-bodied.
A creamy, seductive white from a unique grape.**
Semidano is hardly on every-one's short list of famous grapes,

but it's a wonderfully aromatic variety that produces a deeply fragrant wine. Pears, cream, and minerals from volcanic soils dominate, followed by a floral finish. Explore it with baked poultry and creamy polentas. $17–19
Sardinia
Imported by OmniWines

Palacios Remondo
RIOJA "Placet"
Medium-bodied. Fantastically balanced, aromatic, and supple.
Instead of the oaked, oxidized, heavy, dry wine typical of whites from Rioja, this is devoid of oak, utterly graceful, and clean on the palate. Bewitching aromas of flowers, pears, and fresh hay leave a refreshing finish. Serve it with delicate fish or fowl, crab cakes, or mild cheeses. $18–20
Rioja, Spain
Imported by Rare Wine

Kurt Darting
SCHEUREBE Spätlese "Durkheimer Spielberg"
Medium-bodied. A love-it-or-hate-it wine, with considerable sweetness and oily mouthfeel.
Very apple-cidery, very honeyed, and very seductive, this Scheurebe is outrageously ripe because of its late harvesting. The right food makes the difference, and your glassful will balance with fruit-sauced fatty meats (duck, sausage, and so forth), quell the heat of spicy Szechuan or Indian dishes, and temper the sweetness of mango or tamarind chutney. Food or no food, this Scheurebe tastes rapturously delicious. An adventure! $18–20
Pfalz, Germany
Imported by Michael Skurnik/Terry Theise

Ferrando
ERBALUCE DI CALUSO "Cacina Cariola"
Medium-bodied. An exotic Alpine white with a nutty flair.
A single-vineyard version of a weird and wonderful Piedmontese grape, the Erbaluce. Although Erbaluce wines are usually made as a *passito* (sweet wine from dried grapes), the Cacina Cariola is vinted as a rich, dry white reminiscent of hazelnuts—an interesting alternative to the lemon-fresh whites common in the Piedmont. Serve with robust pastas or salted cod. $18–20
Piedmont, Italy
Imported by Rosenthal

A. & P. de Villaine
BOUZERON DE ALIGOTÉ
Medium- to full-bodied. Prodigious complexity and depth from a grape not known for it.
Aligoté typically makes light apéritif wines. They're traditionally used for the Kir cocktail—but in this case, that would be a waste. This oak-aged, opulent giant is better matched with baked oysters, coquilles St. Jacques, or poached poultry. $18–20
Burgundy, France
Imported by Kermit Lynch

Joseph Högl
GRUNER VELTLINER Federspiel "Ried Schön"
Medium-bodied. A crisp, fine, deceptively powerful dry white.
Högl is a great Wachau producer, as yet little known in the U. S. His Federspiel from the excellent Schön vineyard is crisp, stony, and laserlike in clarity—and lovely with crudités and cooked vegetables alike. The riper **Smaragd "Ried Schön"** ($30–35) is a complex, powerful white in much the same league as Veltliners from Högl's celebrity neighbors

GRÜNER-VELTLINER: THE CHIC AUSTRIAN

On the wine/food front, the grape-of-the-moment harks back to the days of the Austro-Hungarian Empire, with the Emperor Franz Joseph and his courtiers no doubt enjoying its wines in the opulent salons of Vienna. Modern Austria's premier wine grape, Grüner Veltliner is also cultivated in Hungary, the Czech Republic, Slovakia, and Slovenia.

Despite the grandeur inferred from its imperial provenance, Grüner can be refreshingly light and simple—a crisp, slightly spicy white that joins Pinot Grigio and Sauvignon Blanc as an ideal nonthreatening cocktail white and a good match for salads and other light fare. Paradoxically, wines made from this amazingly versatile grape can also be the spiciest—and most monumental—of dry whites.

To start light, try **Loimer Grüner Veltliner "Lois"** ($10–12), from the Austrian wine town of Langenlois in the Kamptal winegrowing area. With its aroma of white pepper and flavors of lemon–lime zest and minerals, it's a fresh and zippy match for omelets, crêpes, and green veggies. *Imported by Vin Divino*

You could then go to the other extreme with the monumental (and much pricier) **Bründlmayer Grüner Veltliner "Ried Lamm"** ($45–50). The Lamm vineyard is at the bottom of a large hill called the Heiligenstein (also in Kamptal), and the wines from this site are exceedingly ripe. In vintages with high acidity, you've got it all: great tingly mouthfeel wedded to rich pear and apple fruit, "woodsy" aromatics, and high alcohol. Either enjoy it now as a formidable fish and lobster partner or cellar it for drinking years hence. *Imported by Michael Skurnik/Terry Theise*

Prager and F. X. Pichler. $18–20
Wachau, Austria
Imported by Weygandt/Metzler

Fefiñanes
ALBARIÑO
Light- to medium-bodied.
Juicy, slender, and refreshing.
Grown in the remote coastal vineyards of Rias Baixas in Galicia, on Spain's north shore, this is an appealing glassful of orchard fruits and flowers. It's particularly handy as a crisp foil for assertively flavored shrimp scampi or tempura. $18–20
Rias Baixas, Spain
Imported by Bayfield

Cornarea
ARNEIS
Medium- to full-bodied.
Concentrated and creamy.
A wondrous dry white made in the Piedmont from Arneis, a local grape that almost disappeared in the 1970s but was revived when it found a solid base of devoted fans. In this extravagant rendition, peaches, pears, and licorice wash over the palate in waves. Explore its charms with a seafood risotto or rich marinated steaks of tuna, swordfish, or shark. $18–20
Piedmont, Italy
Imported by Tesori

PAIRING UNUSUAL WHITES WITH FOOD

So someone gave you a bottle of unfamiliar white wine and you haven't a clue what to serve with it? No problem! Here's an at-a-glance list of lesser known wines, arranged alphabetically by grape (some with two names or sharing a place name), and a simple food-pairing suggestion for each.

Albariño Seafood salad
Aligoté Shellfish
Arneis Seafood risotto
Chasselas (a.k.a. Gutedel) Fondue
Cortese (a.k.a. Gavi) Calamari
Grüner Veltliner
  Grilled vegetables
Italian whites, Southern
  (Fiano, Greco, Lacryma Christi)
  Oily fish
Italian whites, Northern
  (Trebbiano, Vernaccia, Garganega—
  a.k.a. Soave) Pasta primavera
Malvasia Prosciutto with melon
Moschofilero Mezedes (Greek
  appetizers)

Muscadet Oysters
Muscat (fruity) Curries; (dry)
  as an apéritif
Pinot Blanc/Auxerrois
  Creamy soups
Scheurebe Spicy Asian
Seyval/Vidal Cold meats
Tocai Mushrooms; truffles
Verdejo (a.k.a. Rueda) Gazpacho
Verdicchio Pesto; sautéed greens
Vermentino Pesto; mussels
Vinho Verde Picnic food, chips,
  dips, snacks
Viognier Crab, lobster

Mauro Sebaste
ROERO ARNEIS
Medium-bodied. Zesty, with good acidity and clean, modern character.
Sebaste's interpretation of what is now the most renowned white grape in the Piedmont is pleasingly subtle and scented with the variety's typical green apples and anise. At the table, natural partners for this appealing wine are fennel bulb, flaky fish, and savory antipasti. $19–21
Piedmont, Italy
Imported by Opici

Terradora
FIANO DI AVELLINO
"Terre di Dora"
Medium- to full-bodied. Firm and dry, with mild viscosity at the finish.
Perhaps it's the faint honeyed quality of the local Fiano grape

that earned it the moniker "the vine beloved by bees." Like many southern Italian whites, this wine from the Fiano di Avellino DOC is also meaty and earthy. A strong foil for oily sardines, mackerel, and bluefish, it also goes well with Taleggio cheese. $19–21
Campania, Italy
Imported by Vias

Franck Peillot
ROUSSETTE DE BUGEY
"Altesse"
Medium- to full-bodied. Suave and mouthcoating, with a dry finish.
Made near France's Swiss border, this is 100% Roussette, an indigenous white grape more often used for sparkling wines. It's honey and pears all the way in this example, and a match with pork chops with applesauce would be

perfect. It's also an intriguing partner for double- and triple-crème cheeses.
$20–22
Savoie, France
Imported by Louis/Dressner

Lusco do Miño
ALBARIÑO "Lusco"
Medium-bodied. Classy rendition, with lavish aromas and harmonious balance.
Awash in apricot and lemon sorbet scents, this works effortlessly with all kinds of fresh seafood and any preparations of lobster and crab. It's also a clever choice for fusion and Pan-Asian cuisine, which often needs a fragrant white. $20–22
Rias Baixas, Spain
Imported by Classical Wines

Ca' dei Frati
LUGANA "I Frati"
Medium- to full-bodied. A rich wine with soft, luxurious mouthfeel.
The Trebbiano clone planted in Lugana is special—indeed, local growers are trying to legislate the renaming of the subvariety to Lugana to certify its identity. This version is a prime example of Lugana—richly perfumed, pearlike, gently earthy, and very ripe. It's delightful with creamy gnocchi and pastas. $20–22
Veneto, Italy
Imported by Vin Divino

Lucien Albrecht
PINOT AUXERROIS "Cuvée"
Medium-bodied. A dry wine with a surprisingly sweet impression on the palate.
An opulent, honey-textured rarity from thirty- to thirty-five-year-old vines. Amply ripe and well crafted, it smells enticingly of fresh hay, clover honey, and fresh-baked bread. Enjoy it with a simple cow's milk cheese or a bowl of creamy corn chowder and biscuits. $20–22
Alsace, France
Imported by Robert Kacher

Domaine Schoffit
CHASSELAS "Vielles Vignes"
Medium- to full-bodied. Aromatically fascinating and graceful on the palate.
The most esoteric wine from this master vintner—and one of his most enjoyable. While Chasselas (a.k.a. Gutedel in Germany), is mainly used as a blending grape in Alsace, Schoffit took the time and trouble to nurture a parcel of old vines and crafted a fantastic wine in the process. Alluringly scented with pears and roses, it's great with French bistro fare of any kind: pâtés, savory tarts, charcuterie, soft cheeses. It also can't be beat with fondue!
$20–24
Alsace, France
Imported by Weygandt/Metzler

Adegas das Eiras
ALBARIÑO "Terras Gauda"
Medium-bodied.
An especially rich Albariño.
Clearly, this producer is trying to make a more structured, serious wine from Albariño. And he succeeds. Firmly textured, redolent of peaches and apricots, and rather minerally, the Terras Gauda reminds us of a Halbtrocken Riesling from Germany's Rheingau. A splendid salmon steak white. $20–25
Rias Baixas, Spain
Imported by AV Imports

Schloss Gobelsburg
GRÜNER VELTLINER "Steinsetz"
**Medium-bodied. A firm, dry,
filigreed white from gravelly soils.**
Veltliner is Austria's premier grape.
Gobelsburg's Steinsetz is racy at
first sip, then fleshes out in the
mouth with gorgeous fruit and
woodsy, herbal flavors. This is a
serious dinner wine, deserving of
the likes of mushroom-smothered
pork tenderloin or roasted whole
fish. Muskier, fuller, and more in
need of cellaring are Gobelsburg's
Grüner Veltliner "Renner"
($30–32) and **Grüner Veltliner
"Ried Lamm"** ($40–45)—either
a superb choice for roast veal.
$21–23
Langenlois, Austria
*Imported by Michael Skurnik/
Terry Theise*

Ch. W. Bernhard
AUXERROIS Spätlese Halbtrocken
"Frei-Laubersheimer Fels"
**Medium-bodied. Dry,
aromatic, and vibrant.**
The Auxerrois grape, closely akin
to Pinot Blanc, is a German and
Alsatian specialty. Rendered here
in a dry white of startling intensity,
it combines complex floral, apple,
and citrus notes with a savoriness
that works well with richly sauced
veal or vegetable dishes.
$23–25
Rheinhessen, Germany
*Imported by Michael Skurnik/
Terry Theise*

Russiz Superiore
TOCAI FRIULANO
**Full-bodied. Outsized white
wine, powerfully built and
completely dry.**
There's almost something carnal
about a good Tocai, and this is a
formidable example. The nuts,
the flowers, the tingling acidity
are all there, but it's that deep-
down earthiness that makes this

wine so fascinating—especially
with a plate of mushrooms, salt
cod, garlicky pastas, cured meats,
or pungent cheeses.
$23–25
Friuli, Italy
Imported by Polaner

Château Rahoul
GRAVES
**Medium- to full-bodied.
Sparingly oaked, elegant,
and perfectly smooth.**
This distinctive wine is crafted
from 100% Sémillon. Melon melds
with green herbs, Granny Smith
apples, and minerals. A classy dry
white for tuna steaks, grilled
vegetables, or delicate white
meats (rabbit included). $24–26
Bordeaux
Imported by Wine Symphony

Clelia Romano
FIANO DI AVELLINO
"Colli di Lapio"
**Medium-bodied. A firm, dense
white with subtle layers.**
A little nutty, a little honeyed,
very dry, and *not* a quaffing wine,
Fiano is a food-lover's choice for
dishes with strong, salty flavors
(think anchovies or Parmigiano-
Reggiano). $25–28
Campania, Italy
Imported by Marc de Grazia

Domaine Georges Vernay
VIN DE PAYS DES COLLINES
RHODANNIENNES
**Full–bodied. A flamboyant
white with vivid perfume and
gorgeous balance.**
Christine Vernay—daughter of
Georges Vernay, famous for his
Viogniers from the tiny Rhône
appellation of Condrieu—now
makes a wine from vineyards
nearby. A lively tumult of apricots,
honeysuckle, and fresh minerality,
it is lighter than Condrieu Viognier,
with no chemical treatments or

new oak styling marring its purity. (The *vin de pays* in the name indicates a "country wine," the third tier in the French appellation system.) Either a firm fish braised in wine or roast turkey with oyster stuffing would be a great match come dinnertime. $28–30
Rhône, France
Imported by Jandell

Over $30

Tiefenbrunner
MÜLLER-THURGAU
"Feldmarschall von Fenner"
Medium- to full-bodied. Potent, mouthfilling, and dry—yet astonishingly balanced.
Tiefenbrunner, an aristocratic Italian estate, transforms this lowborn German grape into something regal. It's grown at a soaring three-thousand-foot elevation—one of the highest vineyards in Europe. Fermentation and maturation are done in steel, so the wine's primary aromas of apricots, berries, and springwater burst forth unencumbered by wood. Enjoy it with Italian pastas with some sweetness (say, pumpkin tortellini), breaded cutlets, white sausages, and anything garlicky. $30–32
Alto Adige, Italy
Imported by Winebow/
Leonardo LoCascio

Cold Heaven
VIOGNIER "Le Bon Climat"
Full-bodied. Strong, sensuous, and mineral-driven.
Morgan Clendenen's passion for Viognier leads her to craft it as purely as possible—biodynamically from a single cool-climate site and matured in old oak only. The result is a peary, flowery, firm white wine that sings with rich fish or lobster. Collectors prize the luxe **Viognier "Deux C"** ($60–70), which is made in cooperation with Yves Cuilleron, of the Rhône appellation of Condrieu. $30–35
Santa Barbara, California

Müller-Catoir
SCHEUREBE Spätlese
"Haardter Mandelring"
Medium-bodied. Intensely concentrated, succulent, and explosively ripe.
This Scheu offers ripe acidity, a distinctive sweet pink grapefruit character, and strong slate aromas from the soils, plus a unique and bewitching note of currant leaf. In warm vintages, a strong red fruit theme comes to the fore. Enjoy this definitive Scheurebe with a whole stuffed fish, German sausages with mustard, or richly-sauced ham. $40–50
Pfalz, Germany
Imported by Michael Skurnik/
Terry Theise

Schiopetto
TOCAI FRIULANO
Full-bodied. An expansive, powerful white with sensational richness and length.
Renowned as one of Italy's best producers (with price tags to match), Mario Schiopetto makes a profound Tocai that stops conversation at the dinner table. Apples, almonds, a touch of honey, and a *basso continuo* of minerality play through the wine from its start to its long, strong finish. Serve with your best fish and white-meat dishes, a mushroom risotto, or pecorino Romano with a drizzle of truffle oil. $44–48
Friuli, Italy
Imported by Winebow/
Leonardo LoCascio

SO WHAT'S A CRU?

*T*HE LABEL is a wine's "front door," welcoming us in for better or for worse. But wine labels, especially those from Europe, are often sprinkled with unfamiliar words—and the more arcane the word the more likely the wine will be taken seriously by many. One such word is the hallowed *cru*, as in Premier Cru and Grand Cru.

A cru is really just a place where grapes are grown, whether it's a town, a vineyard, or a single estate. The word itself is the past tense of the French verb *croître*, which means "to grow" and is generally translated as "growth."

The cru idea originated in Bordeaux when the organizers of Napoleon III's 1855 Exposition Universelle in Paris asked the region's wine brokers to draw up a list of the wines of the most famous estates, basing the list on price—and, by implication, relative quality. The purpose was to showcase France's cream of the crop at the exposition. Sixty estates from the Médoc and one from Graves were named **Grand Cru Classé**—the great classed growths. The four most expensive wines were named **Premier Cru**, or first growth, while all others were ranked second through fifth. Estates in Sauternes and Barsac were also classified, but on just two levels, with Chateau d'Yquem on top.

A century later, Graves and St. Émilion, which were mostly omitted from the 1855 list, classified their estates. But in St. Émilion, the terminology changed misleadingly: **Premier Grand Cru Classé** came first, then **Grand Cru Classé,** and then simply **Grand Cru.** This last, a revisable catchall category vulnerable to "one-hit wonders," has done little but confuse the public.

Outside Bordeaux, a cru has usually been defined as a vineyard rather than an estate, meaning each cru can have multiple owners. Burgundy, the oldest example, classified its best sites in 1861 as Grand Cru and its second best as Premier Cru. Alsace named its Grand Crus in 1983.

Beaujolais and Champagne, meanwhile, took a different tack. In Beaujolais, ten crus exist, indicating superior wines—but they are named for towns, not vineyards. In Champagne, all 312 winegrowing towns are called crus (!)—but only 17 are Grand and 44 are rated Premier. If this all sounds complicated, it may explain why the cru classifications have been largely overshadowed by modern numerical scoring. In practice, a "98-point wine" from a top magazine or reviewer is worth more these days than the appearance of "Cru" on the label.

CHAPTER FIVE

Champagne and Other Bubblies

Champagne out sparkles its peers in wine lovers' minds and probably always will. Few wines are so rife with symbolism as this top-hat-and-tails bubbly. Fortunately, it isn't necessary to spend a king's ransom to appreciate Champagne's charms, even when you demand the real thing—that is, the versions from its birthplace in France.

Still, other sparkling wines like Cava, Prosecco, and German Sekt outsell Champagne many times over. And that shouldn't come as a surprise. Sometimes a light, frothy sparkler is more appropriate to a brunch or other casual occasion than a fully sparkling, opulent Champagne.

Champagne

Champagne is an icon for the good life because,
like diamonds, it is sparkling and expensive.
It even feels "rich" on the palate.

*T*HE PREMIER sparkling wine's exclusivity is sealed by law, with only wines produced within the boundaries of the Champagne appellation allowed to use the name. Occupying roughly 86,000 acres of chalky slopes ninety miles northeast of Paris and anchored by the towns of Reims, Épernay, and Ay, the region produces about 8% of the world's sparkling wines.

The hierarchy of producers in Champagne was somewhat leveled in the late 1990s, when the *Syndicate des Grande Marques* ("big brands"), created in 1882 by the major houses (the local term for estates), was disbanded and the *grande marques* designation became obsolete. In any event, a better signpost for choosing Champagne nowadays is the fine print at the bottom of a bottle's label—the abbreviations that precede the license number (see "Initials It Pays to Know," page 190).

Today the whole region is planted with the three grapes that form the base of Champagne in combination or singly: red Pinot Noir and Pinot Meunier (a less "noble" but more easily farmed variety), and white Chardonnay. To create what will become Champagne, each house makes anywhere from one to several dozen still wines from grapes either estate–grown or bought. These are carefully blended with a portion of reserve wines held from former years in an effort to achieve a consistent house style. Then begins the winemaking process known as the traditional method, or *la méthode champenoise* (see page 193), which involves *dosage* (the addition of sugar) and a second fermentation in each bottle.

The finished product comes in a particular degree of sweetness, which is designated on the label. From the driest to sweetest, the categories are **Extra Brut** (very, very dry), **Brut** (very dry), **Extra Dry** (off-dry), **Sec** (lightly sweet), **Demi–Sec** (sweet), and **Doux** (very sweet). Knowing the difference is particularly important when pairing Champagne with food. For example, Extra Brut is the best to have with caviar, while Demi–Sec and Doux work best with sweet desserts.

Note: While the following recommendations do not specify Champagne as the place of origin, all of the places lie within its borders.

Under $35

Charles de Cazanove
CHAMPAGNE Brut Azur
**Medium- to full-bodied.
Opulently rich and lengthy.**
Crafted at a tiny, two-hundred-year-old family-run estate in the north of the Champagne district, this *très élégant* Champagne deserves to be better known. Its finish is toasty, almost malty in flavor, and very dry. A stylish partner for soups, poached salmon, and most any dish with a rich cream sauce. $28–30
Épernay, France
Imported by Grand Cru

Pol Roger
CHAMPAGNE Brut
Medium-bodied. Known for its elegance and utter reliability.
Winston Churchill was so taken with this Champagne that he had it made specially for him in pint-size single servings. The blend (roughly half Chardonnay, half Pinot Noir) is vinted in a crisp, balanced style. With its aromas of fresh-baked brioche and a bevy of orchard fruits, it's an excellent choice for cream-laden shellfish dishes. The estate's **Brut "Reserve" Vintage 1996** ($60–70) is a bold, toasty knockout, as are earlier vintages such as '93, '90, and '88 (all of which are drinking well now). The **Brut Rosé Vintage 1995** ($60–70) is one of the very best. $30–35
Épernay, France
Imported by Frederick Wildman

Laurent-Perrier
CHAMPAGNE Brut
**Light- to medium-bodied.
Ethereally fine, dry, and delicate.**
This lacily intricate Champagne is so lightly floral and pale that its high proportion of Pinot Noir comes as a surprise. What's more, the winery is huge yet manages to craft artisanal-tasting Champagnes. The extraordinary **"Cuvée Ultra-Brut"** ($45–50) is bigger-boned and bracingly dry with no *dosage*, making it super for caviar. The **Grand Siecle "La Cuvée"** ($85–110), rich and cellar-worthy, is the *tête de cuvée* (top bottling) Champagne from this house. $32–36
Champagne, France
Imported by Laurent-Perrier

A SECRET SPILLED
The best-kept secret in Champagne? The wines of Paul Goerg, the name for a remarkable co-op in Vertus that sells much of its juice for use by the *grande marques*, including the too-chic-for-words Roederer Cristal. The wines they bottle under their own name are some of the best values in the region.

Made from 60% Chardonnay and 40% Pinot Noir, the fresh, crisp **Paul Goerg Champagne Brut "Tradition" 1er Cru** ($25–30) is subtly elegant, with almond and bread notes in the finish. Try it with crumbly, salty cheeses. The **Brut Blanc de Blancs** ($25–30) is like liquid marzipan—dry, yet somehow confectionery. This one's a natural with Camembert.

The **Brut Rosé** ($30–35) is all strawberries and fresh flowers, bringing a splash of color to exotic hors d'oeuvres or *moules marinière*. Finally, the vibrant, toasty **Brut Vintage 1996** ($30–35) is a tremendous bargain—bright on the palate, very minerally, and almost Riesling-like. It sings even more sweetly with chanterelle mushrooms sautéed in butter. *All wines imported by Mario Rinaldi*

INITIALS IT PAYS TO KNOW

Anyone who wants to ferret out the best Champagnes on the market (and that in no way means the most expensive) will do well to check the abbreviations attached to the license number at the bottom of the label.

Most labels show **NM**—for a *négociant-manipulant* (dealer-producer) who may own vineyards but usually buys most of the grapes. This is the designation you'll find on the Champagnes of all of the mass market houses, meaning that NM Champagnes vary the most in quality.

Small-production, handcrafted Champagnes made from estate-grown fruit are designated **RM** (*récoltant-manipulant*, or grower-producer). It's these initials that should grab your attention, since so-called "grower" Champagnes are always interesting and frequently superb.

MA (for *marque d'acheteur*, or buyer's brand) indicates a brand owned by a third party, such as a restaurant or hotel that orders a private label. These are the cheapest Champagnes, with no guarantee of good quality.

The other two designations are **RC** (*récoltant-coopérateur*), growers who make and sell Champagnes with the help of cooperatives, and **CM** (*coopérative-manipulant*) with some 11,000 growers pooling their resources and marketing approximately 150 of their own brands.

E. Barnaut
CHAMPAGNE BLANC DE NOIRS Extra Brut Grand Cru
Medium- to full-bodied. Deep, bold, and fragrant.

This top-quality RM, or "grower's" Champagne, is made from Pinot Noir. Extremely rich and fine, with a citrusy flair and no *dosage*, it finishes with almost austere dryness. We find it brilliant with all kinds of seafood, from fried oysters to ceviche. The house's magenta-colored **Brut Rosé Grand Cru** ($33–36) is a bubbling swirl of ripe, tangy berries. $33–36
Bouzy, France
Imported by Polaner

Over $35

Guy Larmandier
CHAMPAGNE CÔTES DES BLANCS 1er Cru à Vertus
Medium-bodied. Austerely dry at first, but quickly expands to exquisite richness.

This is a gorgeous, limited production "grower" Champagne from one of our very favorite houses. Profoundly minerally and wickedly dry, it's capped by a delicate essence of fresh pears in the finish. Flawless! Relish it with icy oysters or spoonfuls of sevruga caviar on blini. The powerful **Blanc de Blancs Brut Grand Cru** ($45–50) is a richer, fuller wine with cellaring potential. $35–38
Cramant, France
Imported by Rosenthal

Pierre Gimonnet et Fils
CHAMPAGNE BLANC DE BLANCS Brut 1er Cru
Medium-bodied. Bone-dry and soul-satisfying.

A 100% Chardonnay from a single grower-producer using old vines in three exciting *terroirs,* this is good-as-it-gets Champagne. The very low *dosage* allows the flavors to seem almost crystalline. Citrusy and densely layered with

minerals, it's ideal for caviar. For a great value vintage wine, try **"La Cuvée Gastronome"** ($45–50). $35–40
Cuis/Cramant/Chouilly, France
Imported by Michael Skurnik/
Terry Theise

Gatinois
CHAMPAGNE Brut Grand Cru **"Tradition"**
Medium- to full-bodied. Deeply aromatic, satiny in texture, and gorgeous.
This superb grower sells half his production to Bollinger for

their top cuvées and privately bottles the remainder. Largely Pinot Noir, the wine is a pale straw color—but if you close your eyes, you might think you're smelling red Burgundy. Enjoy this superb dinner partner with roast chicken, salmon, or thinly sliced cold beef. Their **Brut Rosé**

($38–42) is bold-fruited and sensational. $38–40
Ay, France
Imported by Polaner

Bollinger
CHAMPAGNE Brut
"Special Cuvée"
Full-bodied. The deepest, richest, toastiest of all nonvintage Champagnes.
James Bond drinks Bollinger in the movies, so shouldn't you pop the cork to see why 007 and his fellow Brits crave it so? Malty, biscuity, Pinot Noir-driven, and stunning, it teams beautifully at the table with creamy soups and lobster. And then there are those Champagne flutes to clink in a sudsy, candlelit tub . . . Some devotees opt for the **Brut "Grande Année" Vintage** ($100–120), a benchmark bubbly regardless of year. $45–50
Ay, France
Imported by Dreyfus Ashby

René Geoffroy
CHAMPAGNE Brut Grand Cru
Medium-bodied. Fresh, alluring, and extremely creamy.
Jean-Baptiste Geoffroy, a master of detail, produces a lovable cream puff of a Champagne that's so much fun you might miss just how intricate and complex it is. Appley, yeasty, and *terroir*-driven, it makes a fine foil for creamy soups and sauces. His **Brut Rosé** ($45–50), made by the *saignée* ("bled") method typically used for rosés, is a vivid, excellent wine. $40–45
Ambonnay, France
Imported by North Berkeley

Egly-Ouriet
CHAMPAGNE Brut "Tradition– Non Filtré" Grand Cru
Medium-bodied. Made from Pinot Noir in a lush, mouthfilling style.
Die-hard bubbly fans buy this out fast—the reason it's often hard to obtain. Few sparkling wines are as sensuous or primordially satisfying as this Champagne, with its expansive mouthful of vanilla-scented pastry, red fruits, and fresh yet woodsy elements. Enjoy it at brunch with an omelet or cold cuts or at supper with hearty mushroom soup and a baguette. $45–55
Cumières, France
Imported by Michael Skurnik/ Terry Theise

Bruno Paillard
CHAMPAGNE Brut "Chardonnay Reserve Privée"
Medium-bodied. Silken and substantial on the palate, with a long, clean finish.
The bottle looks old-fashioned, but Bruno Paillard (founded 1981) is Champagne's youngest estate. This special cuvée is 100% Chardonnay, rendered in a *pétillant* (frothy) style with significantly less sparkle than traditional Champagne. Buttery, faintly earthy, savory, and smooth, it's particularly alluring with food. Salmon in pastry and triple-crème cheeses are attractive partners. $48–52
Reims, France
Imported by Vintus

Domaine Pierre Moncuit
CHAMPAGNE BLANC DE BLANCS Brut Grand Cru
Full-bodied. Toasty and wonderfully long yet with palate-lifting freshness.
A foodie's Champagne if there ever was one, this 100% Chardonnay is a "grower's" wine from a renowned site. Its rich, mouthwatering character and notes of dried hay, caramel, malt, and minerals make it thrilling with roasted game hens and cold smoked meats. Some tasters prefer it with further bottle age— but who could wait? $48–52
Le Mesnil sur Oger, France
Imported by Polaner

Billecart-Salmon
CHAMPAGNE Brut Rosé
Medium-bodied. Supernally balanced and lightly lingering.
What may be the best rosé from Champagne comes from this two-hundred-year-old family estate. All three Champagne grapes are used, imparting a light-handed quality and great complexity. Raspberries, roses, and minerals suffuse the palate. Serve with carpaccio or sweetbreads. Note: This may be hard to find, as the importer is notoriously selective of his customers. $60–70
Ay, France
Imported by Robert Chadderdon

Other Bubblies

*Before briefly explaining how sparkling wines
are made, let's take a deep breath
and sort out the various kinds.*

*S*PARKLERS given the most pressure during winemaking, like Champagne, are classified as fully sparkling, as opposed to semi-sparkling. They are categorized as *spumante* in Italy and *mousseux* in France ("foaming" or "frothy" in both languages, or "sparkling" when applied to wine). Moderately sparkling *crémant* ("creaming") wines are made with just over half the pressure given Champagne. Then come the lightly effervescent, or semi-sparkling, wines described as *pétillant* in France, *frizzante* in Italy, *spritzig* in Germany, and "crackling" in America. Wines with even less sparkle are called *perlant* in France and *perlwein* in Germany, denoting their pearl-like bubbles.

More technical but easier to keep straight are the two main methods for making sparkling wine. The first is the traditional method, more elegantly called *la méthode champenoise*. After blending and fermentation, the wine is immediately bottled with a starter of yeast and sugar—the *tirage*. A second fermentation then takes place in the bottle, resulting in additional alcohol and the carbon dioxide that gives sparkling wine its effervescence. The new sediment is removed, a dash of sugar called the *dosage* is added to adjust the Champagne's sweetness or dryness, and it is then resealed with a cork and wire cage to protect it from exploding when it is shipped to market.

The other most commonly used bubble-making method, developed just after the turn of the twentieth century by Eugène Charmat in Bordeaux, is much quicker and less expensive. Alternately called the Charmat or bulk process, it uses large tanks to retain the pressure created by carbon dioxide during fermentation. It does not produce wines that benefit from aging, and sparkling wines made by this method often lose their bubbles quickly once they're poured.

One thing to keep in mind: Some sparkling wines do outshine Champagne in their versatility with food. The richness and full sparkle of Champagne limit its ability to complement many things on which you dine or nibble, whereas the gentler textures and varying flavors of other bubblies offer endless variations at the table.

Under $15

Jean-Paul Trocadero
BLANC DE BLANCS Brut
Light-bodied. Crisp, vivacious, and utterly refreshing.
This French sparkler is made from Ugni Blanc (Trebbiano), Chenin Blanc, Macabeo (a Middle Eastern grape that spread to France by way of Spain), and a splash of Chardonnay. A citrusy, bubbling pleasure for mimosas or predinner cocktails. $6–8
Savoie, France
Imported by Lauber

François Montand
BLANC DE BLANCS Brut
Light- to medium-bodied. Dry, but with discernible fruit.
Chardonnay and Ugni Blanc grapes sourced from vineyards across the French countryside are blended in this very appealing sparkling wine. When it's fresh, it's a terrific Champagne alternative. Try it out with chèvre or any other light, creamy cheese. $9–11
Champagne, France
Imported by Stacole

Ermete Medici
REGGIANO "Solo"
Medium-bodied. A deep purple, perfumed, sparkling red apéritif.
If you like Lambrusco, this "deluxe" version, with its rosy mousse and dry palate of jet-black fruits, will stun you. Pair it with *salumi* (salt-cured foods), antipasti, and Parmigiano. $11–13
Emilia-Romagna, Italy
Imported by OmniWines

François Chidaine
MONTLOUIS Brut
Light- to medium-bodied. Very dry, crisp, and aromatic.
This sparkling Chenin Blanc from the Loire sports a fruity fragrance and a lemony, dry finish. It refreshes the mouth

CAVA: CATALONIA'S SPARKLERS

The sparkling wine now called Cava ("cellar") originated in the Catalonian town of San Sadurni de Noy when José Raventos, head of the family firm that grew into the huge sparkling wine producer Codorníu, returned from a visit to France in 1872 and began making *méthode champenoise* wines. Almost all Cava, called Champagña until the early 1970s, is still grown in Catalonia and is made from the grapes Macabeo, Xarel-lo, Paradella, and sometimes Chardonnay, the last in small portions.

A light and refreshing bargain Cava with a fruity, open personality is **Sumarroca Cava Brut "Reserva"** ($9–13), from Penèdes. It is citrusy right off the bat, with a touch of ginger and a clean, brisk finish. It's also a nice alternative to Fino Sherry when you're having tapas. *Imported by Frontier*

More serious is **Juve y Camps Cava Brut Nature "Reserve de la Familia"** ($15–17), one of the new generation of handcrafted, estate-grown Cavas. ("Brut Nature" indicates a wine unsweetened by *dosage*.) Full of nutty complexity and crispy bubbles, it is dry, fairly forceful, and rather Champagne-like. This one makes a rich partner for grilled seafood, fried foods, nuts, and olives. *Imported by Bluegrass-Catalunya*

and cuts through oysters like a razor. $12–14
Loire, France
Imported by House of Fine Wines

Elio Perrone
MOSCATO D'ASTI
Light-bodied. Frothy, fruity, and lively, with a faint hidden richness.
This creamy-textured Moscato, with its strong taste and scent of fresh apricots and spring flowers, is less than 6% alcohol, meaning it won't weigh you or your dinner down. Enjoy icy cold with fresh fruit, tarts, mousses, and crêpes. Also try the delicious pink **Bigaro** ($14–16), a strawberry-redolent blend of half Moscato and half Brachetto. $12–15 (500ml)
Piedmont, Italy
Imported by Rare Wine

Avinyo
CAVA Brut
Light-bodied. Creamy fruit, crisp refreshment.
The label of this artisanal, boutique cava says in Catalan, "with the rigor of a work well crafted"—and justly so. A touch floral, leesy, and a lovely food partner, it's a fitting companion for tapas, fried empanadas, and other Spanish specialties. $13–15
Penèdes, Spain
Imported by De Maison

Gruet
BLANC DE NOIRS
Medium-bodied. A superior American bubbly with a rich, elegant character.
This 100% Pinot is grown in New Mexico at 4,000 feet above sea level by Laurent Gruet, formerly of the Paul Laurent house in Champagne. Its fruit is

a fascinating mix of berries and lemons tempered by earthy, toasty complexity. Brighten up a dull evening with this conversation piece, whose willing partners include sushi, pâté, and croquettes or other fried appetizers. $14–17
New Mexico

Over $15

Eric Bordelet
SYDRE "Doux"
Light- to medium-bodied. Sensuously creamy and fruity—and just 4% alcohol.
This biodynamically grown sparkling apple cider comes from a former Paris wine steward who went home to his orchards. With its Champagne-like feel, it's about as elegant as cider gets. Think of it as something different to serve with cold cuts, farmhouse cheeses, ripe figs, and olives. Bordelet's **Poire "Authentique"** ($12–14) is a deep-gold pear cider that captures the essence of fresh pears. $18–20
Normandy, France
Imported by Daniel Johnnes

Alain Renardat
VIN DU BUGEY CERDON
Light-bodied. Gently sweet, modest in alcohol, and just plain fun.
Here's a 100% sparkling Gamay, the grape of Beaujolais. Raspberry, strawberry, and jasmine trickle across your tongue in this fruity, frothy little bonbon. A winner after dinner with strong triple-crème or blue cheeses, it's also

PROSECCO:
ITALIAN FOR REFRESHMENT

*T*HE INCREASINGLY POPULAR Prosecco could be thought of as Champagne's more casual, yet quite elegant, Italian cousin. A generally dry, refreshing apéritif (*aperitivo* in Italian), it comes in both the *spumante* (fully sparkling) and *frizzante* (semi–sparkling) styles and is usually less expensive than Champagne.

It may be a surprise to many wine drinkers that Prosecco takes its name not from a place or a winemaking technique, but from a grape. All but five percent of production from this Veneto grape is of sparkling wine. The leading DOC is Prosecco di Conegliano–Valdobbiadene, west of the town of Conegliano. (Outside Italy, Prosecco is grown in Argentina, but to a very limited extent.)

Italy's largest Prosecco producer, Mionetto, specializes in the traditional style, making *frizzantes* with about half the sparkle of Champagne. **Mionetto Prosecco** ($10–12) is an appley and vivacious archetype that makes a wonderful warm weather wine. Serve this Prosecco icy cold with antipasti, cold soups, or pasta primavera. *Imported by House of Burgundy*

More Champagne–like than most Proseccos (and, interestingly enough, the café wine of Venice and the traditional base for the Bellini cocktail) is **Nino Franco Prosecco de Valdobbiadene "Rustico"** ($14–16), which shows a bit more staying power than its peers. A pleasure all by itself, it can also be enjoyed with fried appetizers and antipasti. **Franco's "Primo Franco"** ($19–21) is creamier, slightly sweeter, and sexy with a strawberry after dinner. *Both wines imported by Vin Divino*

The exceedingly dry and steely **Bisson Prosecco de Colli Trevigiano** ($13–15) is a quite distinctive version. Crisper and more lemony than most Proseccos, it can handle shellfish and shrimp nicely but is still gentle enough to sip solo. *Imported by Rosenthal*

lovely when served before dinner in Champagne flutes with a garnish of sliced strawberry.
$18–20
Bugey, France
Imported by Louis/Dressner

Ermete Medici
MALVASIA Frizzante Secco "Daphne"
Light- to medium-bodied. Exotically scented and almost bone-dry.
The Malvasia grape expresses itself strongly here, with a pronounced bouquet of apricots and fresh flowers. Yet how can a wine that smells so sweet finish so dry? It's a question worth pondering with an ice-cold bottle and some prosciutto with melon.
$18–21
Emilia-Romagna, Italy
Imported by OmniWines

Foreau
VOUVRAY Brut
Medium- to full-bodied. A powerful Vouvray— but with bubbles!
Drier than most Brut Champagnes, this vivid, sparkling Chenin Blanc from the Loire is a wake-up call. Its tight citrus-peel nose belies a rich palate of baked apples and a complex yeasty character. A bit overwhelming on its own, it makes more sense with food. Seafood (especially crab cakes) brings out its fruit beautifully.
$20–22
Loire, France
Imported by Rosenthal

Dr. Reuter
RIESLING Dry
Light-bodied. A splendid apéritif.
The crisp, citrusy varietal character of Riesling bursts out at you from the first sniff. Lighter than Champagne (and actually drier than many), this bubbly is very food-friendly—an exciting choice for smoked fish, entrée salads, and your most savory or vinegary appetizers.
$20–22
Saar, Germany
Imported by Wines for Food

Schramsberg
BLANC DE BLANCS Brut
Medium-bodied. Elegantly balanced and pure, with a fine bead.

This is the most Champagne-like offering from California, with the finest bead (i. e., smallest bubbles) of almost any *champenoise*-style wine, plus nice, crackery flavors with a bit of leesiness. Enjoy at Thanksgiving as an all-American apéritif or anytime with hors d'oeuvres, pâtés, and seafood salads.
$20–25
California

FIND THAT WINE!

WHY IS IT that you often read of a wine that sounds enticing and different yet you can't find it on the shelves? The answer lies in the sheer number of wines out there—jillions of 'em. With the exception of releases from the largest domestic and international producers alike, the chances of finding what you want at your corner wineshop (or even the mega–mart) are fair to slim at best.

To take things into your own hands, proceed as follows. First e-mail, phone, or visit your trusty local wine retailer, giving the winery's name, what it calls the wine, and, if you're looking for a certain vintage, the year. Your retailer can then order the wine from a wholesale distributor—who, if the wine is in stock, will usually deliver it to the shop the next day. (A hint: Placing orders with a shop's owner or general manager could increase your chances, since some clerks may not be well versed in special ordering.)

If the distributor has to order from the winery, you may have to wait several weeks for delivery. At this point you could try the Internet. Many North American wineries represented in this book sell their wines online (the book's North American wineries, are listed on pages 223–226, complete with contact information). Then there are the wine search sites found on the Internet, several of which are listed on page 231. Advanced searches may require a sign-up fee, but an annual cost that works out to only about $2.50 a month may be well worth it. Also, the Supreme Court's recent ban on direct shipping laws is making online ordering easier.

An alternative is to contact an importer, whose name you'll be lucky to get unless you're searching for a wine from this guide or another publication that specifies importers. How can they help? As often as not, an importer can give you the name of a distributor in your area who can then lead you to a local retailer. Some importers' Web sites provide find-a-wine information in state-by-state directories. If the importer in which you are interested does not provide such a list, a customer service representative reached by phone or e-mail should be able to give you the name of an area distributor.

A potential bonus: Once you've got your hands on a hard-to-locate wine, it just might taste all the sweeter. And what, we ask, could be a more satisfying reward for your successful detective work?

CHAPTER SIX

Fortified and Sweet Wines

In many parts of the world, sipping Port, Madeira, Cream Sherry, or other sweetish fortified wines after dinner has long been de rigueur. But not all fortified wines are sweet, and not all sweet wines are fortified. Simply put, fortified wines have had distilled spirits added during winemaking to strengthen or "fortify" them, while sweet wines come from late-harvested grapes or have had sweet grape must added. Whether you decide to serve them before, during, or after dinner as a dessert wine depends on which kind of wine you've chosen.

Fortified Wines

It has been proved time and again that necessity is the mother of invention, even in winedom. To see the aphorism borne out oenologically, look no further than fortified wine.

FROM THE TIME grapevines were first cultivated and their fruit was transformed into wine, keeping wine from spoiling was a struggle. Greeks extended its life a bit by storing it in amphorae (urns). Romans did the same using oaken barrels. Both civilizations sought to disguise spoilage by flavoring wines with honey, herbs, salt water, and even cheese (!). Exactly when stronger wines or spirits began to be added to wine to preserve it is lost to history, but it worked—and fortified wine was born.

History does record how the fortified wines Port and Madeira came to be. In the late 1600s English wine merchants in Portugal added a little brandy to the dark, astringent red wines they had discovered up the Douro River to ensure that they would arrive in London unspoiled. Eureka! Port. Around the same time, British sailors stopping at Madeira began to stabilize the wines they found there with alcohol to help them survive the long sail back to England, and in the process unwittingly created Madeira (see "Madeira: The Happy Accident," page 206).

Modern-day wines are fortified in one of two ways. Adding grape spirit or other stronger alcohol **during fermentation,** before all the grape sugar has been converted to alcohol, kills the yeast and bacteria and results in longer-lived, higher-alcohol, sweeter wine. The earlier the alcohol is added, the sweeter the wine will be. Alcohol that's added **after fermentation** makes strong, dry wines, with Sherry and the drier Madeiras as two examples. Any sweetness comes from the pre-bottling addition of a sweetener, be it sugar or a mixture of grape juice and spirit.

This complicated vinification, usually coupled with long aging in cask and bottle, ultimately ups the price of fortified wines. (Vermouth is also fortified, but in the United States, Cradle of the Cocktail, it long ago crossed the line from wine to mixer and apéritif.) Nevertheless, the lengthy life of a fortified wine helps offset the cost. That $60 bottle of Vintage Port doesn't look so pricey when it can improve over fifty years and complement a week's worth of dinners. And Madeira is practically immortal. The great unsung bargain is Sherry, which ranges from bone-dry to treacly-sweet and rarely exceeds $40.

SHERRY

Americans may not realize it yet, but Sherry is the perfect apéritif. Its affinity for the snacks we love (pretzels, olives, chips), coupled with its wide range of styles and reasonable prices, would make it a runaway hit if it were marketed better. Its unique and fascinating solera fractional blending system alone makes it appealing. (See "The Solera," page 203.)

Sherry is made in wineries called bodegas at or near the ancient town of Jerez, in the Andalusia region of southern Spain. "Sherry" is the anglicized "Jerez," and "Xérès" is French. All three names appear on the bottle of all true Sherries—those from the three towns in the Jerez DO: Jerez de la Frontera, Sanlúcar de Barrameda, and Puerto de Santa María.

Running the gamut from very dry to very sweet, Sherries are of three types, with subtypes therein. Pale-colored **Fino–style** Sherries are the elegant **Manzanilla** from Sanlúcar, revered for its delicacy and salty tang, and **Fino**—tangily dry, faintly nutty, and refreshing. Both of these should be drunk very fresh and very cold. More complex is the aged, amber Fino called **Amontillado,** which is redolent of smoke and nuts and comes in very dry and slightly sweeter versions. All Fino–style Sherries owe their refinement to protective *flor,* the unique white crust that forms spontaneously on the wine as it develops in the barrel.

Oloroso–type Sherries are darker, fuller, and richer. Because of their higher alcohol content, they remain uninfluenced by *flor* as they age. A standard **Oloroso** is also quite dry, but the version called **Oloroso Dulce** is sweet. **Palo Cortado** is a rare, spontaneously occurring type of Sherry that offers the floral delicacy of Amontillado plus the richness and depth of an Oloroso. The molasses-like **Pedro Ximénez** is made from the grape of the same name and is most often used as a dessert wine or to sweeten dry Sherries. **Cream Sherries** are Olorosos sweetened with Pedro Ximénez, and their degree of sweetness and over-all quality vary widely from producer to producer.

Under $12

Antonio Barbadillo
FINO SHERRY "Pale Dry"
Light-bodied. A piquant, bone-dry, pale, refreshing sherry. Served chilled, this sherry makes the perfect apéritif. With its mouthwatering acidity and faint salty tang, it whets both the appetite and thirst.
$8–10
Jerez, Spain
Imported by Frontier

Antonio Barbadillo
AMONTILLADO SHERRY
"Medium Dry"
Light- to medium-bodied. Essentially dry, with a sweet-salty tang at the finish. Amontillado Sherry is often used for cooking, but if you fill a *copita* with it and start sipping (*copita* is the name for the traditional small sherry glass), you'll find it bracing. The Barbadillo has typical mouthwatering character enhanced by nutty, smoky

aromas. It pairs well with all salty snacks and creamy chowders. $8–10
Jerez, Spain
Imported by Frontier

Antonio Barbadillo
OLOROSO SHERRY
"Full Dry"
**Medium- to full-bodied.
Dry it is, but to some tasters
its richness seems sweet.**
Here's a soul-satisfying Oloroso at an amazing price. As for flavor, just imagine drinking a bowl of chocolate-covered hazelnuts capped by a whiff of smoke. It works well after dinner with a creamy cheese or a handful of nuts. It's also not bad at buffets when sipped with thinly sliced Smithfield ham on biscuits. $8–10
Jerez, Spain
Imported by Frontier

Hidalgo
MANZANILLA SHERRY
"La Gitana"
**Light-bodied. Light and
fragrant, with a savory
(some say salty) tanginess.**
This exquisite dry Sherry has a palate of lemon, citron, and blanched almond. It's a charming partner for green olives, pasta with garlic and olive oil, and smoked fish. $10–13 (500ml)
Sanlúcar de Barrameda, Spain
Imported by Classical Wines

$12 to $25

Emilio Lustau
FINO SHERRY "Jarana"
**Light- to medium-bodied.
One of the richest, most
aromatic, and jazziest Finos.**
Pale straw in color, flowery, nutty, and *dry*, this Fino has exceptionally fresh character and lively alcohol. Serve it chilled

with stuffed olives, shrimp in garlic, smoked cheeses, and your favorite baked shellfish dishes. $14–17
Jerez, Spain
Imported by Europvin

Emilio Lustau
AMONTILLADO SHERRY
"Escuadrilla"
**Medium-bodied. Fragrant and
complex but uncompromisingly
dry—a connoisseur's style.**
Some tasters will be wowed by this totally dry Sherry while others will be puzzled. Salty and tangy, it has earth, coffee, rye, and roasted-nut flavors jet-propelled by acidity. It's best sipped at room temperature with classic tapas: firm cheeses, cured Spanish ham, smoked seafood, and mushrooms sautéed in butter (preferably infused with a few drops of Sherry from the bottle). $20–22
Jerez, Spain
Imported by Europvin

Emilio Lustau
PEDRO XIMÉNEZ "San Emilio"
**Full-bodied. An opaque sherry
that's lavishly sweet and syrupy.**
Blended from stocks of very old wine, this showstopper coats the glass thickly and offers mouthfuls of coffee and molasses with unapologetic zeal. It's a little intense to sip but great poured over a bowl of vanilla ice cream with walnuts, chocolate chunks, and raisins. If you're the daring sort, pour it over pancakes at Sunday brunch. $22–24
Jerez, Spain
Imported by Europvin

Toro Albala
DON PEDRO XIMÉNEZ
"Grande Reserve"
Full-bodied. Sweet and syruplike.
Vintages from the 1970s of this

startling wine are floating around the market, so snap them up. A tidal wave of coffee, caramel, and pralines floods the palate and recedes slowly to a mellow finish. Molten chocolate cake or pecan pie would be a fine partner. $23–25
Montilla-Moriles, Spain
Imported by Classical Wines

Over $25

Emilio Lustau
PALO CORTADO SHERRY
Almacenista **"Vides 1/50"**
Medium-bodied. Deep layers of spice and salt-air complexity propelled by succulent acidity.
The Almacenista line of Sherries is the pinnacle of Sherry production— the reserve wines of the Sherry stockholders themselves. Palo Cortado is the rarest style, an anomaly that occurs spontaneously in the cellars of the bodega and shares qualities of both Amontillado and Oloroso. Profoundly scented with coffee, roasted nuts, and aromas reminiscent of the sea, it can enhance smoked or grilled meats and seafood but provokes the imagination by itself. $32–35
Jerez, Spain
Imported by Europvin

Antonio Barbadillo
PALO CORTADO SHERRY
"Obispo Gascon"
Medium- to full-bodied. Incredibly complex and stimulating on the palate.
In this startling drink, succulent acidity balances the richness and caramelly sweetness, leaving you somewhere between refreshment and satiation. Flavors of butterscotch, toffee, and campfire smoke keep coming and linger. It works with foods as disparate as smoked hams and sausages, crème caramel, and a simple dish of smoked almonds. $34–36
Jerez, Spain
Imported by Frontier

Emilio Lustau
OLOROSO SHERRY Gran Reserva **"Emperatriz Eugenia"**
Medium- to full-bodied. Dry, powerful, and very complex.
In this Gran Reserva, the oldest wines in the solera span many decades. The bouquet smells like a coffee roastery and the texture is firm, juicy, and dense. Try this jewel with aged cheeses or after-dinner biscotti. $36–40
Jerez, Spain
Imported by Europvin

THE SOLERA

A trace of the blend of any Sherry you sip could be as much as two centuries old, thanks to the solera, a unique system of fractional blending. To maintain the historical continuity of their Sherries, winemakers hold the vintages of many different years in rows of old American oak barrels stacked four or five high (the solera), with the oldest Sherries on the bottom. One or more times each year, 10–25% of the wine is taken out of the oldest barrel when Sherry is to be bottled and sent to market. This is replenished with an equal quantity from the next-oldest barrel, and these in turn from younger barrels. At the top, the solera is fed with the wine of the current year, which is known as the *añada.*

Resulting as it does from the continual blending of younger wines into older wines, Sherry isn't the product of any one year—the reason it never carries a vintage date.

203

PORT

True, honest–to–god Port, named for the town of Oporto, comes from the Douro region of northern Portugal. But whether made in Oporto, South Africa, or upstate New York, this brandy–fortified wine is high–alcohol, sweet, full, and practically made for postprandial enjoyment. (The after–dinner pairing of Port and an aromatic wedge of English blue–veined Stilton is a happy legacy of the colonial British Empire.)

So what is it, besides its place of origin, that makes the wine Port? The technique with which it is made. After the grapes have been crushed (a combination of native Portuguese grapes including Touriga Nacional, Tinta Roriz, and Tinta Cão), they are macerated in a tank for about a day. As fermentation begins and the grapes' sugars begin converting to alcohol, fermentation must soon be halted. This is accomplished by pouring the wine into a vat containing clear brandy, the alcohol of which kills the yeast and thus slows fermentation to almost nil. The result is a sweet wine with about 10% residual sugar and up to 20% alcohol.

It takes a long time for Ports to reach full maturity, with the best Vintage Ports left to age for decades. Difference in aging time largely explains the many permutations of the wine, as defined in "A Port Primer," opposite.

Note that all of the Ports recommended here are from Portugal—the idea being that once you've tasted the real thing, you'll have a standard by which to judge those made elsewhere.

Quinta do Infantado
PORT Vintage Character
Medium-bodied.
Moderately sweet, savory, and exquisitely balanced.
This Portuguese-owned estate, of which there aren't many, makes wine the old-fashioned way—and yes, that means stomping on the grapes with bare feet. The Vintage Character is a deep ruby-colored Port with tawny highlights, dominated by fruit but accented with nutmeg, cinnamon, and sandalwood. The **10 Year Tawny** ($35–40) is winey, complex, and distinctively dry for its type. Sip either Port with ginger-bread or cookies. $18–20
Douro, Portugal
Imported by Louis/Dressner

Quinta do Noval
TAWNY PORT 20 Year
Medium- to full-bodied.
Sensuous, generously smooth, and with sweet, lasting flavor.
Imagine a handful of caramel-covered pralines melting slowly into a warm, soothing pool in your mouth. Now extend that sensation for ten minutes or so—about the length of this Port's finish. A great after-dinner sipper from one of the most revered Port houses. $50–55
Douro, Portugal
Imported by William Grant

Warre's
VINTAGE PORT
Full-bodied. A heady, broad style that evolves slowly.
This is first-rate Port from a three-hundred-year-old house at the

top of its game. While the '85 is losing its baby fat and evolving into a spicy, succulent, clove- and currant-scented behemoth, '94 and '97 remain muted and tannic. Warre's are serious, deep, and mysterious wines, so while you're waiting for them, drink the **Late Bottled Vintage 1994** ($24–26), a rich black elixir redolent of blueberries, black cherries, and bittersweet chocolate. $65–90
Douro, Portugal
Imported by Vineyard Brands

Smith Woodhouse
VINTAGE PORT
Full-bodied. Powerful, drier style of Port with a deep, smoky character.

This rich, vastly underrated Vintage Port is loaded with black currant, pipe tobacco, and caramel flavors; look for the '85, a perfect cigar Port. The single-*quinta* **Madalena** ($33–36) seems more opaque and monolithic than the regular vintage and needs time (and some rich cheese) to tame it; look for the '99. The **Late Bottled Vintage Port** ($24–28), which is bottled unfiltered and is aged several years in wood and bottle before release, is sweet, dense, and altogether extraordinary; look for the '94. $65–100
Douro, Portugal
Imported by Premium Port

Dow's
VINTAGE PORT
Full-bodied. Richly layered, and often quite tannic when young.
Owned by the Symington family, whose Scottish ancestor moved to Oporto in 1882 and founded a Port-producing dynasty, Dow

---

A PORT PRIMER

Tawny Port. Vintage Port. Ruby Port. What's the difference between these and the other designations you see on Port labels? From most expensive to least, here are the various styles.

Vintage Ports are wines from a single year's harvest that are blended and bottled after aging two or three years in wood. The customer is expected to cellar them and age them to maturity—often a ten-year-or-more wait. Only a few years in each decade are "declared" a vintage by each house, though in practice certain vintages (like 2000, 1997, and 1994) are universally declared. Vintage Port accounts for only about 1% of all Ports sold. **Late-bottled Vintage Ports** (LBV), dated on their labels but aged a few years in wood and a few more in bottle, are designed to be drinkable on release. **Aged Tawny Ports** are blends of Ports barrel-aged six or more years so that they develop nutty, brown sugar flavors and silky texture. Less expensive versions have no indication of barrel age on the label, suggesting they're under ten years old. The best examples include ten-, twenty-, thirty-, and forty-year Tawnies, referring to the average amount of time spent in wood. The fruity **Ruby Port,** aged for two to three years, is the least complex because it goes almost straight to market after bottling.

Two other Port-related translations: A *quinta* (Portuguese for "farm") is a vineyard site or estate. A **single-*quinta* Port** is blended from grapes grown in the same vineyard.

makes what is considered a comparatively dry style of Vintage Port. Very powerful, fragrant, and saturated with blackberries and cocoa-dusted cherries, it pairs heartily with bread pudding and blue cheeses. Look for '94, '97, and '00 vintages. The rare **Crusted Port** ($22–25) is blended from multiple vintages, left unfiltered, and matured in the bottle before release. The vintage **Quinta do Bonfim** ($38–40) is a single-*quinta* opaque Port with a licoricey, pungent earthiness. $75–85

Douro, Portugal
Imported by Premium Port

Taylor Fladgate
VINTAGE PORT
Full-bodied. Hugely flavorful and fragrant—hedonistic!
Considered by many the best producer, Taylor turns out Ports that are warm, sweet, smooth, and deep. Crammed with black currants and blueberries when young, this wine ages beautifully, developing a wealth of spices and secondary flavors. If food is a must, limit it to nuts and crumbly cheeses. Look for 2000, '97, '94, and the bewitching '83. $95–200 (more for older vintages)

Douro, Portugal
Imported by Kobrand

MADEIRA: THE HAPPY ACCIDENT

The great fortified wine Madeira was accidentally "invented" by the English. En route to the colonies, British ships would stop at the eponymous south Atlantic island and stock up on white wine made from native grapes. Sailors would then fortify the wine with alcohol distilled from cane sugar to help it survive the journey. Tropical temperatures and months of gentle rocking in a ship's hold wrought a miraculous transformation. Rather than being ruined, the cooked, oxidized, shaken wine was found to be the mellowest, nuttiest, most complex beverage imaginable.

Madeira winemakers soon learned to duplicate the conditions of ocean voyages, creating an important export both for Portugal and the English. Madeira was, in fact, the most popular alcoholic beverage in the American colonies during the Revolutionary War era.

Modern Madeira is mostly made from five grapes. Red Tinta Negra Mole makes inexpensive blends; the four whites make the noble wines: Sercial, Verdelho, Bual, and Malmsey, in ascending order of sweetness. **Justino Madeira "Rainwater"** ($10–12) is a light blend—modestly sweet and nutty, very mouthwatering, and enticing with soups and firm cheeses. (*Imported by Monsieur Henri*) The richer **Broadbent Madeira 5-Year "Reserve"** ($18–20) is redolent of roasted nuts, peaches, and orange oil; it makes a versatile after-dinner drink with dates and ripe, aged cheeses. (*Imported by Frederick Wildman*) **Blandy's Malmsey Madeira 15 Year** ($30–35) (500ml) is a cornucopia of dried fruits and treacle—a great partner for sweet cakes and pastries. (*Imported by Premium Port*)

Unfortunately, vintage Madeiras are rarely made in this day and age. Limited stocks are sold, however, through The Rare Wine Company. One triumphant example is **Verdelho d'Oliveiras 1912** ($275+), an alluringly dark, spicy wine that in some ways still seems young.

One of the beauties of Madeira is that you can open a bottle and pour from it for months without worrying about spoilage. The longer you leave it open, the better it gets!

VINS DOUX NATUREL

Though *vin doux naturel* means "naturally sweet wine," the sweetness of these wines actually comes from the process called *mutage*—the addition of spirit halfway through fermentation to halt the conversion of grape sugar to alcohol. Brought forth are very strong, very grapey wines with at least 14% alcohol—not fortified in the usual sense, but close enough.

The high-sugar Muscat and Grenache (white and red, respectively) are the usual grapes, and white *vins doux naturels* are generally sweeter and less alcoholic than the reds. The most famous is Muscat de Beaumes de Venise. If you haven't tried it, you're in luck. The example we recommend is amazingly inexpensive for a dessert wine—a good thing, since you'll probably be coming back for more.

Domaine Beaumalric
MUSCAT DE BEAUMES DE VENISE
Medium-bodied. Deeply
perfumed and pleasant.
Here's the other side of the Port/ Sherry coin. Grapey, flowery, and tender, this Beaumes de Venise offers one of the gentlest palates in the dessert wine kingdom,  hiding its alcohol skillfully under fresh fruit and sweetness. Chill it and pair with a light pudding, panna cotta, or fresh fruit. $14–16
Rhône, France
Imported by Robert Kacher

Domaine Bressy Masson
RASTEAU Vin Doux Naturel
Full-bodied. Very sweet and
satiny on the palate.
This hearty organic version of a Grenache *vin doux naturel* has flavors and aromas of black fruit, milk chocolate, and spiciness underpinned by a little leathery rusticity. Serve it after dinner with blue cheese or dark chocolate-covered nuts.
$15–17
Rhône, France
Imported by
Daniel Johnnes

Mas Amiel
MAURY "Vintage"
Medium-bodied. Soft, suave,
and comforting.
Similar to Tawny Port but more sun-dried in taste, this wine develops flavors of dried apricots, orange peel, and figs as it ages. Vintage Maury is bottled young and aged a year prior to release. Pair it with milk-chocolate candies or fruitcake. The **10 Ans d'Age Cuvée Speciale** ($28–30) is matured from June to June (outdoors!) in seventy-liter *bonbonnes*, or jars. Its creamy, nutty complexity complements blue cheeses. $18–20 (375ml)
Roussillon, France
Imported by North Berkeley

Domaine de la Casa Blanca
BANYULS
"Cuvée de la Saint Martin"
Medium-bodied. Sleek, spicy-tasting, and highly complex.
This hails from the benchmark producer of Banyuls, a wine capable of real longevity. Awhirl with raisin, maple, brown spice, and coffee, it works *with* desserts rather than overpowering them. It is also one of the greatest cheese wines in the world.
$45–50
Roussillon, France
Imported by Vineyard Brands

Sweet Wines

Often misunderstood and even maligned, sweet wines ought to be gaining favor as more wine lovers become interested in dessert wines.

HY IS IT that so many people who love ice cream and sugared soft drinks turn up their noses at sweet wine? Some have probably never tried a high-quality example. Others no doubt were "taught" by wine snobs that only dry wines are worthwhile. Said snobs couldn't be farther off the mark.

Sweet wines are simply wines with "residual sugar," the result of leaving the grapes on the vine until they're super-ripe (hence the labeling of many sweet wines as "late harvest"). Though sweet wines can be made from red grapes, the vast majority are whites. Why? Because white grapes tend to contain higher acidity, which is what balances all that sugar. (For another class of sweet wines, see Vins Doux Naturel on page 207.)

Strangely enough, many of the world's best sweet wines owe their excellence to a fungus. *Botrytis cinerea*—also called "noble rot"—infects grapes left late on the vine and intensifies their sugars and flavors as the grapes' water content drains through the skin. The grapes are painstakingly picked by hand, so the amount of wine ultimately yielded is small—which explains why botrytized wines are so costly. (Note that many of the wines that follow are sold in 500- or 375-milliliter bottles.)

The grapes that lend themselves to sweet winemaking are few in number and more precious for their scarcity. They include the ancient Muscat (Moscato in Italy, Moscatel in Spain); Tokaji, the Hungarian grape that yields some of the best (and priciest) dessert wines; Sémillon, which when "juiced up" with Sauvignon Blanc creates legendary Sauternes in Bordeaux; and Riesling, which makes ambrosial Auslese, Beerenauslese, Trockenbeerenauslese, and Eiswein in Germany.

All these and other sweet wines are frequently used for dessert—but remember that one person's dessert wine is another's apéritif. We pair many of the wines on the following pages with desserts, but plenty of others go beautifully with sweet entrées, full-flavored cheeses, and foie gras. FYI, aging sweet wines reduces their impression of sweetness as the sugars integrate into the wine. Older Ausleses from Germany are hardly sweet at all, yet marvelously lush. Such wines, with their deep and complex flavor, are perhaps the most awe-inspiring to be found.

Under $20

Keo
COMMANDARIA ST. JOHN
Medium-bodied. Said to be
the oldest wine in the world—
and still an amazing bargain.
Produced in Cyprus vineyards
that date from the Crusades, this
sweet curiosity
is made from
sun-dried white
Xynisteri and
red Mavro grapes. Redolent of
dried apricots, pralines, and
caramel, it's an ideal match for
baklava or sheep's milk cheese
drizzled with honey. $8–12
Commandaria St. John, Cyprus
Imported by Athenée

Domaine de la Maletie
MONBAZILLAC
Medium-bodied. Quite sweet
but also tangy, supple, and
easy to enjoy.
If Sauternes is Bordeaux's fair-
haired darling, Monbazillac is the
forgotten stepchild. The good
news is that the wines are
similarly made, with Monbazillac
often as delicious and much
less costly. This example, crafted
from tenderly ripe, late-harvest
Sémillon, is like a liquified
caramel apple. It drinks wonderfully young with pastry and
custards. $13–15
Bergerac, France
Imported by Monsieur Touton

La Sera
MALVASIA DI CASORZO
Light-bodied. A frothy,
fruity, chillable red with
only 5.5% alcohol.
Made from Malvasia Rosso, one
of Italy's classic dessert grapes,
this strawberry-scented red has
a pleasantly astringent snap.
Great for picnics, antipasti, spicy

fare of any sort, or dark-chocolate
mousse. $13–15
Piedmont, Italy
Imported by Matt Brothers

Jaillance
CLAIRETTE DE DIE
"Lou Lou"
Light-bodied.
Frothy, creamy, and
joyously fruity.
Made from 80%
Muscat and 20% Clairette Blanc
(a high-acid, low-alcohol grape),
this unique *pétillant* (frothy)
specialty of the Rhône is just
5.5% alcohol and as fresh as a
late summer peach. It's a cool
after-dinner match for cakes,
trifle, or biscotti. $13–15
Rhône, France
Imported by Wines for Food

Ochoa
MOSCATEL DULCE
Light-bodied.
A pale, lightly
sweet Muscat of
silken delicacy.
A lively cascade of
peaches, tangerines, and white
honey. Sound good? Try it with
a fruit tart and you'll swoon.
$15–18 (375ml)
Navarra, Spain
Imported by Frontier

Ca' del Solo
FREISA Frizzante
Light-bodied. A sweet, sassy,
frothy essence of red berries
with only 5% alcohol.
Soft bubbles, the fragrance of
strawberries, and just enough
sweetness make this a carefree
after-dinner treat with peach
cobbler or with berries in cream.
$16–18
Monterey, California

Selaks
ICE WINE
Light- to medium-bodied. Sweet-tart and enlivening on the palate.
Lime and honeysuckle spring from this tangy, sweet nectar, an interesting South Seas take on Eiswein. Made from varying blends of Riesling and Gewürz, it's a great match for crème caramel or flan. $16–18 (375ml)
Marlborough, New Zealand
Imported by American Estates

Villa Puccini
VIN SANTO
Medium-bodied. Satiny and very nicely concentrated.
The "holy wine" of Tuscany is made from the concentrated essence of sun-dried grapes and aged in special small oak barrels called *caratelli*. This bargain example, redolent of caramel and candied almonds, is a plunge into pleasure with a rich baklava, nut pastries, or biscotti. $16–18 (500ml)
Tuscany
Imported by Verdoni

Domaine de l'Ancienne Cure
MONBAZILLAC
Light- to medium-bodied. A rich, honeyed character suggestive of a Sauternes.
This late-harvest Sémillon is grown upstream from Sauternes and is similar in style to that region's famous wines: honeyed, soft, caramel-scented, and pleasantly tangy. It's a reasonably priced, reasonably sweet white for biscotti, cakes, and apple tarts. $18–20 (375ml)
Bergerac, France
Imported by Bayfield

Domaine Bourillon–Dorleans
VOUVRAY Demi-Sec
"La Coulée d'Argent"
Medium-bodied. Half-savory, half-sweet, it's drinkable
during or after a meal.
The Demi-Sec on the label implies a wine with noticeable sweetness, but bracing acidity keeps

this one in perfect balance as a food partner. Flavors of fresh cream, apple, and caramelized lemon virtually quiver on the palate. Think sweetly rich dishes like sweet-and-sour fish or a pork roast stuffed with apricots. For dessert, go for something a little less sweet—say, lemon cookies or panettone. $18–20
Loire, France
Imported by Europvin

Rivetti
MOSCATO D'ASTI
"La Spinetta"
Light-bodied. *Frizzante*, creamy, and delightfully sweet.
Here's a frothy and aromatic semi-sparkling white from the hills near Asti in Italy's Piedmont region. Its low alcohol and billowing aromas of peach and melon make it a delightful picnic partner or a fine after-dinner drink with fresh fruit. On self-indulgent Sunday mornings it's a decadent treat with smoked whitefish and bagels with cream cheese. $18–20
Piedmont, Italy
Imported by Europvin

$20 to $40

Bonny Doon
MUSCAT "Vin de Glacière"
Medium-bodied. Very sweet.
Vintner Randall Grahm's quirky take on Eiswein, Vin de Glacière ("wine of the icebox") captures the essence of frozen, late-harvested grapes. Plump, peachy, and practically perfect,

it's a pretty partner for poached pears and plum cakes.
$20–22 (375ml)
California

Vasse Felix
NOBLE RIESLING
Medium-bodied. A flamboyant "stickie" from Australia.
Sourced from the Forest Hill vineyard in the remote state of Western Australia, this rich Riesling combines sultry, earthy, sun-ripened fruit with a nice lemon crème acidity. Like many sweet Rieslings, it owes its honeyed character to noble rot. Serve with apricot or peach tarts, grilled fruit, or pumpkin pie.
$20–22 (375ml)
Western Australia
Imported by Old Bridge Cellars

Château La Faurie–Peyraguey
SAUTERNES
Medium-bodied. Concentrated, smooth, and fragrant.
Easily the best value out there for Sauternes lovers! This opulent wine from an opulent thirteenth-century château practically drapes the mouth with satiny sheets of honey. One order of tarte tatin, please. $20–30
Bordeaux
Imported by Diageo

Saucelito Canyon
LATE HARVEST ZINFANDEL
Full-bodied. Intensely flavorful and concentrated with smooth texture.
This winery turns out great Zin practically every vintage from carefully tended hundred-year-old rootstock planted near San Luis Obispo. The LH is a mind-boggling mix of raspberry, chocolate, and plum compote. It's great with blue cheeses or a pear poached in red wine. $22–24 (375ml)
Arroyo Grande, California

Gutiérrez de la Vega
ALICANTE MUSCAT "Casta Diva"
Medium- to full-bodied. Strong, musky, slick, and very sweet.
Imagine a mouthful of honey, marmalade, and dried apricot purée swirled together in a smooth elixir. Now think of enjoying it with bananas flambé or any rich, caramelized dessert. Decadent and exciting!
$25–30 (500ml)
Alicante, Spain
Imported by Classical Wines

Château Pierre Bise
COTEAUX DU LAYON BEAULIEU "L'Anclaie"
Medium-bodied. Creamy yet lively on the palate, with a long and juicy finish.
The flavor of apple dominates in this smooth, sensuous Chenin Blanc, accented by clover honey and a nice leafy "greenness." Super-fantastic with apple pie, it's also an original choice for foie gras. $25–30 (375ml)
Loire, France
Imported by Louis/Dressner

Olivares
DULCE MONASTRELL
Full-bodied. A luscious purple, powerful dessert wine.
Pruney, very sweet, and intensely concentrated, this wine made from the grape Monastrell (a.k.a. Mourvèdre) tastes like a pan-seared reduction of red wine sweetened with chocolate and lavender. Serve it with Spanish blue cheeses like Cabrales and Idiazabal, dried plums or prunes, or a dark-chocolate cake with blueberries. $25–35 (500ml)
Alicante, Spain
Imported by Rare Wine

ICE WINES

*S*OME DESSERT WINES get their sweetness from grapes that were botrytized with noble rot (as defined on page 208), but in other cases the same concentration of sugar and acidity is brought about when grapes freeze on the vine. These Eisweins (anglicized from the German to "ice wines") date only from the early 1960s, when the first Eiswein vintage in Germany was released. Four decades later they gain steam with each passing year in spite of their high cost. (Two less expensive ice wines, both of them made outside Germany, can be found on page 210.)

The frozen grapes for Eiswein are picked and pressed immediately so that most of the water in the grapes separates out as ice. The sweet, concentrated juice left over (grape juice has a lower freezing point than water) is the basis of Eiswein.

An affordable example of this chilly delicacy, **Fitz–Ritter Riesling Eiswein "Durkheimer Hochbenn"** ($50–55 for 500ml), is opulently sweet and vibrant when young and becomes more plush as it matures. Its pineapple, mango, and other tropical flavors are given a freshening lift from buzzing, limelike acidity. It's a gorgeous partner for key lime pie. *Imported by Chapin Cellars*

One of the raciest is **Karlsmühle Riesling Eiswein "Lorenzhofer"** ($85–100 for 375ml). Bursting with fresh ginger, lemon blossoms, key limes, and coriander, it pulls off a fantastic balancing act of ripe fruit and delicacy. Serve it with a grilled pear and slivers of a salty blue cheese. If the cost of this jewel is prohibitive, drink the exquisite **Karlsmühle Riesling Auslese "Lorenzhofer,"** less sweet and half the price. *Imported by Michael Skurnik/Terry Theise*

Dr. F. Weins–Prüm Riesling Eiswein "Bernkasteler Johannisbrunnchen" ($100–125) is a bountifully rich example from the Mosel. Flavors hit the palate with clarity and force—tropical fruit, lemon custard, wet stones, and sugar–glazed flowers are just a few of many. Cellar this one or serve it with fruity desserts and creamy pastries. Finally, for those who prefer absolute power and vigor (and for whom price is no object), there is no better wine we know than the **Robert Weil Riesling Eiswein "Kiedrich Grafenberg"** ($300–400 for 375 ml). High levels of residual sugars and acid allow this wine to age beautifully when it is properly cellared. *Imported by Cellars International*

Selbach–Oster
RIESLING Auslese
"Zeltinger Himmelreich"
Medium-bodied.
Great finesse and length.
This is vintner Johannes Selbach's best, with its zingy, peachy palate and a solid slate foundation. These wines get very diesely for the first five or six years of cellaring, then settle down and become smooth and pleasing. When it's ready, enjoy it with cheeses or custards. $28–30
Mosel, Germany
Imported by Michael Skurnik/ Terry Theise

Château Raymond–Lafon
SAUTERNES
Medium-bodied. A model of grace and balance, and a very fine cellar candidate.
In 1972 Pierre Meslier, the manager of Château d'Yquem, purchased the neighboring estate of Raymond-Lafon. The wine he now makes there is a gem, honeyed and caramelly in its youth, and supported by a bit of lemony acidity. Pair it with light desserts like pound cake or meringues. It also goes well with foie gras. $30–35
Bordeaux
Imported by French Prestige

Domaine Baumard
COTEAUX DU LAYON
"Cuvée Le Paon"
Medium-bodied. Plump and creamy but not too sweet.
In this wine the vibrant Chenin Blanc flavors of spiced apple and banana and the delicate scents of minerals are nicely amplified by sweetness. *Paon* means peacock— as in a peacock's tail of flavors fanning out on your palate. It's fruit-saturated and appealing when young, though some fans like to cellar it.

Serve at a holiday party with apple tart or pound cake with lemon crème frosting.
$33–35
Loire, France
Imported by Monsieur Touton

Von Buhl
RIESLING Auslese GoldKap
"Forster Ungeheuer"
Medium-bodied. Mind-bendingly ripe and honeyed.
Enjoy a ladling of clover honey, berries, and broiled peaches in the abundantly fruit-saturated style this producer is known for. The bracing acidity that keeps it from cloying also keeps it alive in the cellar for thirty (even forty) years. It's a treat with a dish of candied fruits, pineapple cake, or no food whatsoever. $34–36 (375ml)
Pfalz, Germany
Imported by Cellars International

Von Hovel
RIESLING Auslese
"Oberemmeler Hutte"
Light- to medium-bodied. An exceedingly delicate Riesling with distinctive freshness.
Baron Eberhard von Kunow typically produces winsome Rieslings—one being this glassy, pure Auslese cascading with minerals, green apples, and wildflowers. It's grown in the pebbly, steep Hutte vineyard, a source for refined sweet wines occasionally honeyed by noble rot. Sip this one after dinner with pastry or madeleines. $35–40
Saar, Germany
Imported by Cellars International

Over $40

Château Rieussec
SAUTERNES
Medium- to full-bodied.
Quintessential Sauternes—
thick, sweet, fabulous.
Unless you feel the need to spend hundreds more on Yquem, this is top drawer Sauternes. Ancient hillside vineyards on the misty banks of the Ciron River see the ideal combination of warm sunshine and humidity to incur botrytis. From there, ruthless selection and long aging in barrel do the rest. Caramelly, viscous, and long-lived, this is the Roquefort and foie gras wine foodies are talking about. $40–60
Bordeaux
Imported by Diageo

Bert Simon
RIESLING BA
"Serringer Herrenberg"
Medium- to full-bodied.
Delicate minerality married to intense sweetness.
One of the only reasonably priced Beerenauslesen (BA), this exquisite dessert wine is lacy and intricate, an extreme version of all the captivating wines from this estate. Its aromas, magnified exponentially by sweetness, conjure up wet stones and crisp autumn apples. The wine ages well but drinks wonderfully young with cobblers and trifle. $45–50 (375ml)
Saar, Germany
Imported by Cellars International

Fritz Haag
RIESLING Auslese
"Brauneberger
Juffer–Sonnenuhr"
Medium-bodied. Certainly sweet, but the acidity wakes up your palate.
Herb-kissed limes and lemons, ginger, vanilla, and an elusive saltiness from minerality persist on the palate of this Auslese. In warm, wet years, noble rot adds a honeyed and almost woodsy element. Cellar this wine and wait for a most auspicious occasion before serving it. In some years, Haag makes an even riper, more profound **Riesling Goldkap Auslese** ($80–90). $45–55
Mosel, Germany
Imported by Cellars International

H. Dönnhoff
RIESLING Auslese
"Niederhauser Hermannshöhle"
Light- to medium-bodied. Great clarity and purity of flavor.
This wine astonishes in every vintage. Suggestions of tangerines, peaches, tea leaves, and rain-wet pebbles waft from each sip. It's a long-term cellar candidate (20+ years) and a sublime match for fresh foie gras or the sticky black sesame buns of Szechuan cuisine. $45–60 (375ml)
Nahe, Germany
Imported by Michael Skurnik/ Terry Theise

Domaine Zind–Humbrecht
RIESLING Vendange Tardive
"Brand"
Full-bodied. Rich in everything— sugar, alcohol, and sheer force of flavor.
This masterful late-harvest Riesling is a powerhouse from ancient vines. Redolent of caramel, broiled peaches, and lemon drops, it is sweet but not overly so, and its deep earthiness rebounds on the finish. It is traditional with seared slices of foie gras (especially with a fruit element) or the pungent Alsatian Münster, a cheese intimidating to lesser wines. $50–55
Alsace, France
Imported by Kermit Lynch

C. von Schubert
RIESLING Auslese "Maximin Grünhauser Abtsberg"
Medium-bodied. Practically glowing with fruit when young.
Baron Carl von Schubert's Auslese, from selected bunches of late-ripened, botrytized grapes, boasts dozens of exotic fruit notes and a minerally aroma that reflects the *terroir*. As the wine ages, it drops much of its sweetness and becomes a sipping wine, albeit a very complex one. Cream cakes would be a fun pairing if the wine is young; after more bottle age, sip it solo. $50–60
Ruwer, Germany
Imported by Valckenberg

Tommaso Bussola
RECIOTO DELLA VALPOLICELLA "bg"
Full-bodied. A deeply sweet, thick, sensuous red of extravagant proportions.
From one of Italy's most revered producers comes this Recioto, a wine whose grapes have been specially selected and partially dried to concentrate their flavors. The result is Portlike but not as alcoholic; winelike but more raisiny; liqueurlike but more complex—in other words, a perfect after-dinner pleasure. Try it with a chocolate biscotti or a fresh hunk of Parmigiano-Reggiano. The rarer and pricier "tb" ($90–100) is pursued by collectors. $50–60
Veneto, Italy
Imported by Rare Wine

Bodegas Oremus
TOKAJI ASZU "5 Puttonyos"
Medium- to full-bodied. Sweet and completely mouthfilling.
The legendary dessert wine of Hungary, Tokaji (the "j" is silent) is crafted from indigenous grapes, mainly Furmint and Harslevelu. *Puttonyos* are basketfuls of dried, late-harvested grapes added to the base wine to increase its sweetness (six *puttonyos* is the maximum). Its concentrated core of dried peach, apricot, and nut fondant will develop for decades in the cellar. Serve it on its own or with biscotti, rich cakes, cobblers, or even foie gras. $55–60 (500ml)
Tokay-Hegyalia, Hungary
Imported by Europvin

J. J. Christoffel Erben
RIESLING Auslese "Ürziger Würzgarten"
Light- to medium-bodied. Enticing sweetness balanced by shimmeringly fresh acidity.
Hans Leo Christoffel releases several Ausleses every year, labeling different cuvées with one, two, or three stars. Though subtly different, all serve as vehicles for the slate, honey, and pungent florality of the Würzgarten ("spice garden"). Wines this delicate and contemplation-worthy are best tasted by themselves rather than with food. $68–70
Mosel, Germany
Imported by Michael Skurnik/ Terry Theise

Gunderloch
RIESLING TBA "Nackenheimer Rothenberg"
Full-bodied. Sweet insanity.
The shock isn't how sweet this wine is, but rather how complex it still tastes underneath all the sugar. Pungent red slate aromas help you glimpse the vineyard's soul through gulps of maple syrup, glazed pear, and crème caramel. This TBA (short for Trockenbeerenauslese) needs no dessert—it's perfect on its own. Scarcity, international fame, and unflagging quality account for the sky-hgh price. $350–400 (375ml)
Rheinhessen, Germany
Imported by Cellars International

STORING WINE

OST WINE LOVERS don't waste too much energy worrying about wine storage, nor should they. At the same time, they'd do well to acquaint themselves with the basics.

Luckily, learning how to store a wine properly to make sure it maintains or reaches optimum drinkability doesn't require a class or seminar. All it takes is noting a few facts: First, wine deteriorates when it's exposed to sunlight or gets "too hot," meaning a temperature over 77° F or so. Second, wines meant to be stored for a year or more should be kept in a place with reasonable humidity; otherwise, the cork could dry out, shrink, and let air seep in. Third, if wine gets cold enough to freeze, it will expand and force the cork to pop out.

The type of wine is another consideration. Most white wines and inexpensive to moderately priced reds are meant to be drunk right away, and won't suffer from standing on a counter for a few days. If you wait longer before enjoying your latest purchase, give some thought as to how to store it; this is essential if you have a certain red you want to keep for a longer period of time.

How important is it to store the bottle horizontally or angled rather than standing up? For short-term storage (anything under a couple of months), not very. Long-term storage is another matter: Horizontal is the answer, since the cork needs to be kept moist so it won't shrink and let in oxygen—the reason wine racks were invented.

"Cellaring"

The word *cellaring* may call to mind an Irish lord poking around in the castle's musty depths, but it's simply wine lingo for long-term storage. Your "cellar" could be anything from a kitchen cupboard to the floor of a closet to a spare dresser drawer. The temperature (ideally around 65°F) is your primary consideration. Also make sure the bottles won't be disturbed: Vibrations or anything else that shakes a wine up even slightly can throw off the precious balance of its elements.

Leftover Wine

The party's over, so what do you do with that half-bottle of Chablis or Bordeaux you're loath to pour down the drain? First, be aware that the fuller-bodied the wine, the longer it lasts. To keep oxygen out of leftover wine, plastic levered stoppers, rubber stoppers (often part of a vacuum kit), or a chrome, rubber-lined winestopper with a handle are preferable to shoving the cork back in. For an anti-oxidation double whammy, store the stoppered wine in the fridge, which will prolong its drinkability. Generally speaking, reds should stay drinkable for up to four days, whites for two to three days.

Another tip for the wine lover: The more air space there is in a leftover wine, the faster the wine will oxidize. Pouring it into a smaller screw-top container—say, a club-soda or tonic-water bottle from a six-pack—could mean an extra day or two of drinkability.

GLOSSARY

abundant *See* generous.

acidity The acid content of a wine (largely tartaric acid, which occurs naturally in grapes). Acidity makes wine "juicy" in the mouth—imperative in white wines. Acidity also allows certain white wines to cellar well.

AOC Abbreviation for *Appellation d'Origine Contrôlée* ("protected place of origin"), the French system that sets standards for three categories of wine. In order of quality, the categories are *Vins d'Apellation d'Origine Contrôlée* (AOC); *Vins Délimités de Qualité Supérieure* (VDQS); and *Vins de Pays* (country wines).

appellation The name of the place from which a wine originates, determined by a country's laws, and often a part of the wine's name. *See also* AOC, DO, DOC, DOCG.

astringent Describes the puckering effect that tannins or acids in wine have on the mouth. Not necessarily a pejorative term.

balance The relative proportions of a wine's structural elements, such as alcohol, residual sugar, acid, fruit, and tannin. In a well-balanced wine, no one component stands out.

barnyard(y) An aroma that is the quintessence of Burgundy and positive in connotation. Characterized by the aroma of stables, including loam and damp hay.

barrel-aged Used to describe wines (usually white) that have spent time in wood barrels after fermentation. The wines receive oxygen through the barrels, turning them darker, softer, and frequently sweeter. *See also* oak.

barrel-fermented Describes wines fermented in wood barrels, most often of oak. The result is a richer wine, often sweeter and higher in alcohol.

barrique A small new oak barrel (225 liters, or nearly 60 gallons) used for aging and storing wine. Originally a Bordeaux design, now in global use.

big Describes wines that are especially full or intense. *See also* full; intense.

biodynamism System of organic grape growing and winemaking based on the holistic principles of Austrian philosopher Rudolph Steiner. Known as *biodynamie* in France, it combines principles of astronomy and homeopathy with total avoidance of conventional fertilizers, herbicides, or pesticides in the vineyard.

blend A wine made from the juice of different grape varieties or the wines of different vineyards, regions, or vintages.

blush wine A wine made pink when the skins of black grapes are left to briefly soak in the fermenting must.

body Impression of a wine's weight in the mouth—light, medium, or full.

botrytis *See* noble rot.

bouquet Aromas of a wine. Also called nose.

bready *See* yeasty.

bright Describes a wine whose aroma, or flavor, is vividly perceived.

buttery A term used to describe wines—usually whites that have undergone malolactic fermentation—that 1) taste like butter from the resulting diacetyl compounds or 2) feel "buttery-smooth" from the softening of acidity.

carbonic maceration A fermentation method in which bunches of whole grapes are placed in a closed tank so that the weight of the top bunches crushes those at the bottom.

Fermentation then takes place inside each grape of the top bunches, leading to extremely fruity wines such as those of Beaujolais. Also called whole–berry fermentation.

character The personality or overall impression a wine makes on the taster—"serious," "fun," "insipid," etc.

château The French word for "castle", most commonly referring to estates in Bordeaux. Despite the translation, a château can be a single small building.

chewy Mouthfeel term for a wine so rich and concentrated that it creates the impression of chewiness; often applied to highly tannic wines.

clos French term for a vineyard surrounded by a wall.

compact Describes wines that are not "big" but give the impression of intensity. *See also* big; intense.

complex, complexity Describes a wine with several aromas and flavors; often a product of maturation in the bottle.

concentration The perceived or actual density of a wine.

co–op Short for cooperative. A consortium of growers who pool their resources to produce a single wine or brand of wines.

crackling Describes wine with a light sparkle.

crisp Said of a wine (usually young), with pleasant tartness; opposite of soft.

cru French for both "growth" and "vineyard," used to designate a vineyard often classified as high–quality. Grand Cru ("great growth") is the highest designation in Burgundy, Alsace, and Champagne. Premier Cru ("first growth") is the highest in Bordeaux.

cuvée A special bottling made separately from an estate's regular wine.

depth Attributed to full-bodied wines with multiple layers of flavor. *See also* intensity, complexity.

descriptor(s) The word(s) used to describe the flavors or aromas of a wine, usually comparative. Typical nouns include herbs, berries, flowers, or generalized references to orchard fruits (apples, pears, quince) or brown spices (cloves, nutmeg, cinnamon). Often–used adjectives include buttery, citrusy, cedary, plummy. Some descriptors, like weedy or musty, are considered pejorative. *See also* barnyard(y); earthy; floral; fruity; minerally; woody.

DO Abbreviation for *Denominación de Origen*, the Spanish equivalent of France's AOC.

DOC Abbreviation for Spain's *Denominación de Origen Calificada*, the highest classification; Portuguese *Denominaçao de Origen Contralad*; or Italian *Denominazione di Origine Controllata*, all the equivalent of France's AOC.

DOCG Abbreviation for *Denominazione di Origine Controllata e Garantita*, Italy's highest classification.

domaine The French word for a winemaking estate (especially in Burgundy, the Loire, and Alsace) that owns one vineyard or parts of many.

dry Describes a wine in which all or most of the sugars have been converted to alcohol during fermentation. Little or no sweetness is perceived. A dry wine with a slight touch of sweetness is variously described as off-dry, medium–dry, or semi–dry.

earthy, earthiness Describes a nice flavor or aroma evocative of the soil. *See also terroir.*

elegant, elegance Most often used to describe a well–balanced, high–quality wine with evident finesse.

enology. *See* oenology.

estate The physical holdings of a winery, including all facilities.

estate-bottled In America, this term refers to a wine that has been grown at vineyards the winery owns and vinified and bottled at the winery itself. Other countries' definitions are looser.

fat Said of wine that is fruit-saturated and weighty on the palate, but not necessarily tannic.

fermentation The complex process by which yeasts devour the sugars in grape juice, producing the by-products ethyl alcohol and carbon dioxide.

filtering The process by which winemakers remove unwanted solid matter from their wines prior to bottling. This is often accomplished with layers of porous fabric or cardboard. Controversy has arisen over whether this partially strips the finished wine of flavors.

fining The clarification of wine by removing its volatile or unstable molecules. The traditional clarifying agent, egg white, is now often replaced with minerals, clays, or proteins.

finish In simplest terms, the aftertaste of a wine; more technically, the impression of flavor and texture that remains after a wine has been swallowed or spit.

firm An impression of solidity or "chewable" texture in a wine, caused by structural elements such as tannin or acidity. *See also* chewy.

first growth *See* cru.

flabby Said of a wine that lacks adequate acidity.

floral, flowery Describes a wine with aromas of nonspecific flowers.

frizzante Italian for lightly sparkling. Often applied to Prosecco, Lambrusco, and Moscato wines.

fruity Describes a wine whose primary aroma or flavor is that of fresh fruit. Typical fruity wines include Beaujolais (Gamay), Riesling, Muscat, Zinfandel, and Barbera among others.

full Describes the body of a wine with an abundance of extract, alcohol, and/or tannin; a texture that seems to fill up the mouth. *See also* body.

generous Said of wines with characteristics that are full-flavored in the mouth or are expressive enough to be easily perceived. Synonyms include abundant and giving.

giving *See* generous.

Grand Cru *See* cru.

harmonious An old-fashioned term, more in use in Europe today, that describes a wine of particularly appealing balance. *See also* balance.

intense, intensity Describes a wine with a strong character, one that cannot be ignored. Not a pejorative, although often perceived as so by consumers.

late harvest (abbr. LH) Applied to wines made from very ripe grapes picked late in the growing season. Usually very sweet, late harvest wines are often used as dessert wines.

lees The spent matter left over from fermentation, including dead yeast cells, skins, and other grape fragments. Wines aged on their lees are often richer in flavor and texture.

length The amount of time a wine's flavor remains in the mouth after it has been spit or swallowed. *See also* finish.

light Describes the body of a wine that feels delicate or airy in the mouth. Not a pejorative, "light" is sometimes a great compliment, since wine can feel light yet offer abundant flavor. Light wines with little flavor are critiqued as thin. *See also* thin.

lively Said of a wine that is tingly on the tongue, whether because of acidity or carbonation.

luxurious Describes particularly lush, flavorful wines, usually with soft mouthfeel.

malolactic fermentation The secondary fermentation, often artificially induced, that converts naturally occurring malic acid (the acid in apples) into lactic acid (the acid in milk), giving wine a creamy mouthfeel.

medium–dry *See* dry.

medium–sweet Often used to describe dessert–grade and fortified wines, including Sherry and Madeira, whose sugars remain in balance.

minerally, mineral, minerality An aromatic suggestion of stones, wet rocks, or flint. Many tasters recognize it as the smell of a clean sidewalk just after a rain. A source of complexity, particularly in white wine. *See also terroir.*

mouthfeel The combined sensation of all aspects of a wine on the tongue, gums, and palate—one of the most important criteria by which a wine's quality is judged. Also called texture.

must The fermenting juice, skins, seeds, pulp, etc., of grapes.

négociant French for "merchant." A person or firm that purchases fruit or finished wine, then blends, bottles, and ships it under his or her own label. Those who work with the growers and take an artisanal approach are known colloquially as *petit négociants.*

noble rot A beneficial fungus (*Botrytis cinerea*), the mold of which penetrates grape skins and saps water from the juice. The concentration of sugar, flavor, and acid in the grapes results in very sweet, complex wines.

nonvintage A wine blended from grapes that were picked in more than one year. Also the largest category of Champagne.

nose *See* bouquet.

oak The wood from which most wine barrels are made, varying in provenance. American white oak, from the eastern United States, is used for many California Zinfandels and Australian and Spanish wines, while more expensive French oak (from designated forests such as Limousin, Nevers, and Tronçais) is used for Bordeaux, Burgundy, and many prestigious wines from around the world. Oak barrels also vary in age, with **new oak** imparting strong flavors and tannins and **old oak** (previously used) imparting none. Some unfinished barrels are given a "toast" or "char" over fires that partly burn their interiors, thus caramelizing the sugars in the wood; a heavily charred barrel imparts strong, sweet, or smoky flavors to the wine. Not all oak influence comes from barrels: Cost-conscious wineries may buy oak chips in nylon sacks (the chips come in light, medium, or heavy char), which they dip like giant tea bags into fermenting or aging wines to impart the desired oaky flavor—very typical of Californian and Australian wines costing less than $10. Less scrupulous wineries add oakiness with powders, essences, and artificial flavorings.

oenology The study or science of wines and winemaking. Also spelled enology.

off–dry *See* dry.

palate Literally the soft, fleshy surfaces at the top and bottom of the mouth. In wine parlance the palate has come to mean 1) the physical tasting platform of the mouth—as in, "That wine feels great on the palate" and 2) the natural ability of the taster to judge the quality of wines as in, "He's got a very sophisticated palate."

petit négociant *See négociant.*

phylloxera Plant-eating louse native to North America that migrated and devastated European vineyards in the nineteenth century, then rebounded in American vineyards at the end of the twentieth. Planting in sandy soils or grafting vines onto genetically resistant rootstock have thus far been the only defense against this persistent pest, which burrows in the soil and feeds on the roots of vine plants.

plush Describes wine that is texturally luxurious on the tongue.

Premier Cru *See* cru.

release A wine that is commercially available from a winery, or the official offering of that wine for sale.

reserve Supposedly the best (or better) cuvée from a winery, "reserved" for special customers or the winemakers themselves. In practice, use of the term usually describes a wine that has spent more time in oak, for better or worse. Reserve wines are more expensive than a winery's regular offerings.

rich Said of wine with particularly pronounced flavor, texture, or both.

round Describes a wine that feels smooth and ample in the mouth, lacking sharpness or "edges."

Schloss The German word for castle, similar to *château* in France.

second label A wine priced lower, bottled separately, and given a different name and label than a winery's regular offerings.

silky Refers either to a wine's mouthfeel or the quality of its tannins. Suggests a seductive softness reminiscent of the feel of spun silk.

single-vineyard A wine whose grapes were grown in one vineyard, often named on its label. *See also* cru.

smooth Describes a wine that glides easily and pleasingly over the palate.

soft A mouthfeel term used to describe a wine whose acidity and/or tannins are minimal. Can imply "gentle" in a positive context or "insipid" in a negative one; opposite of crisp.

spritzy Describes a wine with either lively sparkle or the high acidity that creates a sparkling impression.

spumante A catchall term for Italian wines that sparkle.

structure, structural components The combination of all a wine's physical elements that constitute its mouthfeel: acidity, sugar, alcohol, extract, tannin (if any), oak (if any), etc. A poorly structured wine is one exhibiting an imbalance in these elements; a well-structured or "well-crafted" one is balanced—and, by implication, likely to age well.

supple Describes a wine that simply feels good in the mouth, offering ample fruit and a gentle enough structure that it can be enjoyed at its current state of development.

sur lie The French term for a wine aged on its lees. *See also* lees.

sweetness The perceived sensation of sugar in a wine—not to be confused with actual sugar content. A wine with less sugar and low acidity can actually taste sweeter than a wine with a bit more sugar but much higher acidity; it's all in the balance. Sweetness, which implies ripeness, is inherently good. A technically dry red, like a red Zinfandel, can have fruit so ripe-tasting that it seems "sweet," and saying that such a wine has "beautiful sweetness" is high praise.

tannin(s) A complex group of chemical compounds found in tree bark, tea, and the skins of many fruits, including grapes. They play a major role in the aging of wine—particularly red wines, the pigmented tannins of which impart color and sensory qualities. In the mouth, astringent (drying) tannins taste slightly bitter and cause a puckering sensation.

terroir A French term that encompasses the climatic, geographic, geologic, and environmental aspects of a vineyard. A wine that reflects the character of the place from which it comes is said to be *terroir*-driven or expressive of its *terroir*. Some wine writers use the term, for which there is no English equivalent, as a synonym for *earthy* or *minerally*.

texture An alternate word for *mouthfeel*.

thin Pejorative term describing wines that lack concentration or flavor.

tight Describes a wine whose tannins need time to settle down, meaning it is too young to enjoy. Synonyms include *closed*, *mute*, and *dumb*.

unfiltered *See* filtering.

unfined *See* fining.

unripe, underripe Said of a wine whose grapes were picked before they were fully ripe and thus usually have more acidity and less character.

varietal Term for a wine named after the dominant grape variety from which it is made. An adjective, it is commonly misused as a noun.

VDQS *See* AOC.

vegetal Describes a family of flavors reminiscent of green vegetables. The term is often used as a synonym for *unripe*.

vendage tardive French for "late harvest." An official label designation in Alsace. Sometimes appears in plural form.

vin de pays French for "wine from the country." A category of the French appellation system, it is also a catchall term for inexpensive French wines. *See also* AOC.

vins doux naturel French for "naturally sweet wines." The sweetness, however, comes from the fortifying process called *mutage*—the addition of spirit halfway through fermentation to halt the conversion of grape sugar to alcohol. The resulting wine is semi-, rather than fully, fortified.

vinification The process of winemaking.

vintage The year in which the grapes for a wine were picked. Vintage wines tend to be more highly regarded than nonvintage wines.

viticulture The growing of grapes for the purpose of winemaking.

weight *See* body.

weingut German for "winery."

whole-berry fermentation A nontechnical term for carbonic maceration. *See also* carbonic maceration.

woody A term, usually pejorative, for wines whose oak flavors are particularly evident.

yeasty Describes wines with pungent, floral aromatics derived from time spent on their lees; *bready* is a common synonym.

THE NORTH AMERICAN WINERIES

Some of the wineries whose wines were chosen for this book maintain Web sites that leave no stone unturned, providing contact information, retail store locations, and sometimes selling their wines online. (Note: Browsing wineries' Web sites is also a fun diversion, giving you a glimpse of the personal side of winemaking.) You can get in touch with some other wineries only by phone—or better still, a prearranged visit should you happen to be in their neck of the woods.

California

ALBAN VINEYARDS
www.albanvineyards.com

ALEXANDER VALLEY VINEYARDS
www.avvwine.com

AU BON CLIMAT WINERY
www.aubonclimat.com

AVILA WINERY
www.avilawine.com

BAREFOOT CELLARS
www.barefootwine.com

BARNWOOD VINEYARDS
www.barnwoodwine.com

BARON HERZOG WINERY
www.baronherzog.com

BELVEDERE VINEYARDS AND WINERY
www.belvederewinery.com

BENSON FERRY VINEYARDS
www.bensonferry.com

BERNARDUS WINERY AND VINEYARD
www.bernardus.com

BLACKSTONE WINERY
www.blackstonewinery.com

BLOCKHEADIA WINERY
www.blockheadia.com

BOGLE VINEYARDS
www.boglewinery.com

BONNY DOON VINEYARD
www.bonnydoonvineyard.com

BOUCHAINE VINEYARDS
www.bouchaine.com

CA' DEL SOLO WINES
See Bonny Doon Vineyard

CALERA WINE COMPANY
www.calerawine.com

CAPAY VALLEY VINEYARDS
www.capayvalleyvineyards.com

CAPIAUX CELLARS
www.capiauxcellars.com

CARNEROS CREEK WINERY
www.carneros-creek.com

CARTLIDGE & BROWNE WINERY
www.cartlidgebrowne.com

CASTLE ROCK WINERY
www.castlerockwinery.com

CAYMUS VINEYARDS
www.caymus.com

CLAY STATION
See Delicato Family Vineyards

CLINE CELLARS
www.clinecellars.com

CLOS DU BOIS WINERY
www.closdubois.com

CLOS LA CHANCE WINERY
www.closlachance.com

CLOS MIMI WINERY
www.closmimi.com

CLOS PEGASE WINERY
www.clospegase.com

COLD HEAVEN
www.coldheavencellars.com

COSENTINO WINERY
www.cosentinowinery.com

COTURRI NATURAL WINES
www.coturriwinery.com

DARIOUSH WINERY
www.darioush.com

DAVID BRUCE WINERY
www.davidbrucewinery.com

DELICATO FAMILY VINEYARDS
www.delicato.com

DE LOACH VINEYARDS
www.deloachvineyards.com

DUCKHORN WINE COMPANY
www.duckhorn.com

EASTON WINERY
See Terre Rouge/Easton Winery

EDMEADES WINERY
www.edmeades.com

EDMUNDS ST. JOHN WINERY
www.edmundsstjohn.com

**FESS PARKER WINERY AND
VINEYARD**
www.fessparker.com

FIFE VINEYARDS
www.fifevineyards.com

FORMAN VINEYARDS
www.formanvineyard.com

FOXEN VINEYARDS
805-937-4251

**GARY FARRELL VINEYARDS
AND WINERY**
www.garyfarrell.com

GIRARD WINERY
www.girardwinery.com

GRGICH HILLS CELLAR
www.grgich.com

HRM REX GOLIATH
See Wimbledon Wine Company

HAGAFEN CELLARS
www.hagafen.com

HAHN ESTATES WINERY
See Wimbledon Wine Company

HAVENS WINE CELLARS
www.havenswine.com

HEITZ CELLARS
www.heitzcellar.com

JORY WINERY
www.jorywinery.com

JOSEPH PHELPS VINEYARDS
www.jpvwines.com

LANE TANNER WINERY
www.lanetanner.com

MCMANIS FAMILY VINEYARD
www.mcmanisfamilyvineyards.com

**MACROSTIE WINERY
AND VINEYARDS**
www.macrostiewinery.com

MARIETTA CELLARS
www.mariettacellars.com

MARTINE'S WINES
www.mwines.com

MIDNIGHT CELLARS
www.midnightcellars.com

MIETZ CELLARS
www.mietzcellars.com

MONTERRA WINERY
www.monterrawine.com

MOSS BRIDGE WINERY
www.mossbridgewinery.com

MOUNT EDEN VINEYARDS
www.mounteden.com

MURPHY-GOODE ESTATE WINERY
www.murphygoodewinery.com

NEWTON VINEYARD
www.clicquotinc.com

OJAI VINEYARD, THE
www.ojaivineyard.com

PAGOR/ROLLING HILLS
VINEYARDS
805-484-8100

PHILLIPE-LORRAINE VINEYARDS
707-963-0121

RAMSAY WINES
www.kentrasmussenwinery.com

RANCHO ZABACO WINERY
www.ranchozabaco.com

RENWOOD WINERY
www.renwood.com

SAUCELITO CANYON VINEYARD
AND WINERY
www.saucelitocanyon.com

SCHRAMSBERG VINEYARDS
www.schramsberg.com

SEAN H. THACKREY
www.wine-maker.com

SEGHESIO FAMILY VINEYARDS
www.seghesio.com

SHENANDOAH VINEYARDS
www.sobonwine.com

SHOOTING STAR
See Steele Wines

SPELLETICH CELLARS WINERY
www.spellwine.com

SPRING MOUNTAIN VINEYARD
www.springmtn.com

STEELE WINES
www.steelewines.com

SUMMERS WINERY AND VINEYARDS
www.summerswinery.com

TALBOTT VINEYARDS
www.talbottvineyards.com

TAURIAN VINEYARDS
www.taurianvineyards.com

TERRE ROUGE/EASTON WINERY
www.terrerougewines.com

TOAD HOLLOW VINEYARDS
www.toadhollow.com

TRENTADUE
www.trentadue.com

VINUM CELLARS
www.vinumcellars.com

WATERSTONE
Z Wine Company
707-253-2511

WIMBLEDON WINE COMPANY
www.wimbledonwine.com

WYATT WINES
www.polanerselections.com

Canada

HENRY OF PELHAM FAMILY
VINEYARD
www.henryofpelham.com

Connecticut

SHARPE HILL VINEYARD
www.sharpehill.com

Mexico

L. A. CETTO WINERY
www.lacetto.com

New Mexico

GRUET WINERY
www.gruetwinery.com

New York State

DR. KONSTANTIN FRANK'S
VINIFERA WINE CELLARS
www.drfrankwines.com

MILLBROOK VINEYARDS
AND WINERY
www.millbrookwine.com

PAUMANOK VINEYARDS
www.paumanok.com

PELLEGRINI VINEYARDS
www.pellegrinivineyards.com

RED NEWT CELLARS
www.rednewt.com

SCHNEIDER VINEYARDS
www.schneidervineyards.com

TERNHAVEN CELLARS
www.ternhaven.com

WARWICK VALLEY WINERY
www.wvwinery.com

WÖLFFER ESTATE
www.wolffer.com

Oregon

ADELSHEIM VINEYARD
www.adelsheim.com

ARGYLE WINERY
www.argylewinery.com

CRISTOM VINEYARDS
www.cristomwines.com

DOMAINE DROUHIN
www.domainedrouhin.com

ELVENGLADE WINERY
www.elvenglade.com

LANGE ESTATE WINERY &
VINEYARDS
www.langewinery.com

PATRICIA GREEN CELLARS
503-554-0821
winery@patriciagreencellars.com

RANSOM WINES
503-868-9415

WILLAKENZIE ESTATE WINERY
www.willakenzie.com

WILLAMETTE VALLEY VINEYARDS
www.wvv.com

Texas

PHEASANT RIDGE WINERY
www.pheasantridgewinery.com

Washington

L'ECOLE NO. 41
www.lecole.com

PEPPER BRIDGE
www.pepperbridge.com

POWERS WINERY
www.badgermtnvineyard.com

WOODWARD CANYON WINERY
www.woodwardcanyon.com

IMPORTERS OF FOREIGN WINES

Wines can have more than one importer nationally, so the one we specify for a featured wine may or may not be the source for it in your area.
Also bear in mind that wines carried by an importer change constantly
as producer/importer relationships and contracts are altered.

The level of information found on an importer's Web site varies.
Importers without Web sites can be reached by phone or e-mail.

AV IMPORTS
www.avimports.com

ABARBANEL
www.kosher-wine.com

ALLIED DOMECQ
www.kosher-wine.com

ALLIED IMPORTERS USA
www.alliedimporters.com

AMERICAN ESTATE WINES
908-273-5060;
wines@allieddomecq.com

ARTISAN WINES
800-847-2780; arttwine@snet.net

ATHENÉE IMPORTERS
www.atheneeimporters.com

AVATAR WINE MARKETING
www.avatarwinemarketing.com

BACCHANAL WINE IMPORTERS
www.bacchanalwines.com

BARON FRANÇOIS LTD.
www.baronfrancois.com

BAYFIELD IMPORTING LTD.
natebayfield@aol.com

BLUEGRASS-CATALUNYA
www.bluegrasscatalunya.com

BOISSET AMERICA
www.boissetamerica.com

BROADBENT SELECTIONS
www.broadbent-wines.com

CADET WINES LTD.
www.cadetwines.com

CAPE CLASSICS
www.capeclassics.com

**CELLARS INTERNATIONAL/
RUDI WIEST**
www.germanwine.net

CHADDERDON, ROBERT
212-332-4999

CHAPIN CELLARS
www.billingtonwines.com

CLASSICAL WINES
www.classicalwines.com

CLICQUOT, INC.
www.clicquotinc.com

COMMONWEALTH WINES
www.commwine.com

DALLA TERRA
www.dallaterra.com

DAVID BOWLER WINE
212-807-1680;
amanda@bowlerwine.com

DE GRAZIA SELECTIONS, MARC
www.marcdegrazia.com

DE MAISON SELECTIONS
www.demaisonselections.com

DIAGEO CHATEAU & ESTATE
www.aboutwines.com

DISTINCT EXPRESSIONS, INC.
www.distinctexpressions.com

IMPORTERS OF FOREIGN WINES

DOMAINE SELECT WINE ESTATES
www.domaineselect.com

DREYFUS, ASHBY & COMPANY
www.dreyfusashby.com

EDWARD WINES LTD., T.
www.tedwardwines.com

EMPSON USA
703-684-0900

ENOTEC IMPORTS
www.enotec.net

EPIC WINES
www.epic-wines.com

EPICUREAN WINES
www.epicureanwines.com

EUROPEAN CELLARS/
ERIC SOLOMON
www.europeancellars.com

EUROPVIN/CHRISTOPHER
CANNAN
Europvin@europvin.com

EVATON INC.
www.evaton.net

F & F FINE WINES
www.fwiwines.net

FRENCH PRESTIGE WINES
415-296-7798

FRONTIER WINES
973-328-4500;
wineimport@optonline.net

GIVEN WINES, JOHN
www.jgwines.com

GRAND CRU IMPORTS
www.grandcruimports.com

GRANT, WILLIAM
www.grantusa.com

GRATEFUL PALATE, THE
888-472-5283;
info@gratefulpalate.com

HOUSE OF BURGUNDY
914-937-6330

HOUSE OF FINE WINES
212-828-1500; hofw@nyc.rr.com

IMPORTICOS
www.importicos.com

INTERNATIONAL CELLARS
www.pacwine.com

INTERNATIONAL GOURMET
www.intlgourmet.com

INTERNATIONAL IMPORTERS/
HARVEY BRONSTEIN
516-429-5427;
hbcettowine@aol.com

JANDELL SELECTIONS
516-364-9889;
dhayes@jandelselections.com

JOHNNES WINES, DANIEL
www.danieljohnneswines.com

JUNGUENET, ALAIN
908-654-6173; junguenet@aol.com

KACHER SELECTIONS, ROBERT
www.robertkacherselections.com

KERMIT LYNCH
510-524-1524; klwmjt@aol.com

KOBRAND CORPORATION
www.kobrand.com

LANGDON SHIVERICK IMPORTS
www.shiverick.com

LAUBER IMPORTS, LTD.
www.lauberimports.com

LAURENT-PERRIER
www.laurent-perrier.com

LOUIS/DRESSNER SELECTIONS
www.louisdressner.com

MARTIN SCOTT WINES LTD.
516-327-0808;
sesposito@martinscottwines.net

MATT BROTHERS & COMPANY
www.mattbrothers.com

METROPOLIS
212-581-2051; invinoveritas@cs.com

MIONETTO USA, INC.
www.mionettousa.com

MOËT HENNESSY
212-251-8200

MONSIEUR HENRI
www.monsieurhenri.com

MONSIEUR TOUTON
212-255-0674;
guillaume@mtouton.com

MOORE BROTHERS WINE
www.moorebrosnj.com

NEAL SELECTIONS, CHARLES
www.charlesnealselections.com

NÉGOCIANTS USA
www.negociants.com

NEW CASTLE IMPORTS
www.newcastleimports.com

NORTH BERKELEY
www.northberkeleyimports.com

OLD BRIDGE CELLARS
www.oldbridgecellars.com

OMNIWINES
www.omniwines.com

OPICI IMPORT COMPANY
www.opici.com

ORGANIC VINTAGES
www.organicvintages.com

ORIENTATE IMPORTS
www.orientateimports.com

PALM BAY IMPORTS
www.palmbayimports.com

PANEBIANCO
www.panebiancollc.com

PASTERNAK WINE IMPORTS
www.pasternakwine.com

PATERNO WINES INTERNATIONAL
www.paternowines.com

PLEASANT IMPORTERS, INC.
718-842-7201;
pleasant-importers@verizon.net

POLANER SELECTIONS
www.polanerselections.com

PREMIUM PORT WINES INC.
www.premiumport.com

RARE WINE COMPANY
www.rarewineco.com

RAVENSVALE IMPORTS
203-552-9275;
ravensvale@aol.com

RÉMY AMERIQUE
212-399-4200

RINALDI, MARIO
212-787-6156;
mconsultant@noirgroup.org

ROBERTO COHEN WINES
roberto@2kosherwine.com

ROSENTHAL WINE MERCHANT
www.madrose.com

ROYAL WINE CORPORATION
www.royalwines.com

SELECTED ESTATES OF EUROPE
www.selectedestates.com

SERGE DORÉ SELECTIONS LTD.
914-861-9206;
serge@sergedoreselections.com

SIGNATURE WINES INC.
503-730-7655

SKURNIK WINES LTD., MICHAEL
www.skurnikwines.com

SOUTHCORP WINES/AMERICAS
www.devils-lair.com

SOUTHERN STARZ INC.
www.southernstarz.com

SPAIN WINE COLLECTION INC.
845-268-2622

STACOLE FINE WINES
www.stacolewines.com

STONEPRESS WINE IMPORTS
www.stonepresswine.com

SUMMA VITIS
www.summavitis.net

SUPREME WINES
www.supremewines.net

SUSSEX WINE MERCHANTS
856-608-9644

TGIC
www.wineofakind.com

TEMPRANILLO INC.
914-576-9190; vinos.antonio@att.net

TESORI WINES
www.tesoriwines.com

THINK GLOBAL
www.thinkglobal-wine.com

TRICANA
www.tricana.com

TRI-VIN
www.tri-vin.com

UNIQCO
256-534-6758; fio@ro.com

VALCKENBERG, P. J.
www.valckenberg.com

VERDONI IMPORTS
www.verdoniimports.com

VIAS IMPORTS LTD.
www.viaswine.com

VILLAGE WINES
212-866-4266;
mpetrillo1@hotmail.com

VILLA ITALIA/LORENZO SCARPONE
www.villaitaliawines.com

VIÑA LA ROSA
www.larosa.cl

VIN DIVINO
www.vindivino.com

VINEYARD BRANDS
www.vineyardbrands.com

VINIFERA
631-467-5907;
info@viniferaimportsltd.com

VINOS AND GOURMET
www.vinosandgourmet.com

VINTUS
914-759-3000

VIVA VINO WINES
www.vivavino.com

VOS SELECTIONS
www.vosselections.com

WEYGANDT/METZLER
www.weygandtmetzler.com

WILDMAN, FREDERICK
www.frederickwildman.com

WILLETTE WINES
liz@willettewines.com

WILSON DANIELS LTD.
www.wilsondaniels.com

WINEBOW
www.winebow.com

WINE SYMPHONY
212-226-8283;
andrewbell@bellwines.com

WINES FOR FOOD
www.winesforfood.com

WINES WE ARE IMPORTERS
888-680-8244

WINGARA WINE GROUP
www.wingara.com.au

WORLD WIDE WINE, LTD./
JENNY & FRANÇOIS
SELECTIONS
www.worldwidewine.net

ONLINE SUPPLIERS

Consumers in many of the fifty states have long been unable to order and receive direct shipments of wines from out-of-state wineries and online wine merchants—the result of laws left over from the Prohibition era. In short, online shoppers in Michigan, New York, and some twenty other states couldn't order a Zin or Merlot from a California winery that had caught their attention. But a new day is dawning. On May 16, 2005 the Supreme Court ruled that states cannot ban interstate wine sales while allowing in-state direct-to-consumer sales; these discriminatory laws violate the Commerce Clause of the Constitution. The next step is for legislators in the affected states to pass direct-shipping bills.

Online suppliers like those shown below generally list the states to which they are currently allowed to ship wine. You can also stay up-to-date on direct-shipping legislation by checking out these two sites:
- Direct Wine Shipments (www.wineinstitute.org/shipwine)
- Free the Grapes (www.freethegrapes.org).

67 WINE
www.67wine.com

B-21
www.b-21.com

BEVMO.COM
www.bevmo.com

BROWN DERBY.COM
www.brownderby.com

CAROLINA WINE COMPANY
www.carolinawine.com

K & L WINE MERCHANTS
www.klwines.com

MacARTHUR BEVERAGES
www.bassins.com

MORRELL
www.morrellwine.com

PJ WINE.COM
www.pjwine.com

PREMIER CRU
www.premiercru.net

RARE WINE COMPANY, THE
www.rarewineco.com

SAM'S WINES AND SPIRITS
www.samswine.com

SHERRY LEHMANN WINE & SPIRITS
www.sherry-lehmann.com

WINE.COM
www.wine.com

WINE ACCESS.COM
www.wineaccess.com

WINE EXCHANGE
www.winex.com

WINE-SEARCHER.COM
www.wine-searcher.com

WOODLAND HILLS WINE COMPANY
www.whwineco.com

ZACHYS WINE ONLINE
www.zachys.com

COUNTRY AND REGION INDEX

If you're partial to wines from certain countries or specific regions (say, Bordeaux), then this is the index for you. Just don't be flummoxed by some of the regional assignments, which are often determined by law. For example, wines sourced from various appellations of California are designated merely as California, not Napa, Sonoma, or any other well-defined region. Likewise, the designation South Eastern Australia transcends state boundaries, just as the French designation Southwestern France is not as geographically tidy as Languedoc or the Loire. Also note that wines made from grapes sourced from multiple vineyards have less specific appelations—for example, "California" or "Oregon."

VICTORIA
Mount Langi Ghiran Cliff Edge 71
Mount Langi Ghiran Shiraz 71

Western Australia
FRANKLAND RIVER
Ferngrove Chardonnay 118

MARGARET RIVER
Beckett's Flat Shiraz 72
Cape Mentelle Cabernet
    Sauvignon/Merlot 20
Devil's Lair Cabernet Blend 21

WESTERN AUSTRALIA
Vasse Felix Noble Riesling 211

Austria
Burgenland
Bayer Weissburgunder 170
Liegenfeld Ottonella 171
Sommer Grüner Veltliner Kabinett
    Dry 172

Kamptal
Bründlmayer Grüner Veltliner 181
Bründlmayer Riesling 151
Josef Hirsch Riesling 152
Loimer Grüner Veltliner 181
Schloss Gobelsburg Grüner
    Veltliner 184
Schloss Gobelsburg Riesling 143

Kremstal
Fritz Salomon Grüner Veltliner 175
Nigl Grüner Veltliner 179

Sudsteiermark
Tement Temento 176

Wachau
Franz Prager Riesling Federspiel 150
Joseph Högl Grüner Veltliner
    Federspiel 180
Joseph Högl Grüner Veltliner
    Smaragd 180

Canada
Niagara, Ontario
Henry of Pelham Baco Noir 91

Chile
Casablanca
William Cole Pinot Noir 50
William Cole Sauvignon Blanc 154

Colchagua
Casa Lapostolle Merlot 41

Maule
Aresti Merlot 38
Carta Vieja Cabernet Sauvignon 18
Carta Vieja Chardonnay 117
Carta Vieja Merlot 38
Carta Vieja Sauvignon Blanc 154
Terranoble Carmenère Reserva 94

Rapel
Viña La Rosa Cabernet
    Sauvignon/Merlot 18

Santa Cruz
Montes Cabernet
    Sauvignon/Carmenère 99
Montes Merlot 42

Cyprus
Commandaria St. John
Keo Commandaria St. John 209

France
Alsace
Domaine Albert Mann Gewürztraminer
    Grand Cru 135
Domaine Albert Mann Pinot Gris Grand
    Cru 139
Domaine Schoffit Chasselas 183
Domaine Schoffit Gewürztraminer 134
Domaine Schoffit Riesling Grand Cru
    152
Domaine Schoffit Pinot Gris Grand
    Cru 139
Domaine Trimbach Gewürztraminer
    133
Domaine Trimbach Pinot Gris 138
Domaine Weinbach Gewürztraminer
    135
Domaine Zind-Humbrecht
    Gewürztraminer 135
Domaine Zind-Humbrecht Riesling 151
Domaine Zind-Humbrecht Riesling
    Vendange Tardive 214

Pierre Boniface Vin de Savoie 170

Southwest France
Château Boucassé Madiran 110
Château La Caminade Cahors 97
Château Montus Madiran 111
Cosse Maisonneuve Cahors 97
Domaine de la Chanade Côtes du
Tarn 87
Domaine de la Chanade Loin de
L'Oeil 165
Domaine de Lagrezette Cahors 105
Domaine Mouréou Madiran 96
Elian Daros Côtes du Marmandais
102

Germany
Baden
Hugelheim Gewürztraminer 133
Joachim Heger Pinot Gris Trocken
139
Von Franckenstein Gewürztraminer
Kabinett 133

Franken
Am Stein Müller-Thurgau 169

Mittelrhein
Ratzenberger Riesling Spätlese
Trocken 148

Mosel
C. von Schubert Riesling 146
Dr. F. Weins-Prüm Riesling Eiswein
212
Dr. F. Weins-Prüm Riesling
Halbtrocken 143
Dr. F. Weins-Prüm Riesling Kabinett
145
Dr. F. Weins-Prüm Riesling Spätlese
143
Dr. Loosen Riesling 142
Franzen Elbling Dry 171
Freiherr von Schleinitz Riesling Dry
142
Fritz Haag Riesling Auslese 214
Fritz Haag Riesling Goldkap
Auslese 214
Fritz Haag Riesling Kabinett 150
Fritz Haag Riesling Spätlese 150
J. J. Christoffel Erben Riesling
Auslese 149, 215
J. J. Christoffel Erben Riesling
Kabinett 149

J. J. Christoffel Erben Riesling
Spätlese 149
Joh. Jos. Prüm Riesling Kabinett
148
Joh. Jos. Prüm Riesling Spätlese
149
Joh. Haart Riesling Kabinett 143
Max Ferdinand Richter Riesling 141
Max Ferdinand Richter Riesling
Kabinett 141
Max Ferdinand Richter Riesling
Spätlese 141
Meulenhof Riesling Erdener
Treppchen Spätlese 145
Meulenhof Riesling Kabinett 145
Mönchhof Riesling 145
Mönchhof Riesling Spätlese 145
Reinhold Haart Riesling Kabinett
149
Selbach-Oster Riesling Auslese 213
Willi Schaefer Riesling 146

Nahe
H. Dönnhoff Riesling Auslese 214
H. Dönnhoff Riesling Kabinett 150
H. Dönnhoff Riesling Spätlese 151
Kruger-Rumpf Riesling Spätlese 149
Schafer-Frohlich Riesling 151

Pfalz
Auggen Gutedel Trocken 166
Dr. Bürklin-Wolf Riesling 152
Fitz-Ritter Chardonnay Spätlese
Trocken 119
Fitz-Ritter Gewürztraminer
Spätlese 134
Fitz-Ritter Riesling Eiswein 212
Jul. Ferd. Kimich Riesling Kabinett
Trocken 141
Kurt Darting Muskateller Kabinett
174
Kurt Darting Riesling Kabinett 145
Kurt Darting Scheurebe Spätlese
180
Müller-Catoir Scheurebe Kabinett
185
Von Buhl Riesling Auslese Goldkap
213

Rheingau
Franz Künstler Riesling 148
Franz Künstler Riesling Kabinett 148
Georg Breuer Riesling 148
Joachim Flick Pinot Gris 137

WINES FOR FOOD

Wondering what sort of wine would be a good match for your porterhouse steak tonight? Or even a take-out pizza? This index provides some answers to "What would go well with this?" From the thousand-plus wines in this book come our picks for everything from barbecue to blue cheese, pork loin to paella. Just be sure to read the tasting note for each wine we recommend to make sure you've got the full name. Another tip: If you're unable to find the exact wine we suggest, you could always ask your wine merchant for the closest match.

Note: When the food categories are as ordinary as steak or chicken, the assumption is that the dish will be fairly plain. If your dish will be highly seasoned or sauced, refer to the categories that seem to be the best fit—Curries, say, or Sweet 'n' Saucy Barbecue. In those cases, seasoning and preparation—not the main ingredient—guides the match.

ANTIPASTI
Cavalchina Bianco de Custoza 175
Di Majo Norante Sangiovese 61
Ermete Medici Reggiano 194
Giuseppe Mascarello Freisa 101
Mauro Sebaste Roero Arneis 182
Monte del Fra Bardolino 92
Nino Franco Prosecco 196
Pecchenino Dolcetto 104
Scarbolo Tocai Fruilano 170

BARBECUE, DRY RUBBED
Girard Petite Sirah 108
Jory Winery Red Zeppelin 70
Pheasant Ridge Cabernet
 Sauvignon 20
Simon Hackett "Gatekeeper"
 Shiraz 68
Tim Adams Cabernet
 Sauvignon 21

BARBECUE, SWEET 'N' SAUCY
Bleasdale Cabernet Sauvignon 20
Charles Melton Nine Popes 36
Coturri Zinfandel 82
Franz Künstler Riesling 147
Marquis Philips Shiraz 69
Meulenhof Riesling Spätlese 145
Summers Charbono 107

BEEF, FATTY
Allain Graillot Crozes Hermitage 72
Chateau Pontet-Canet Paulliac 24
Clos Roche Blanche Touraine Rouge
 14
Monchiero Carbone Barolo 47
Newton Merlot 43
Pellegrini Cabernet Franc 14
Penley Estate Cabernet Sauvignon 23
Valdipiatta Vino Nobile di
 Montepulciano 64

THE VERSATILE ROAST CHICKEN
If there's a food more wine-friendly than roast chicken, we don't know of it. Like wine, its styles run from one pleasant extreme to the other. From fatty, crusty rotisserie chickens to slow-baked, delicate poussins (baby chickens) to fiery, Peruvian pollo a la Brasa, there's a bird for every taste—and practically every wine in this book. Use your intuition. Pair rich reds like Syrah and Grenache with saucy, bold-flavored chicken; serve crisp, herby whites with delicate, herbed hens; try rich, smooth wines—white or red—with Mom's oven-stuffers. When in doubt, use the tabula rasa of a plain, baked chicken to show off the subtleties of any mature, complex, or otherwise precious bottling you've got tucked away. We bet you'll never be disappointed.

BEEF, LEAN
Barnwood Cabernet Sauvignon 22
Bernardus Marinus 23
Cartlidge & Brown Syrah 67
Château Grand Pey Lescours St.
    Émilion Grand Cru 41
Ercole Velenosi Rosso Piceno 111
Heitz Cellars Cabernet Sauvignon
    22

CAVIAR
Guy Larmandier Côtes de Blanc
    1er Cru 190
Pierre Gimonnet & Fils Blanc de
    Blancs Brut 1er Cru 190
Laurent-Perrier "Ultra Brut" 189

CHEESE
See Fondue; Wine and Cheese,
    page 253

CHICKEN, FRIED
Bogle Vineyards Merlot 39
Elian Daros Côtes du Marmandais
    102
Hardy's Chardonnay 117
Marietta Cellars Old Vine Red 96
Ramsay Pinot Noir 51

CHICKEN, ROAST
See "The Versatile Roast Chicken,"
    page 247

CHICKEN, SAUTÉED/
BRAISED/POACHED
Capay Valley Viognier 176
Domaine de Mauvan Côtes de
    Provence 169
Domaine du Clos du Fief
    Juliénas 30
Marc Brocot Marsannay 52
Philippe Raimbault Sancerre 159
Selaks Sauvignon Blanc 157
Wyatt Chardonnay 117

CHILI
Aveleda Estremadura 92
L. A. Cetto Petite Sirah 88
Pierre et Paul Durdilly Beaujolais 28

COLD CUTS AND SANDWICHES
Château Aiguilloux Corbières 88
Didier Fornerol Côte de Nuits-
    Villages 52

Domaine de Cassagnoles Côtes
    de Gascogne 165
Domaine du Roncée Chinon 13
Eric Bordelet Sydre 195
Graffigna Malbec 91
Max Ferdinand Richter Riesling 141
Viña La Rosa Cabernet Sauvignon/
    Merlot 18

CURRIES
Alexander Valley Vineyards
    Gewürztraminer 133
Château de la Guimonière Rosé
    112
Franz Künstler Riesling 147
Liegenfeld Ottonella 171
Mas Amiel Maury 207
Red Newt White 169

DUCK
Château Boucassé Madiran 110
Coturri Syrah 69
Domaine le Sang des Cailloux
    Vacqueyras 35
Marietta Cellars Petite Sirah 106
Robert Weil Riesling Spätlese 150

FISH, FIRM/STEAKS
Adegas das Eiras Albariño 183
Giovanni Struzziero Greco di Tufo
    175
Hugelheim Gewürztraminer 133
Millbrook Pinot Noir 53
Roberto Cohen Pouilly-Fuissé 120
Selaks Sauvignon Blanc 157

FISH, FLAKY/LIGHT
André Rampon Régnié 30
Château Tour de Goupin
    Bordeaux Blanc 154
Egon Müller Riesling Kabinett 151
Pierre Boniface Vin de Savoie 170
Stefano Massone Gavi 172
Thelema Sauvignon Blanc 157
Verget Chablis 121
(See also Fish, Firm/Steaks; Grills,
    Fish; Oysters; Shellfish; Sushi)

FOIE GRAS
Château Pierre Bise Côteaux du
    Layon Beaulieu 211
Château Rieussec Sauternes 214
Château Raymond-Lafon
    Sauternes 213

THREE GO-WITH-EVERYTHING REDS

For the sake of convenience, here are three reds that, from our experience, just seem to please everybody and go with almost any food you put on the table—no mean feat! They hail from France, Italy, and California, and all of them are reasonably priced, costing less than $20. **Château Aiguilloux Corbières** ($7–9) from the Languedoc region, is described on page 88; **La Tunella Cabernet Franc** ($12–14) on page 13; and **Au Bon Climat Pinot Noir "Santa Barbera"** ($18–20) on page 56. Whether you're a seasoned or novice foodie who has yet to buy wine by the case, now is your time to start.

Coturri Zinfandel 82
Domaine Albert Mann
  Gewürztraminer 135
(See also Pâtés and Terrines)

FONDUE
Domaine Les Grands Bois Côtes du
  Rhône "Cuvée Gabrielle" 33
Domaine Schoffit Chasselas 183
Pierre Boniface Roussette 170

GAME
Allegrini Amarone della Valpolicella
  109
Best's Wines Cabernet Sauvignon
  22
Domaine Bressy Masson Rasteau 34
Domaine Henri Gouges Nuits-St.
  Georges 1er Cru 57
Fattoria Le Pupille Morellino
  di Scansano 63
Muri-Gries Lagrein Dunkel 103
Philippe Alliet Chinon 16
Spelletich Cellars Zinfandel 83

GAME BIRDS
Bollinger Champagne Brut 191
Domaine François Lamarche
  Vosne-Romanée 58
François Buffet Volnay 1er Cru 57
Penley Estate Cabernet Sauvignon
  23
Tommaso Bussola Valpolicella
  Classico 101

GRILLS, FISH
As Laxas Albariño 179
Au Bon Climat Pinot Noir 54
Emilio Lustau Palo Cortado Sherry
  203
Keller Riesling Kabinett 147
Saucelito Canyon Zinfandel 83

Zerbina Sangiovese di Romagna 62
(See also Fish, Firm/Steaks; Fish,
  Flaky; Oysters; Shellfish)

GRILLS, MEAT
Cantina Zaccagnini Montepulciano
  d'Abruzzo 100
Château Mourgues du Gres
  Costières de Nimes Rosé 113
Cosentino Zinfandel 83
Pagor Cabernet Sauvignon 19
Palacios Remondo Rioja 77

GRILLS, VEGETABLE
Argiolas Vermentino de Sardegna
  169
Clos Roche Blanche Touraine Rouge
  14
Fritz Salomon Grüner Veltliner 175
Koura Bay Sauvignon Blanc 159
Ransom Pinot Noir 53
Villa Giada Barbera d'Asti 93

HAM
Argyle Pinot Noir 56
Cellers Unió Priorat 108
Domaine Bart Marsannay Rosé 113
Trimbach Gewürztraminer 133
François Raquillet Mercurey 54
Franz Küntsler Riesling Kabinett 147

LAMB
Bodegas Castano Yecla Rosé 113
Bonny Doon Old Telegram 110
Brancott Vineyards Sauvignon Blanc
  158
Château Gruaud Larose St. Julien 24
Domaine Mosse Anjou Rouge 20
Giuseppe Mascarello Barolo 48
Phillipe-Lorraine Cabernet
  Sauvignon 21
Yannick Amirault Bourgueil 16

LASAGNA/BAKED PASTAS
Appollonio Copertino Rosso 92
Ca' dei Frati Lugana 183
D'Angelo Aglianico del Vulture 103
Foradori Teroldego Rotaliano 105
Giuseppe Mascarello Barbera d'Alba 108
Montes Cabernet Sauvignon/ Carmenère 99
Pecchenino Dolcetto di Dogliani 104

LIVER, SWEETBREADS, AND OTHER ORGAN MEATS
Dr. Bürklin-Wolf Riesling 152
Gary Farrell Pinot Noir 55
Henry of Pelham Baco Noir 91
Tommaso Bussola Valpolicella Classico 101

MEAT, RED
See Barbecue; Beef; Cold Cuts; Duck; Fois Gras; Game; Game Birds; Grills, Meat; Pâtés and Terrines; Pot Roasts/Slow-Cooked Meats; Ribs, Short; Sausage; Stews, Red Meat

MEAT, WHITE
See Barbecue; Cold Cuts; Chicken; Ham; Pork; Turkey; Veal

MUSHROOM DISHES
Castello di Bossi Chianti 65
Château Les Barraillots Margaux 22
Emilio Lustau Amontillado Sherry 202
La Vis Lagrein 101
Marziano & Enrico Abbona Nebbiolo d'Alba 46
Schiopetto Tocai Friulano 185

OMELETS, QUICHES, AND FRITTATAS
Domaine du Pavillon Côte Roannaise 28
Domaine Jean Touzot Mâcon Villages 117
Domaine Saint Vincent Saumur-Champigny 13
Loimer Grüner Veltliner 181
William Cole Pinot Noir 50

OYSTERS
Domaine Billaud-Simon Chablis 119
Domaine de la Pepière Muscadet Clos des Briords 171
François Chidane Montlouis Brut 194
Guy Larmandier Champagne Côtes des Blancs 1er Cru 190
Quinta da Romeira Bucelas 166
Stephan Reuter Riesling Dry 142
Txomin Etxariz Txakolina de Gataria 178
(See also Shellfish; Sushi)

PAELLA/RISOTTO/JAMBALAYA
Aveleda Vinho Verde 172
Bodegas Pucho Bierzo 94
Broglia Gavi di Gavi 178
Burgans Albariño 166
Foradori Teroldego Rotaliano 105
Marotti Campi Verdicchio dei Castelli di Jesi 173
Marziano & Enrico Abbona Nebbiolo d'Alba 46
Pagor Tempranillo 79

PASTA WITH BUTTER/OIL OR WHITE SAUCE
Château Lamothe de Haux Bordeaux Blanc 154
Gini Soave Classico 177
Hidalgo Manzanilla Sherry 202
San Rustico Valpolicella 102
Tiefenbrunner Müller-Thurgau 185

PASTA WITH RED SAUCE
Badia a Coltibuono Chianti 61
Battistotti Marzemino 99
Coturri Syrah 69
Due Tigli Maestro del Pomodoro Sangiovese di Romagna 61
Gallino Barbera d'Alba 89
Le Terrazze Rosso Conero 103
Midnight Cellars Zinfandel 82

PÂTÉS AND TERRINES
Château de Ribebon Bordeaux 18
Domaine du Tariquet Côtes de Gascogne 167
Domaine Hervé Sigaut Chambolle-Musigny 56
Domaine Olivier Dumaine Crozes Hermitage 71
Kir-Yianni Akakies Rosé 113
(See also Foie Gras)

THREE GO–WITH–EVERYTHING WHITES
A Vouvray from France, a Sauvignon Blanc from New Zealand, and a Riesling from an ancient German vineyard are so versatile with food that it's almost impossible to go wrong with these three. Check out **Château de Montfort Vouvray** ($8–10) on page 127, **Vavasour Sauvignon Blanc "Dashwood"** ($12–14), on page 156, and **C. von Schubert Riesling "Maximin Grünhauser"** ($16–18), on page 146. Then settle into a comfy chair and start browsing your cookbooks.

PIZZA BIANCO (TOMATOLESS)
Château de la Presle Touraine Blanc 154
Marco Felluga Pinot Grigio 138
Sessa Lacryma Christi Bianco Del Vesuvio 173

PIZZA, PLAIN OR VEGETARIAN
Mionetto Cabernet Franc del Piave 13
Renzo Masi Chianti Rufina 62
Villa Diana Sangiovese 61

PIZZA WITH MEAT
Campo de Borja Borsao Red 32
Cataldo Nero d'Avola 87
Gianni Gagliardo Dolcetto d'Alba 104
Miranda "Firefly" Shiraz 67
Warwick Valley Black Dirt Red 92

PORK
Au Bon Climat Chardonnay 121
Avide Cerasuolo di Vittoria 96
Karthäuserhof Riesling Spätlese 150
Kruger-Rumpf Riesling Spätlese 149
Ramblilla Tempranillo 77
Seghesio Zinfandel 81
Vinicola del Priorat Onix Priorat 32
Domaine Zind Humbrecht Gewürztraminer 135

POT ROASTS/ SLOW-COOKED MEATS
Aurelio Settimo Nebbiolo Langhe 47
Clos l'Eglise Pomerol 44
Domaine de la Pousse d'Or Volnay 1er Cru 58
Girard Petite Sirah 108
La Vis Lagrein 101
Valdinara Nebbiolo d'Alba 46
(See also Stews, Red Meat)

RIBS, SHORT
Capiaux Pinot Noir 55
Chateau Talbott St. Julien 23
Clos l'Église Pomerol 44
Domaine Jean-Luc Joillot Pommard 56
Viñedos Agapito Rico Carchelo 90

SALADS, CHICKEN/SEAFOOD
Domaine Gaujal de Saint-Bon Picpoul de Pinet 166
Joachim Flick Pinot Gris 137
Martin Codax Albariño 166
Mönchhof Riesling 145
Mount Eden Chardonnay 120
Rockbare Chardonnay 119

SALADS, GREEN
Allan Scott Sauvignon Blanc 158
Château de Chesnaie Muscadet 167
Fritz Salomon Grüner Veltliner 175
William Cole Sauvignon Blanc 154

SAUSAGE
Bisci Verdicchio Matelica 168
Cosse Maisonneuve Cahors 97
Giuseppe Mascarello Dolcetto d'Alba 102
Henry of Pelham Baco Noir 91
Lucien Albrecht Gewürztraminer 133
Muri-Gries Lagrein Rosato 113
Villa Fanelli Primitivo 87

SHELLFISH
Capay Valley Viognier 176
Didier Fornerol Aligoté 177
Domaine Bourillon-Dorléans Vouvray Sec Vielles Vignes 129
Foreau Vouvray Brut 197
Franzen Elbling Dry 171
Pierre Boniface Vin de Savoie 170

Stoneleigh Sauvignon Blanc 156
Verget Chablis 121
(See also Oysters; Sushi)

SPICY-HOT DISHES
Ca' del Solo Big House White 170
Château de la Guimonière Rosé
    d'Anjou 112
Château de Montfort Vouvray 127
Josef Leitz Riesling 143
Kurt Darting Riesling Kabinett 145
Kurt Darting Scheurbe
    Spätlese 180
Red Newt Cellars White 169
Sharpe Hill Ballet of Angels 168

STEWS, FISH
Babich Sauvignon Blanc 156
Les Lauzeraies Tavel Rosé 113
Moncaro Esino Bianco 167

STEWS, RED MEAT
Caves Alianca Alentejo 90
Domaine Tempier Bandol Rosé 113
Easton Zinfandel 82
Guilhem Durand Syrah 68
(See also Pot Roasts/Slow-
    Cooked Meats)

SUSHI
Domaine de Mauvan Côtes de
    Provence 169
Domaine l'Ameillaud Cairanne 33
Franzen Elbling Dry 171
Fritz Salomon Grüner Veltliner 175
Gruet Blanc de Noirs 195
H. Dönnhoff Riesling Kabinett 150
Johannes Ohlig Riesling Dry 142
Vissoux Beaujolais 28

TAPAS
Antonio Barbadillo Amontillado
    Sherry 201
Avinyo Cava Brut 195
Coop. del Masroig Montsant 95
Pinord Reynal Rosé 112
Tilenus Bierzo Roble 94

TARTS AND PIES, SAVORY
Clos La Chance Merlot 41
Domaine de Mauvan Côtes de
    Provence 169
Domaine Schofitt Chasselas 183
Girard Sauvignon Blanc 158

Goisot Sauvignon de St. Bris 157
Martin Zahn Gewürztraminer 133

TURKEY
Blockheadia Winery Zinfandel 81
Bonny Doon Le Cigare Volant 35
Capay Valley Viognier 176
ElvenGlade Pinot Gris 139
François Raquillet Mercurey 54
Lake Breeze Bernoota 71

VEAL
Beni di Batasiolo Barbera d'Asti 94
Caparzo Rosso di Montalcino 64
Domaine Le Mas de Collines
    Gigondas 34
Domaine Schoffitt
    Gewürztraminer 134
Franz Prager Riesling
    Federspiel 150
Gunderloch Riesling Kabinett 147
Warwick Valley Winery
    Pinot Noir 51

VEGETABLES, LEAF AND GREEN
Blanco Nieva Sauvignon Blanc 155
Jacky et Fabrice Gasnier
    Chinon 13
Marotti Campi Verdicchio dei
    Castelli di Jesi 173
Mionetto Cabernet Franc
    del Piave 13
Villa Maria Sauvignon Blanc 157

VEGETABLES, ROOT
Arnaldo-Caprai Montefalco Rosso
    107
Bayer Weissburgunder 170
Domaine Saint Antonin
    Faugères 95
François d'Allaines Montagny 123
Kurt Darting Muskateller
    Kabinett 174
Ratzenberger Riesling Spätlese
    Trocken 148

**VEGETABLES, WINTER
AND SQUASHES**
Coturri Merlot 41
Domaine Chaume-Arnaud
    Vinosobres 34
Domaine de Vaufuget Vouvray 127
François Chidaine Montlouis 129
Piero Busso Barbaresco 47

WINE AND CHEESE

Wine and cheese go so naturally together that the idea of selectively pairing them may seem unnecessary. But you can turn good match-ups into great ones if you consider these guidelines before tearing off into the, well, bleu:

- Pair wines with cheeses from the same region
- White wines work more often with more kinds of cheese than red
- Match sweet wines with rich cheese
- Match light wines with mild cheese
- Fortified wines like Port and Madeira are terrific with most cheeses

Some of the reliable wine-and-cheese pairings shown here (cheese first, with a few examples) are old reliables, while others are new discoveries made by today's *sommeliers* and *fromagers*—the result of the cheese plate's comeback in American restaurants.

BLOOMY RIND
(Brie, Camembert)
Rosés; creamy dry whites
(Chardonnay, Pinot Blanc);
medium-bodied dry reds (Merlot,
Bordeaux, most Spanish reds)

BLUE, AGED
(Maytag Blue, Stilton, Cabrales)
Fortified wines (Port of all kinds;
Madeira; sweet sherry; vins doux
naturel); strongest dry reds
(Amarone)

BLUE, CREAMY
(Roquefort, Saga Blue, Cambozola,
Gorgonzola)
Sweet white (Sauternes; late-
harvest Chenin Blanc); sweet reds
(late-harvest Zinfandel)

FETA
(Greek, Bulgarian, French)
Dry Riesling; dry Greek whites

FIRM/PRESSED
(Cheddar, Manchego, Gruyère,
Gouda, Emmenthaler)
Medium and full-bodied dry reds
(Bordeaux; Cabernet Sauvignon;
Chianti Classico; most Spanish reds)

FIRM/PRESSED, AGED
(Parmigiano-Reggiano, Pecorino
Romano, Dry Jack)
Strongest dry reds (Amarone);
fortified wines (Tawny Port,
Madeira); vintage Champagne

GOAT CHEESE, AGED
(Monte Enebro, Selles-sur-Cher)
Cabernet Franc; richer Sauvignon
Blanc

GOAT CHEESE, FRESH
(Montrachet, Petit Billy,
Humboldt Fog)
Light and medium-bodied
Sauvignon Blanc

SEMI-SOFT/PRESSED
(Fontina, Havarti, Jack, Morbier,
Raclette)
Fruity reds (Beaujolais, Pinot Noir,
Valpolicella)

SMOKED
(Cheddar, Gouda)
Rich, smoky reds (Montepulciano
d'Abruzzo, Syrah)

TRIPLE CRÈME
(St. André, Explorateur)
Fortified wines (Tawny Port,
Madeira); sweet whites
(Sauternes, late-harvest Riesling);
Champagne (for some tastes)

WASHED RIND
(Taleggio, Limburger, Reblochon,
Vacherin Mont d'Or)
Strong dry reds (Barolo, Aglianico,
richest red Burgundy); earthy
whites (Tocai)

INDEX

M

BIBLIOGRAPHY

Brook, Stephen. *The Wines of Germany.* London: Mitchell Beasley (Octopus Publishing Group), 2003

Clarke, Oz. *Oz Clarke's New Encyclopedia of Wine.* New York: Harcourt, 2003

Diel, Armin, and Joel Payne. *German Wine Guide.* New York: Abbeville Press, 1999

Gluckstern, Willie. *The Wine Avenger.* New York: Simon & Schuster, 1998

Hazan, Victor. *Italian Wine.* New York: Alfred A. Knopf, 1982

Herbst, Ron and Sharon Tyler Herbst. *The New Wine Lover's Companion.* New York: Barron's, 2003

Jefford, Andrew. *Wine Tastes, Wine Styles.* London: Ryland, Peters & Small, 2000

Johnnes, Daniel. *Daniel Johnnes's Top 200 Wines.* New York: Penguin Books, 1996

Johnson, Hugh. *Hugh Johnson's Pocket Wine Book 2004.* London: Mitchell Beasley (Octopus Publishing Group), 2003

Johnson, Hugh. *The World Atlas of Wine (4th Edition).* New York: Simon & Schuster, 1994

Joseph, Robert. *French Wines.* New York: DK Publishing, 1999

MacNeil, Karen. *The Wine Bible.* New York: Workman Publishing Company, Inc., 2001

Morrell, Peter. *I'm In the Wine Store, Now What?* New York: Silver Lining Books, 2002

Osborne, Lawrence. *The Accidental Connoisseur.* New York: North Point Press, 2004

Robinson, Janis. *The Oxford Companion to Wine.* New York: Oxford University Press, 1999

Root, Waverly. *The Food of France.* New York: Vintage Books, 1992

Root, Waverly. *The Food of Italy.* New York: Vintage Books, 1992

Wilson, James. *Terroir.* San Francisco: The Wine Appreciation Guild, 1999

Zraly, Kevin: *Windows on the World Complete Wine Course.* New York: Sterling Publishing Company, Inc., 2000

http://www.erobertparker.com

http://www.wineloverspage.com/site

http://www.wine–searcher.com

http://www.winespectator.com

ACKNOWLEDGMENTS

The Ultimate Wine Lover's Guide was born of the work of many. Foremost thanks are due to the intrepid staff (past and present) of Nancy's Wines for Food: Ben Crumlich, Peter, Wayne, Max, Johnny, Stephen, Mark, Tom, Ben F., Steve O., Steve K., Kent, Katy, Jeannine, Louise, Leah, Beth, and the entire crew. Thanks, too, to Willie Gluckstern, who filled the store with wine, taught us how to taste, and wrote the manifesto. And special thanks to Jason Spingarn (a. k. a. "The Tongue"), whose infallible palate and integrity have made him a New York wine-world legend.

Thanks, too, to those who were always ready with answers and often with labels: Shirley Alpert, Nate Archibald, David Baer, Emanuel Berk, Cyril Bonetski, Abigail Boyd, Bridget Burgos, Roberto Cohen, Tim Coles, Sheila Doherty, Sheila Esposito, Anne Faurot, John Given, David Glass, Cathy Kitch, Jenny Lefcourt, Robert Mackin, Corrie Malas, Amanda Miller, Kelly Moore, Barry Olivier, José Pastor, Mario Rinaldi, Judy Sandland, Peter Speck, and Cecile Vielle.

We are also grateful for the practical, culinary, and sundry advice volunteered by Linda Ambrose, Polly DuBose, Charlotte and Tom Foster, Jack Heifner, Marsha and Sam Horowitz, Karen Nelson, Kate ("The Cheese Queen") Spingarn, and Kate and Peter Tomassi.

PHOTO CREDITS